THE COMPANY OF
APOSTOLIC
WOMEN

Their Own Stories in Their Own
Words

Compiled by:

Candi MacAlpine

Cover by www.davidmunozart.com

Paperback: 9780999783757

7710-T Cherry Park Dr, Ste 224

Houston, TX 77095 713-766-4271

Contents

Dedicated to the women in every nation yet to realize
they have been created to be an apostolic woman.
The world is waiting for you, step into your destiny.

Foreword by

Dr. Bill Hamon

Candi MacAlpine has blessed the Body of Christ with the understanding that there are women in the Church that have an apostolic anointing to accomplish great things for Jesus and His Church. Some are even called to be one of the 5-fold ministers with the calling and commissioning of an Apostle.

This is revolutionary thinking to an evangelical dispensationalist theologian for prior to 1948, 99% of the Christian world did not believe that there were any active Apostles or Prophets in the present day-Church. A few centuries ago, those dispensational theologians developed the doctrine that the ministry of the apostle and prophet were depleted after the function of the Church was established and the Bible was written. Nevertheless, the restoration movement that was birthed in 1948 received revelation and taught that Apostles and Prophets were still part of the fivefold ministry that Jesus gave to equip and mature the Church to Christ's ministry and maturity. A few years back a major Pentecostal organization put out a white paper to all their ministers directing them that they could say they were prophetic or apostolic, but they were not to call themselves a "Prophet or Apostle." One of their ministers shared that with me because he knew that I had been recognized as a Prophet for 60 years and as an Apostle for 24 years. I asked the fellow minister, does that mean you can call yourself pastoral but can't call yourself a Pastor, evangelistic but not an Evangelist.

Eph. 4:11-13 reveals that Jesus gave all five of His ascension gift ministries to the Church and they are to function until the mortal Church becomes the immortal, eternal Church. Nowhere in scripture does it say that any of the five were to be depleted from the Church. Nor does scripture say that they could only be given to the male part of the redeemed mankind race. After writing my three books on Prophets and the prophetic ministry, I wrote my book called "Apostles, Prophets, and the Coming Moves of God ". It covers the history of prophets and apostles, and the part they play in building the Church that Jesus had in mind when He said, "I WILL BUILD MY CHURCH." The book gives understanding concerning how a Christian can determine their participation in the prophetic and apostolic. The Bible declares that those who are in Christ are members of one body called the "One Universal Many Membered Corporate Body of Christ." There is no difference between male or female or Jew or Gentile when it comes to God's call or ministry. The Holy Spirit does not look at whether a Christian is Jew or Gentile male or female when He calls and anoints them to be an Apostle or Prophet, Evangelist, Pastor, or Teacher.

I believe a woman can be any ministry that Jesus has established in His Church. Balance and wisdom must be maintained in using the title of Apostle and Prophet. The first prophecy in the Bible is God prophesying to Adam, Eve, and the Serpent. God prophesied that the serpent would bruise the heal of the woman, but the woman would stomp on the head of the serpent. Every time another anointed woman goes into her God given ministry the devil gets an awful migraine headache. If you receive a prophecy declaring that you will have a prophetic or apostolic anointing/mantle/ ministry or work, it is not necessarily saying that you are going to be ordained as a fivefold

7

Prophet or apostle minister. You can have an anointing of one of the five-fold ministers, but it isn't declaring you are to become an ordained five-fold minister. If you receive a personal prophecy or a revelation that you are "called to be" you do not immediately print business cards saying I am an Apostle will govern, or Prophet will prophecy, or Pastors will shepherd you. If a thirteen-year-old girl received a prophecy that she would be a good mother, she wouldn't start calling herself a mother until she gets married and has her own child.

I say let God's Apostolic women arise and fulfill their ministries even though some old order ministers may not recognize them as such.

After the Prophetic movement was established in the 1980's and then the Apostolic movement in the 1990's. I had our local church start addressing their husband and wife, team pastors as Apostle Tom and Apostle Jane. Because my son and his wife Jane have the dual calling of Prophet and Apostle like their natural father and spiritual Bishop. The purpose was to make the ministry of the apostle as accepted and recognized in the Church as the other Fivefold ministers. Our Christian International Apostolic Network ministers who were apostles took on the name Apostle to make it known and more accepted in the church world. The CI home Church members refer to them as their Pastors but formally call them Apostle Tom and Apostle Jane.

During my 68 years of ministry, I have prophesied to over 75,000 individuals, saints, and ministers. About 20,000 of those received prophetic words that they had a fivefold calling and identified which one it was. During the first ten years I prophesied to women that they were called to be a teacher in the Body of Christ, some an evangelist, pastor, and prophetess, but I couldn't prophesy---called to be an apostle. God started talking to me concerning His fivefold ministers.

He asked me, why do you feel free to prophesy to women every fivefold ministry except that of the Apostle? I answered, I guess it is because of the teaching I received from some of the older men apostles. He said all My gifts are for all My people and I make no distinction between male and female. However, through the Holy Spirit I choose which of my people receive one of My fivefold headship ministries. May this book inspire many Christian women to fulfill their calling. You few who do have the calling to be apostolic or even called to be an apostle do not allow any religious critic to hinder you from being all that your Lord and Savior Jesus Christ has personally called you to be.

Dr. Bill Hamon

Bishop: Christian International Apostolic-Global Network

Author of: *The Eternal Church; Prophets & Personal Prophecy; Prophets & the Prophetic Movement; Prophets, Pitfalls, & Principles; Apostles/Prophets & the Coming Moves of God; The Day of the Saints; Who Am I & Why Am I Here; The Prophetic Scriptures Yet to Be Fulfilled; 70 Reasons for Speaking in Tongues; How Can These Things Be?; God's Weapons of War, Your Highest Calling;* and *The Final Reformation & Great Awakening.*

Introduction

Candi MacAlpine

Where do I begin?

For an author you know the diligence, the time, the sacrifice, rewriting repeatedly. It is not about money, because authoring books is not a money maker. It is about your audience. It is the ability to impact their lives via the printed (or Kindle or Audible) form. It's about people you will never meet face to face.

I had received a number of prophetic words for the last few years in regard to writing another book. I had already published 4 books over the last 15 years so this was a known path of my life. To be honest I had no idea of the subject matter and most of what I would write about had already been published and on the shelves of bookstores and digital, etc, forms. I didn't think another one was necessary. I've been around that mountain thinking that MY book would impact the world, etc, LOL

This book is different and came in such a beautiful way. The revelation came through a comment made by one of my spiritual daughters, Elizabeth Hawker. My spirit exploded knowing this was IT, the book prophesied for the last couple of years, and its Mother's Day 2021. What a perfect day for the God of the universe to release His plan on this day, on behalf of thousands of spiritual mothers who have persevered, prayed, stomped their feet, pressed through and never given up no matter what obstacles they had to confront including every mountain of doubt and rejection they had to encounter.

This is not a feel-good book, but you will laugh and you will cry. It is a truth book and like the mighty women of the bible who did impact their sphere of influence and their world at that time; of great influence and of small influence. It's not about greatness, but about the greatness of Father God and the destiny of the daughters of Eve.

This company of women is fierce, strong, loving, compassionate and all with a spirit of excellence. It is not for the faint hearted or the squeamish. Yes, there are beautiful testimonies and you will read many in this work. It is sacrificing on so many levels I cannot even write it all here. It is walking in realms and opportunities you NEVER thought were possible for you. It is not about women who are gorgeous, even though many are. It is not about education, position, power, being articulate or any other attribute, even though many are. It is our spiritual and physical DNA, which was put there when we were created in our mother's wombs. And little did we know that it takes many years of life and preparation before we can step over that threshold into this destiny. I pray as you walk through our journeys you will be uplifted, see yourself in our personalities, our stories and see yourself in our journey.

These women are as young as 30 and as 'mature' in the 70's and every age in between. They are black, white, Native American, children of immigrants, Asian, married, single, divorced, widowed. They are mothers and grandmothers. There are some whose DNA is 100% a people group and some like me who are, English, Irish, Dutch, and to my amazement Ashkenazi Jew. Some of their ancestors were part of the foundation of this nation, some part of the host people of this North American continent. Some are born here while others emigrated from China, South America, Korea, Europe or Eastern nations, Africa and all across the earth.

They are each magnificently individual with amazing personalities and who have one thing in common; they love Jesus Christ with all their heart. They are all intercessors and prayer is a major component in their lives.

They serve the Kingdom in such diversity. These mighty women serve in local congregations, in political offices, doctors, authors, teachers, some speak on major platforms, and some serve in their city or state. Some are in the business mountain and are CEO's, CFO's of corporations. Some work in the streets of the worst cities in the United States, all preparing for the King of Glory to return to this earth having established His Kingdom wherever we go. I know you will enjoy each one and will find yourselves in more than 1 of their journeys. Each one I know personally so I know some of their stories. I invited them to be a part of this project because of our relationship and because the Lord said give them a voice along with others that will impact every woman who picks up this title and reads it.

Chapter 1

Jane Hamon

As a young sixteen year old girl, recently saved and filled with the Holy Spirit, I had an encounter with the Lord that changed my life. I was in my bedroom praying one afternoon, when I heard the audible voice of God speak to me and call me into ministry. At that time in my Christian walk I had never been exposed to a woman preaching or ministering so I asked the Lord to show me an example of someone doing what I was called to do. The Lord's response to me was "There is no one yet doing what I have called you to do, for I will be doing a new thing in the earth."

Fast forward over forty years and we are now living amid this "new thing" God was speaking to me about all those years ago. Not only has God restored women to a full place of function and purpose in ministry in the church, but He is also mightily using women to impact the social structure through their influence in business, government and other aspects of culture and society. This "new thing" also involves the restoration of the ministry of apostles and prophets which have emerged to bring kingdom transformation in the midst of the earth.

Today we see that God is raising up apostolic men and women in every sphere of influence within society. What does it mean to be apostolic? The word "apostle" means "*one sent into a region to bring transformation*." It was a government term conferred on those within the Roman system who carried great authority in aligning conquered territories to the Roman way of doing things. It also became a descriptive term given to the early Church disciples who later became the leaders of the movement who were "sent ones" to take the Gospel to the ends of the earth, introducing Kingdom culture everywhere they went. These early apostles changed cities and nations as they were sent by God and demonstrated His reality and power to those they touched. These early church apostles knew how to heal the sick, move in signs and wonders, raise the dead, cast out devils and bring transformation to the cities to which they were sent. Every where they went they carried the transforming power of the Kingdom of God.

In Roman's 16:7 we are told of Andronicus and Junia who are "notable *among the apostles*". Junia was a woman's name. The Jewish historian, Josephus, says that Junia was the wife of Andronicus and that they were apostles of Rome who went about doing the works of the apostles. Today many modern day Junias are being released to apostolically impact the earth. Let's look at some of the characteristics of this apostolic company of women.

Anointed to Lead

Apostolic women are anointed to be leaders. Judges 5:6-7 says, *"In the days of Shamgar, ... the highways were deserted, and the travelers walked along the byways. Village life ceased, it ceased in Israel, until I, Deborah, arose, arose a mother in Israel."* Deborah is a great example of an apostolic woman who brought impact to her nation and her generation at a critical hour in Israel's history. Deborah was called "a mother in Israel" as she stepped into the leadership role of being the only woman judge in the nation's history. This was an apostolic calling from which she would change the course of history and set a nation free.

God is raising up women leaders both in both secular and spiritual environments today. It is no longer "a man's world". Women are taking their place in culture to be used by God to confront the oppressive systems that hold nations and generations in captivity. Leaders are willing to count the cost and determined to pay the price to see change that will pave the way for future generations to run.

Anointed with Vision

Apostolic women are women of vision and full of revelation from the Spirit of God. Judges 4:4 says *"And Deborah, a prophetess, the wife of Lapidoth, she judged Israel at that time."* Deborah was a woman called by God as a prophetess. She received divine revelation and insight that enabled her to effectively govern her nation and to release strategies to other leaders to bring Israel into a place of freedom. She was a woman of vision, evidenced by the fact that she was able to hear the voice of God for Israel during a time of tremendous bondage and oppression, and to release the battle plan that would secure Israel's liberty.

Because she was a woman of vision, Deborah was able to look past the seemingly impossible situation which her nation faced, and lay hold of the hope of God's promise of deliverance and find His strategies for freedom. Someone once said of people who have vision:

> *"People of vision see the invisible, hear the inaudible, believe the incredible, think the unthinkable and do the impossible!" (Unknown)*

It is imperative that we rise as women of vision and begin to speak life to this generation which seems to have lost its way. As we release vision and a sense of destiny and purpose, we will confront hopelessness, discouragement and fear. We will take people from a place of perishing to a place of flourishing, from a place of death to life!

Anointed with Wisdom

Apostolic women have a tremendous capacity for wisdom and implementing the government of the Kingdom of God in the earth. Deborah is the fourth in a list of twelve judges that ruled in Israel during a critical period of their history. She was a woman of influence and great wisdom who effectively led her nation to victory. God is raising up apostolic women throughout the earth today with the same wisdom and governmental leadership qualities that can bring God's transforming power into their communities and even nations.

This word judge is the Hebrew word *"sapat"* meaning, *"one who judges, governs, passes down divine judgment, pronounces sentence, and decides matters."* This word would imply every aspect of the function of government. This position was much more than simply settling disputes. Old Testament judges were basically the governors of the land and would rule in all judicial, legislative and military matters. They were the executive, military and religious leaders of the land, and because of their divine appointment by God, were the ultimate authority in ruling the people. They were respected and honored for their wisdom in judgment and ability to bring the people of God from a place of oppression and cursing to a place of rest and blessing.

For us to truly operate in divine wisdom and Kingdom government we must understand that God has released this ability to us by His Spirit. The Apostle Paul prayed for the Church at Ephesus that God would grant them the spirit of wisdom and revelation and that the eyes of their understanding would be enlightened and they would know the hope of their calling... (Eph. 1:17-18). We must realize that having vision and revelation is imperative, however, without the wisdom to implement the revelation our lives will be frustrated and fruitless.

We must draw on the wisdom of the Word of God and its principles rather than basing our judgments out of our emotions or soul nature. We must be wise in our discernment; that we are truly discerning by the Spirit of God, and not after the flesh. We must be wise with our emotions. We must walk in full pursuit of wholeness in Christ, not as victims but as victors. We must be wise with our words for "life and death are in the power of the tongue." Women of God, let's allow our conversations to be life giving rather than death dealing.

It is time to receive the impartation of divine wisdom to enable us to legislate God's agendas in the earth. Let us marry the anointings of revelation and wisdom within us that we might be fully equipped to effectively minister truth to our generation. Let us be women who can discern the times as did the sons of Issachar. Let us receive the gifts from the Spirit that will enable us to properly discern between good and evil. Let us put aside all criticism and judgment and walk righteously before God and man in love. Let us be the women of wisdom we are called to be, for this day and hour!

Anointed with Balance

Apostolic women have their lives ordered in such a way that they can balance family responsibilities and their destiny calling. Deborah was not only a respected prophetess and judge in the land of Israel, but she also exemplified being a woman of balance by being a wife and maintaining a home. This is part of our calling that cannot be neglected or trivialized in order to fulfill other aspects of our ministry call. I have seen women who have sacrificed their calling to only focus on their family. I have also seen women who have sacrificed their families to only focus on the call of God. How sad! As God is raising up apostolic women, we will be those who have ordered our lives in such a way as to succeed in business, career, government, and ministry without losing our most important area of influence, our families.

The scriptures paint a clear picture of a woman who can raise a family and still run a business, minister to others, be a successful wife, and manage a household, all at the same time. "The Virtuous Woman" from Proverbs 31 was a woman who did it all. This word that has been translated "virtuous" has a very different meaning when looking at the original Hebrew. The same word translated in Proverbs 31 as "virtuous" when referring to a woman is translated everywhere else as "valor" or "valiant" when referring to a man. We need to make a shift in our identity to realize that we are to be as the Proverbs 31 "Valiant Woman" to accomplish all God is saying in this strategic time.

Anointed for Breakthrough

Apostolic women know how to achieve breakthrough in whatever situation they may encounter. Breakthrough is actually a military term. Websters defines it as *"A Military movement or advance all the way through and beyond an enemy's front line defense; an act or instance of removing an obstruction or restriction; the overcoming of a stalemate; any significant or sudden advance, development, achievement or increase that removes a barrier to progress."* Apostolic women know how to pray with power, how to decree God's purposes, and how to stand in faith until the breakthrough comes. They understand that if things are going to change in their families, schools, cities and even nations, it will be because someone determines to make a righteous stand and begins to release the power of spiritual breakthrough which results in transformation.

God is calling us to be risk takers who boldly pursue the things of the Spirit and pioneer a new path for the daughters of the next generation. God is looking for women of courage who will bring forth breakthrough in every battle.

Courage is not the absence of fear but the "*capacity to meet danger without giving way to fear.*" One should not feel condemned because fear is present; it is what you do in the face of fear that counts. Do you press through to freedom and victory, or do you give in, give up and retreat? In order to embrace the fullness of our calling we must be willing to face our fears. The term "fear not" appears over one hundred times in scripture. Why? Because God knew that we would have cause and reason to feel afraid. We must learn to identify, confront and destroy our fears in order to be all God has called us to be.

I have a real passion to see women overcome their fears and become women of courage. Fear will rob from you, accuse you, and cause you to feel helpless, hopeless and defeated. I know. One of my greatest personal battles has been in overcoming fear. I know firsthand how fears can affect your life and try to dissuade you from pursuing destiny. I thank God that His power delivered me from the bondage of fear so that I could be who God called me to be.

God is raising up warriors! Apostolic women must be full of the Holy Ghost anointing, free from our own fears and determined to persist in the face of adversity. We need to realize that our warfare is not only about receiving our own freedom but also releasing that victory to others. Jesus has already won the victory for us and passed sentence on the forces of darkness, but it is up to us to execute the vengeance that He has written. (Psalms 149:6-9).

Anointed through Passion

Deborah was a worshiper! Her heart overflowed with praise for the greatness of God, His might, power and majesty. Judges chapter four tells us the facts regarding Israel's victory over Sisera and his armies, but Judges chapter five passionately re-tells the story through poetry and song. This song was an expressive declaration that flowed out of hearts of worship from Deborah and Barak. They weren't just warriors, they were worshipers!

Those who will be a part of this apostolic company of women will be those who have learned to passionately embrace worshiping the Most High God. Unless we learn to truly live lives of worship before the Lord and press into His presence in prayer, we will never fully understand the greatness of His power. By worshiping God and spending time in His presence, we begin to comprehend how big He is, and how big He is in us.

True worship will cause us to desire His will above our will, His plan above our plan, His way above our way. Having hearts of true worship will cause us to live our lives of obedience to the One we love. It will cause us to yield ourselves completely and utterly to Him. **In this manner, every act of obedience becomes an act of worship.**

Apostolic women will be free from dead religion and from empty form and ritual. Apostolic women will be full of life, passion and excitement for their Lord and King! To do so we must meditate on His words to us, listen to His voice and spend intimate time with Him in prayer. Through the depth of our relationship with Him we can stir up a desire that will overcome every desire of the flesh.

When we love Him that intensely and that passionately, there will be nothing we will not be willing to do for Him. No price will be too great. Our lives become consumed with Him and His purposes in the earth. This is the place of greatest victory. This is the place of highest calling!

Apostolic Women – Arise!

God is raising up a new breed of apostolic women in the earth today. These women are not single dimensional in nature, but have many facets of giftings, talents, abilities and influence. Like a priceless gem mined from the mountain, God will take them through the process of cutting and polishing them until each facet shines with brilliance and clarity. Rise up apostolic women of God. This is your time to shine!

Apostle Jane Hamon

Vision Church @ Christian International

Santa Rosa Beach, FL

Author of *Dreams and Visions, The Deborah Company, The Cyrus Decree, Discernment* and *Declarations for Breakthrough*

Chapter 2

Dr. Candi MacAlpine

I love hearing stories about people's lives, especially women. It seems we have the capacity to navigate through so many different seasons and situations. As the different stories began to come into my email I found myself laughing, crying, and rejoicing because of these women. As I begin my story I pray it will land on people who are also in the path of being in this company of apostolic women.

As I received each woman's story I cried through most of them, had moments of amazement and was encouraged and faith increased by the stories of these women in my circle of friends. Some I have known for decades, and some just a few years. They have already impacted my life even before I knew "the rest of the story".

Beginning

My story begins before I was conceived. She was widowed at age 32, with no children and was living the Hollywood life like many in those days, circa 1940 or about there.

She and her husband Cliff attended Whittier College in California. It was about 1936 or so. She had been gifted with the ability to paint on anything. She, like the others in the group from Whittier College, was studying in the art department. They were just living their lives in their 20's when a man came to them. He shared his dream but had very little money. He suggested to them if they wanted to follow him and his dream it could be fun and would utilize the tremendous artistic gifts they all had. His name was Walt Disney and he had a dream, way beyond most men in that time to entertain the world through the medium of film, and oh so much more. He needed artists, because he was not one. He needed artists who could take his dream and his ideas and put them on an art material called celluloid and bring to life stories that had been around for decades.

A few years later, pre–World War II, they were living life with gusto, and this new dream they decided to embark on was fun. They were young, most with no children and they were ready to take the world by the horns and see what the results would be. As Disney studios started, she loved her job being one of the first animators of those first films that Walt Disney produced. It was long hours but the results were amazing. Her husband worked in the film department and in a time where their life was going great, but then tragedy and he died, leaving her with grief that was unbearable. She had been drinking since the age of 16 and became addicted to a life of alcoholism. This was just typical for the Hollywood scene at the time. She also was becoming quite well known for her innovative art murals on black velvet. No Elvis was not even alive so no velvet Elvis paintings.

She was devastated at the loss of her beloved husband, who could not have children. She was totally alone.

A few years later World War 11 was impacting the United States and Europe and there were lots of opportunities for party time with military personnel. She met a dashing young sergeant from the Air Force and in quick time they were involved.

I did not know until my oldest daughter was three that she had become pregnant with me. She was 34 and thrilled to finally bear a child. Mary Edmonds DeMent was my mother. I happened onto a wedding announcement in some of her boxes of stuff one day while visiting her at her home in Bakersfield! There in front of me was a date that did not coordinate with my birth date of April 26, 1944. She had been ashamed and never told me.

He did marry her and immediately left for England and the war. He did not return until I was 17 months old. We lived with my maternal grandparents until his return and then moved into one of the three houses my grandfather owned on a corner property in the city of Madera. We were only 25 minutes from my grandparents' ranch in Raymond.

If it had not been for my grandparents, I do not know what would have been my ultimate circumstances. They were my salvation, in a sense, the tools the Lord blessed me with to fashion part of my destiny as a woman leader in the decades ahead. My grandmother was a lover of Jesus. She would write poetry in her Bible next to certain passages. She also told me of the angel who would come to the foot of her bed.

I grew up in the foothills of Raymond California, on the amazing ranch of my grandparents. There were secret places all over the big wonderful two story ranch house for dreaming of what my life would be. Grandma would share about her Jesus with me. It planted seeds in me that took many decades before they began to sprout even the tiniest leaf of life. She wasn't able to attend a church service much as they lived seven miles from town. Groceries were brought to the ranch once a week after a phone call to the local grocery store in town. Electricity was not available in that location. Outside a distance from the main house was the wash house. It was a small structure that housed a huge noisy generator. The generator was only to be started up at 5 pm in the evening. The other appliances in the large country kitchen were run on propane, including the refrigerator, water heater, and other needed appliances. It was of no concern to me as everything was provided by my grandparents. I had no idea of the sacrifices' they made to live there. This is another story for another time. Leave it to say my childhood was beautiful when I was with them.

The life with my parents ended in divorce when I was less than 5 and it was just mom and me for the rest of my growing up years. From that point forward it was a very different story. You might call it a horror story in many ways.

Life Changes

By the time I was less than five the marriage had deteriorated drastically. Alcohol and adultery being the key components. Two people with bondages that consumed them came crashing down on this little girl. My mother's alcohol addiction took on a whole new life. My father's drinking, gambling, womanizing, and sadly sexual, physical and verbal abuse of me came to an end when he left for another woman. She was just one in a line of many women taking my mother's place. A psychologist once told me many years ago that about age 3 I became a parent and my mother became a child. Little did I know that what the enemy of my soul meant for destruction the Lord would change to good in His time.

I didn't see much of my father, except for occasional phone calls or showing up on the doorstep for a day or two. Years would go by without knowing or hearing where he was.

My mother's continual addiction continued throughout her and my life at home till her death at 74. Despite her damaged life Father God in his grace and mercy saved her in her 70th year and even baptized her in His spirit. She spent the last years of her life in convalescent care.

As a child we moved every year because she could not keep her teaching job in the school districts that hired her. This kept me from forming any lasting friendships and as teen years came around, I was in charge. In the summer months she would be drunk in her bedroom for weeks at a time. I did attend a Lutheran church due to my mother spending a short time in the AA program that met weekly. I was confirmed and baptized in the Lutheran church, but I had never heard a gospel message of the saving power of Jesus Christ and personal relationship with him.

Teen years of rebellion and sin established strongholds in my life. Despite my personal choices Father God knew one day he would redeem me and restore me to the right relationship with him. My grandmother's prayers during those teen years were the key to so many things that should have happened to me but did not because she was holding me up before the Lord every day.

According to Psalm 139 His design for us even before we were conceived will prevail as others are called to intercede on our behalf. It also eventually brings us to that place where we realize Jesus is the only hope of surviving and having a life of value.

Many more seasons of sin, brokenness, fear, strongholds being established in my life. Bad choices were the norm of my life at that time. My will was in opposition to Father God's. He used those years and seasons to mold and prepare me for His Kingdom in my life. My pain and fear eventually brought me to salvation at the age of 27. It set me on another path to be the person He destined me to be. I always felt guilty in every sin, but it wasn't until years later that He sought me out and brought me out of bondages that were destroying my life. Strongholds of fear and rejection, especially self-rejection plagued me every day. Without a relationship with Jesus, sins will destroy others and yourself.

The Glory Begins

It really begins at the moment, even before the moment we are conceived according to Psalm 139:13-16:

For you formed my inward parts; you knitted me together in my mother's womb.[14] I praise you, for I am fearfully and wonderfully made. Wonderful are your works; my soul knows it very well. [15] My frame was not hidden from you, when I was being made in secret, intricately woven in the depths of the earth. [16] Your eyes saw my unformed substance; in your book were written, every one of them, the days that were formed for me, when as yet there was none of them. [1]

I spent a lot of time studying and researching this passage. The key in the passage is before our conception He (Father God) had already decided who we would be and what His design and purpose was when there was nothing of us physically at that time.

We are created by a master planner, one who has the ultimate creative gift and has so many ideas of who people will be as He decides when

---

[1] *The Holy Bible: English Standard Version*. (2016). (Ps 139:13–16). Wheaton, IL: Crossway Bibles.

they will be conceived, and eventually come forth from their mother's womb. Just ponder that a bit, maybe even more than a bit. It should blow your mind in realizing who we are. No wonder there has been such a battle for our destinies.

So from this place Father God infused my DNA with His glory to be released at certain times in my life. They would propel me into my destiny in Him,

My childhood was wrought with alcoholism, adultery, abandonment, rejection, abuse, sexual and emotional. I really did have to raise myself. Father God would use it to build me into His daughter that would glorify Him. I could spend pages and pages giving you all the gory details, but I do not think that is necessary. So many of the other stories have similar circumstances in their lives, it just shows Father's promise "all things work together for our good for those called according to His purpose".

My teen years in 'church' were in that Lutheran Church and even though I went through their catechism, no offer of salvation was offered, and I did not know Him on any kind of personal deep level. The only level I had was from my maternal grandmother Vera Odessa Edmonds. She had this amazing personal relationship with Jesus that she shared with me, her only granddaughter, and favorite of all three grandchildren of course. LOL.

She and my grandfather were my salvation in those early years and no doubt my grandmothers' prayers were what kept me from so many circumstances like not becoming pregnant, not dying, not becoming a drug addict or any number of results of life without Jesus. I was 17 when she passed away. I was distraught. I spent a considerable amount of time continuing to live a life of bad choices and more bad choices.

By the time I was 19 I was living on my own in an apartment and working for the Bakersfield Californian newspaper as a teletype setter. A very bad relationship, that was on track to marriage, got sidetracked, thank the Lord. Even though I did not know Him, the lover of my soul stepped in. It would take another 20 pages to tell it all but I was introduced to a sweet man by the name of Don MacAlpine, 12 years my senior. This was in August 1964, by January 1, 1965; he had told his younger brother that he was going to marry me. The fact we hadn't even talked on the phone was not a deterrent to him.

On our first date January 4, 1965, he proposed to me, and I said yes and we were married in 6 weeks. Well, they said it would never last, but 55 years and nine months later we were still in love. I was there as he stepped into Jesus' arms November 23, 2020.

Now there is a story and laughter here to be told. Don had been in our care in our home for the last five years with dementia, PTSD, and other issues. He was in Hospice care via VA mid 2020. He was a disabled veteran of the Korean Conflict. He was one of the original jet fighter pilots and was stationed in Hawaii in the 50'.

The night before he passed away (not knowing he was going to pass away) I asked the Lord to let me be there when he left for heaven. Well, I was two hours late getting to the facility where we had finally had to take him for care just a few days before that Monday. I arrived and went into his room. He was not conscious, so I told him sorry I was late and that I loved him so much. He was breathing when I arrived. It was less than 10 minutes, and I sensed him to say "well you got your desire, I waited for you to get here, but I have to go now, see you later Honey". I had to laugh and think of all the times of the last 55 years when I had made him late. He was always so patient, even to his very last breath. It was so gentle and holy as he gently stepped into Jesus arms, peace filled the room, and I knew he was gone.

Now with Jesus' arms around me and Holy Spirit comforting me each day I am learning to live without the man who loved me unconditionally, laughed with and at me for almost 56 years. He was an amazing gentle man who blessed me in more ways that I could ever expect. We loved being together. When he retired from Madera Police Dept after 20 years of service, I was excited to have him around all the time.

To back up a bit, after marrying our first daughter arrived. I wanted my child to be in church. The only thing I knew was the Lutheran denomination so that is where I went. Let me make sure you understand that God can work in your heart drawing you to him no matter what or where the circumstances exist. A hunger for him began to grow in my heart. A few years later Don said, "Well if I did go to church I'd go to the Presbyterian Church," where he had attended as a child. After attending the Presbyterian Church for a season, it was announced one Sunday that a family camp was coming up in the mountains above our town and I wanted to attend. By then our second daughter had been born and was just a year old. Don was on duty and couldn't attend with us, but he agreed we could attend. It was there on the mountain at Calvin Crest Christian Camp that He came to me and I met Him in a most dramatic way and I have never looked back.

A New Era

A few years at Madera Pres and my hunger for the Lord continued to grow and we and four other couples decided to plant a community non-denominational church. It had started as a bible study in our home. Grace Community church is still thriving as an evangelical community church and K-12 school to this day. We did not know of apostolic or prophetic or companies of leaders at that time. Father did so gently, and sometimes not so gently, thrust us forward into the fullness of His kingdom and our destinies.

Understand that our stories are not of man's glory, or speaking in front of thousands, or traveling the world to minister, even though many have experienced those opportunities. It has been a journey of day-to-day living, walking in faith, in spite of all circumstances. Walking with Jesus is exactly what He said.

24 Then Jesus told his disciples, "If anyone would come after me, let him deny himself and take up his cross and follow me. 25 For whoever would save his life will lose it, but whoever loses his life for my sake will find it. (Matthew 16:24-25)

Initially that can sound like Joan of Arc. I suggest that you watch the movie to understand what I am saying. Reality is the key to walking in the fullness of our destiny and becoming a woman of an apostolic company. We are ordinary women who follow an unordinary God who promised He would walk with us all the days of our lives and would fill us with His spirit if we would allow Him to mold and make us into the people of God He designed from the foundations of the earth.

In my case the idea of 'ministry' was as far as the east is from the west. I never even considered it until I was introduced to the prophetic movement. I didn't go looking for it, but Father God lifted me up by the nape of my neck and sat me down amid prophetic men and women. They began the process of teaching and imparting to me what they had received from the Lord.

I experienced a simple process of attending a lot of conferences. I am an avid reader. Another leader in the body saw prophetically the call of God in my life and was the catalyst that brought us into the amazing father of the Prophetic Movement, Dr. Bill Hamon. In a very short time frame my husband and I were ordained with Christian International Ministries in 1997, and we were off to the races, so to speak, prophetically and apostolically.

I did not go into full time ministry until both of our daughters were married. I felt I couldn't give the time needed to ministry until then. It was from this place that Bishop Hamon prophesied to me that I would raise up a training center to equip the saints for the work of the ministry. We have done that for the last 21 years. It wasn't just in our location but all over California and beyond.

It wasn't until sitting at my desk one day studying that an angel showed up and I heard prepare and doctorate. It seemed quite foolish to do the doctorate thing for lots of reasons. Within two years I was a member of the ministry and intercessory team of Dr. Peter Wagner and his ministry. We were in Oklahoma City, Oklahoma, doing a Prayer and Spiritual Warfare Conference. Peter got up and dropped a bombshell on us all. He had left Fuller Seminar and given up all his retirement and followed the Lord's direction to raise up an end time seminary like no other, and not like traditional education. Wagner Leadership Institute, later to be renamed Wagner University was born that day. I knew I had missed it when the Lord told me to train and pursue a doctorate. I immediately repented and went and signed up. I was student #6. I was credited with past experience, etc. and began halfway through the master's program. I graduated in the first graduating class of Wagner in May of 2000. I continued with my doctorate studies, and graduated in the second graduating class with my doctorate and was now Dr. Candi MacAlpine. Never did I imagine His plan for me. I would never have come this far without the prophetic word implanted in my life.

The years since that time have held many joys, growing in Him and the knowledge of His plan to be an ambassador for Christ in the earth. He has allowed me to participate in healing the sick, raising the dead, casting out demons, and making disciples of nations. I never would have gotten close to the incredible people, places and opportunities without the prophetic voices speaking into my life. They also spent considerable time teaching, activating, and mentoring me in the ways of God's Kingdom.

Prayer the Priority

Prayer became my friend many years ago. I did not know it was my training ground to be a prayer leader in California and beyond. It became a passion during difficult circumstances and situations. I did not know how to navigate in life, in family, children, jobs, everything thrown in the pot. The only answer was prayer. It took some time for me to realize that. In the whirlwind of life, I began to speak on prayer at different speaking engagements and had built a small three-part series on prayer. The pastor of one of the churches I was asked to speak at with their leaders and youth told me "Candi, you need to write a syllabus for this school of prayer and add to it". It really shook me. I had no idea it was that significant. He had been a pastor for over 20 years and ministered in many nations.

It took me about 10 years to develop my "School of Prayer, Invitation to Intimacy." At one of my seminars, one of the attendees asked if he could record it. I am not internet, computer savvy and said, "Sure." When the class was finished, we said goodbye. A few weeks later he called me and said, "I want you to come to my studio. We need to do some introductions to the seminar and each session. The school now includes eight sessions with activations. I had no idea this man was a professional, one who did Ted Talk-type videos and more. Wow! And it was all given as a blessing. He spent many hours making a first-class video series, including the extensive syllabus included in the first DVD that the person can download as many copies as needed. I believe everything I do is from the Lord and does not belong to me, so I tell people if you come to the school the syllabus is five dollars a person. If you buy the DVD series at $65 you get the syllabus for free and can make as many copies as you need to help teach others. I could not get to every place the Lord wants this school, so the "DVD series" makes it possible for anyone to use it, teach it, and share it. I have taught it all over California, across the country, in Washington, DC, in Italy and other locations. It is truly a compilation of so many other prayer leaders. We can always pray and intercede no matter the circumstances. There isn't sufficient time to share the myriad of stories and testimonies from each School of Prayer. It would be pages and pages.

I have been privileged to lead teams to nations to pray and watched dramatic results from our time in the nations. I have made prayer journeys and strategic prayer a priority in my life.

I love to pray anywhere and with anyone for any situation. It is my lifeblood for sure.

A New Season

About five years ago, after just being diligent enough to share my life and my spiritual family of *Christian International Apostolic Ministry*, the CI leadership asked me to be Director of California's CI churches and ministers. I was honored to receive such a responsibility. It became another release of the Lord to build on another level and it was swift in coming. I have been so honored to be the "momma" of CI in California.

Family is so important in this company of apostolic women. We may be living across the earth but we stand together as one on behalf of women across the entire earth to rise up into the full destiny as women of God.

Part of the new seasons of life that I had always desired to do was to write books. It was again prophetic words that began to be spoken over me regarding publishing a book. I knew through the confirmation of that word over and over by different believers that I had been given a mandate. My first book was published almost 15 years ago. It is called "Take Back the Night". It is of course about intercession in the night hours. The Lord had shown me that the enemy had stolen the night for his purposes, and we were to take it back because He did more activity, including angelic actions in the night hours. It somehow got into a few prisons, and I got letters from prisoners, male and female that it had changed their lives. Wow, never did I realize this would be an audience to this book. Three more books over the last 10 years have been published and their stories again would take too many pages. Peter the Pebble, Peter the Rock, the journey of our destiny has helped many walk the journey to be apostolic and prophetic people. The last two were devotionals focused on prophetic words I did weekly called Monday Manna. They are named "Adding Depth to Your Destiny"

Vol. 1, a 40-day devotional. "Adding Depth to your Destiny" Vol. 2 was a 50-day devotional focusing on Jubilee in the life of the individual.

It is interesting that for the last two years I received numerous words about another book. I must admit I had no idea what the subject matter would be. As you know from the introduction, on Mother's Day 2021, the Lord exploded my Spirit for this book. The title He gave immediately "A Company of Apostolic Women." It was not for me to write but the actual company of apostolic women that I have encountered for many years. It is time for the 'company 'to arise across the earth and the apostolic women of God to Arise. So, ladies, it is time for you to arise into your destiny as an apostolic woman. I know without a doubt this is not just about this book. There is so much more God will do to expand this dynamic, because He is the one who desired it, prepared the women, and will fulfill His desire.

This brand-new life is strange and different, but He has it all in order. I had no idea what it would look like. I know my life and times are in His hands and yours is also. As we each move forward we will share our stories over and over again and see the impact on other women who have been waiting for these testimonies and stories. The life of ordinary women with extraordinary destinies is here.

Becoming an Apostolic Woman

Apostolic women are pioneers by nature. We don't always fit the mold of the world around us. We go where others don't want to go just to see what is there. Many times, there is absolute bareness, nothing there and that is what gets our juices flowing. I know for myself I love new territory. In fact, after something is up and running, well, I can get bored and happy to hand whatever it is off to the next ones called to continue to build. I love seeing nothing but dirt and receiving vision to begin the foundation of whatever the dream is. For many of the women like me, we seem always ready to try something new and we, or at least myself, are ready to learn a new thing just because we don't know how to do it. It could be quilting, or decorating, or cooking, or traveling to different places I have never been before.

I may be strange, but I think there are more like me that like change. I love change. I am always looking for something to change, even if it is my living room furniture that just needs to be moved to the other side of the room. I get a thrill with new whatever it might be.

I also know that pioneering is not for wimps. It takes a lot of falling and skinning your knees, but it also means getting up with those skinned knees and getting 'back on the horse' that just bucked you off. I don't want to take the time or words to rag on those people we encounter that just can't handle a 'strong' woman. It isn't that she is not insecure in areas of her life, but it is a determination to go where no man (figuratively) has gone before and to conquer and build something out of nothing. I know so many areas of my life have repeated this scenario over and over again. I think it really began through the story I told you about my husband proposing to me on our first date and marrying six weeks later. It was new territory. It really shouldn't have worked, considering the baggage we were both carrying, but God in his grace built us into a family that not only survived but thrived. Our two daughters have followed that pattern in their lives, marriages, children, and businesses and gifting.

Carrying the mantle of being apostolic is not something that we know; it is something that we are, even when we do not know it ourselves. It is something that takes years of Father God's influence in every area of our lives. There does come a day when we suddenly realize what we carried and what many times was a struggle and seemed to take so long before a 'thing' was accomplished that we realized we were apostolic. Of course, it also took the timing of the Lord in His restoration movements in history to bring those of His kingdom into that place of revelation of the apostolic and prophetic movements and the present-day truths needed to navigate the changing times.

For me I did not have a frame or even an idea of the prophetic and apostolic revelation because I was not in congregations who had any idea of these terms or as we say present day truth. The Lord had to literally plop me down in the middle of people who were hearing from him about the anointing and movements. I am so thankful for the men and women who saw something in me that I did not see in myself. They taught and mentored me, despite my immaturity. There are so many I am thankful for impacting my life year after year. My time of preparation into being an apostolic woman took longer than many I believe. I've said for some time "I'm the trinity's pet project". In reality though as I look at the matriarchs and patriarchs of the Bible, I realized it was just that they lived much longer than we do today but it took years and years of walking out life that was selected just for them and for us to become apostolic and prophetic.

I remember the time Chuck Pierce called me and told me about the dream for The World Prayer Center in Colorado Springs, Colorado. He said 'we would like you to be part of the intercessors from the dirt up as the dream unfolds'. I was so excited to intercede over dirt and watch miraculously as The World Prayer Center began to become a reality and not just a dream. When it was completed, it was so exciting to see and be a part of the birth of a dream that had originally just been dirt. To this day it is an amazing place where the presence of God is tangible especially in the main room with the revolving earth that is about 12' across!

It would take far too long to share all the journeys, sorrows, victories, and visions that have brought me to this place today, getting to be part of this company of apostolic women. Please know we do not stand arm in arm alone. There were so many people along the way, from fathers, mothers, teachers, friends, spouses and just every part supplying their part in the body of Christ. So many spiritual fathers and mothers guided us on our path, and sometimes had to pull us, and especially me, back from a path that was not the plan of God and put me back on the destiny path of my life.

I pray my story and the stories of all these other incredible women will impact your lives and as we carry you on our shoulders and walk arm in arm with one another to see God's Kingdom advance onward into eternity. Be brave because you can. No matter what your eyes see before you it is possible. You don't have to walk along. Others will walk with you. You just might have to look awhile until you find them, but you will learn much on that path. Be strong in the Lord and in the power of His might.

Finally

Yes, finally in closing I believe with all my heart, that a company of apostolic women all over the world are about to arise and be a key element in the shifting of first America and then to the uttermost parts of the world. It is time, says the Lord. We have our houses, our relationships and our destiny in the place they belong, and we are ready for the warfare, the criticism if it comes, and it will come. So be it. We have our spouses, our children, and friends and the rest of Ecclesia by our side as we storm the gates of hell to take back what the enemy stole centuries ago. No longer will he reign on this planet and be the prince of the power of the air, but will go down. At the right time Father will throw him into the lake of fire along with every demon/fallen angel who also made a bad choice. Now the consequences of their choices will come back upon their heads. Jesus is Lord over heaven and earth, and we are His army and we will prevail and we will win the victory. It was already won at the cross, and we will prevail to complete the spiritual warfare. Many who came before us held the line. Now it is our time to hold the line, and walk boldly into the king's palace and say, "You are not rightful heir and ruler. Jesus the Christ is. We are His appointed and anointed army to dethrone you and your company, and take back all you have stolen from us the family of God.

Dr. Candi MacAlpine

www.destinytraining.org

rhemanow12@gmail.com

Chapter 3

Corrine B. Cardoza

I'm A Part of a Company Apostolic? Who am I? I can think of a number of women I know who fit that description perfectly. But truthfully, I wouldn't have put myself in that category. Isn't it amazing how God will call you out? He will use someone to make a declaration over your life and suddenly you enter a new door, and a whole new perspective opens up to you.

That's what happened when Candi asked me to participate in this book. I actually thought I was only agreeing with her that she should do this project. After all, 'A Company of Apostolic Women', how cool is that title! I would read that book. Little did I know I was agreeing to write a chapter for it? Yes, our Father has people in our life that see things in us we don't see yet. Now I want to be clear. I am not saying I'm an Apostle. But I have come to see and accept that I am apostolic, that I have an apostolic call on my life. That has opened up a whole new perspective of self - realization for me. When it finally dawned on me that I had agreed to write this I called two people immediately. They are two of my closest friends.

Carla is a professional, published writer and a Grammy winner. I could write a chapter just on all her accomplishments. In so many ways she is apostolic in her life and ministry. Her approval and encouragement gave me courage to pursue this. Carla helped confirm a vision that I actually had something to contribute. She also gave me practical steps to help me begin to put words down. Thank you, dear friend! I also called my friend Anita. Now Anita actually is an Apostle and a prophet.

We have known each other since 1977. You know how you have some relationships where you can get away with saying things so frank that you couldn't say to anyone else. Well Anita is one of those friends. We have been prayer partners for 25 years. The thing is I have been the pestering voice reminding her of the writing projects she's supposed to do. So when I called her about this assignment she just laughed! I don't mean in a bad way. I mean she laughed because it was payback. In one of our monthly prayer meetings, just the week before Candi's call, she had told me that God was about to open some new doors and I was not to question it or hesitate but go through them. This project was one of three that opened up that next week.

These friends helped me to look with fresh eyes at the Apostolic. They began to speak in terms that took Apostolic out of the religious hierarchy box. Really, they were things I already knew and personally things I believed. Those things I had seen in others but failed to connect with how God had used me throughout my life. I like to refer to it as 'the diversity of operations.' That is a story for another day, but it's a reference to 1 Corinthians 12:4-6 and how God opened my eyes to widen my perspective of His spiritual operations. A Company of Apostolic Women Each of these three things mean something specific and special to me; a company, apostolic, and women. As I said earlier I don't really see myself in the office of an Apostle, but I do however completely identify, and very strongly, with being a part of a company of women that are doing apostolic things in the earth today. Now that gets me very excited.

It's easy for me to affirm the call and office of the pastor and teacher. I have been in full time ministry since 1980. My husband Richard and I have helped pioneer three churches. We have served as both Associate Pastors as well as Senior pastors for 40+ years. I have ministered at our church as well as women's retreats and conferences, both in the States and abroad. I love teaching the Word of God and I love pastoring people.

A Company *"And being let go, they went to their own company, and reported all that the chief priests and elders had said unto them."* Acts 4:23 KJV

Several years ago my husband Richard and I were invited to a church in our city of Sacramento. They were having a well known guest speaker and quite a few ministers and pastors had been invited. What stood out the most to me was that I only knew one other pastor there that night and this was in my city. How could that be? There was a room full of ministers and I didn't know any of them. We all had a common faith perspective, we even lived and ministered in close proximity to each other yet I had no relationship with these people. I kept wondering how we were of like minded faith, yet I didn't know or fellowship with any of them. That really bothered me. That night changed my life. I began to pray about that. I asked the Lord to open doors for me to know and develop relationships with other ministers and people in my city. I really wanted to get to know other camps and associations outside my own company. My eyes had been opened to just how myopic we all can be.

We can get very comfortable in our own pond, and I wanted to be stretched. Or as my Apostle friend Anita once said, "The Lord wants us to learn how to be comfortable in uncomfortable situations." Richard and I had been directors for our Ministerial Association in Northern California for 17 years. It was an honor and privilege, and we loved our roots and spiritual heritage. But I realized, as open as we had always been to ministers outside our faith family, we still had a far way to go in developing connections within the whole body of Christ. I prayed for open doors. I mean I really prayed about it and sought it out. I watched for those doors to open with expectancy. Ask and it will be given. Seek and you shall find. Knock and the door will be opened. And that's what began to happen. I thought of how Richard and I first met Candi. We had been invited to a prayer rally through a mutual connection at the State Capital in Sacramento. The whole reason we were even there was because we had been open to a new company of believers. What an amazing connection this has been for us. We have learned and received from Candi and her company. Now our streams are merged in a precious friendship that has enriched our lives so much. When Candi began to share her vision for this book, what excited me the most was participating with so many amazing women, a company of women, who were in some way right in the middle of what God was doing. How did I know that when I had not met any of them? Because I knew Candi I knew if she was in this company then we shared a lot more than our mutual camaraderie with her. We shared a common purpose and passion and I'm all in. We came up under Kenneth E Hagin and so many times we would mention the importance of having a company. I mean a spiritual family of likeminded believers that hold the same doctrinal foundations. The number one being was and is the Lordship of Jesus through the new birth. Wherever I've been in the world, and we share that common faith we are in our own company. It's at those times you need prayer, when you need to be built up and encouraged, or just want to worship with like believers, that's when you go to your own company. I've never bought into the lie that the "world treats you better than the Church." No, it's just that the Church, the assembled, called out Body of Christ, is made up of people. Those people are not perfected. They are in varied stages of their spiritual growth. He who began a good work in us will complete it. He is working for us to will and do His good pleasure. (Philippians 1:6; 2:13) These are two of my favorite scriptures that remind me of His finished work and His finishing work for us.

Companies are made up of people and no company is perfect. They can be broken down into even more close and intimate groups. When you get married the two become one. You are the most intimate special ops company on earth! Where two or three are gathered in His names He is in the midst! There is power in your agreement. As you are blessed with children, and they begin to participate with you then your company expands. I can think of different companies of relationships I'm a part of through friends, church members, prayer partners and organizations.

Today with phone conferences, Zoom and live feeds on the internet we are interconnected with each other and form companies of Believers on so many levels. I recently preached to village women in Pakistan and joined live prayer in Iran. I've been a part of two prayer companies via the phone since 2012 and another one since in 2016, all from my own home. Don't misunderstand; I would prefer face to face. I love going to the nations, but God has been expanding our vision. Just think of Rahab when she saved the two spies in Jericho. Her brief encounter with those two men opened a connection with Jehovah God that ended up saving her whole family. That scarlet ribbon they gave her was tied outside her window and with her faith she brought salvation to all of them. Rahab's entire Gentile family was grafted into God's covenant people. Her family became a part of that company of faith. (Hebrews 11:31)

When my husband's great grandmother turned 100, we started a once-a-year celebration with her that lasted until she went home to be with the Lord at age 108. What a gathering of family that first time we all got together. Most of us didn't even know each other. It didn't seem to matter because we were united in our bond with Grandma Luis. Many had married outside their Portuguese roots, but we were still family. We were a "company." Something many of them didn't know was Grandma prayed daily for all of us, down through the six generations living at that time. Many had received the Lord Jesus in a personal way amidst our strong Catholic roots. The same thing happened when my sister and I took our mom to Italy to meet our family there. What a joy to be met at the airport with a sign of the family name, "Salvatorelli". My sister still has that sign. When we arrived at the home of one of our relatives, we found that all the family had gathered from the entire region to greet us. Then we all sat down together in that living room with all the furniture pushed aside to the walls just to fit all those tables into that cramped space. And what did we do? You probably guessed it. We ate. After all, we are Italian! We spent the next week going from house to house, eating, and laughing and looking at family photos. Each individual family wanted us to share a meal with their children and grandchildren. Young and old, it made no difference. We had all just met each other. We really didn't even know each other. We couldn't speak the same language, but we were with our own company, and we were family. I have found this true no matter where in the world I have gone. There is an amazing connection with the family of God, especially in persecuted areas, or in hard times. Those differences that can create barriers seem to not matter as much, whether doctrine or language or culture. We are one body and one faith. That's when you go to your own company. After all, we are family. Apostolic "And God has appointed these in the church: first apostles, second prophets, third teachers, after that miracles, then gifts of healings, helps, administrations, varieties of tongues." (1 Corinthians 12:28 NKJV)

Just after I agreed to write this chapter I was listening to a message and I heard a statement that spoke loud and clear to me, "First's break barriers." That really resonated with me and it took me back to a moment a number of years ago when the Lord had me get out a piece of paper and begin to write down all the times I was involved in something that was a first. As I looked back over the years, I recalled time and time again when people would say they were having something for the first time and the Lord wanted me to be involved. As I pondered that list, I could see a pattern of how God had used me. I noticed how this 'first's' list had grown through the years since He first brought it to my attention. Then I thought of times I had initiated for the first time myself. At the time I had not linked any of these things together in a pattern. But now I could see what He was showing me. I realize now that it was a part of what I call a diversity of operations. In this case a diversity of the Apostolic. God uses different people in different ways to cooperate with Him in His spiritual operations.

I'm a part of breaking barriers and pioneering new things. That's what Apostles do, and that's what an Apostolic Company does. Now I may not have a huge part, but I might be that link in the chain of connections that bring about an establishing moment. Like many of us, we can be used in delivering a word at the right time to the right person. We might pray all night or in the dark of the early morning hours to stand in the gap, or even birth something new. It's in the connections with people and places and time. I like to think of it like a teaspoon of salt. Yes, a small ingredient but essential in the mix. Just leave it out of a recipe and see what happens or in some cases doesn't happen.

The Lord has been teaching me in this last decade of His amazing diversity in the Body of Christ. I mean we are all aware of how different we are as people, our backgrounds, looks, abilities, and so forth. But those things are more superficial. I'm referring to the diversity of operations of how God uses us. It's all those different and unique ways of how it all works together in the assembly and building up of the Body of Christ. That is such a beautiful thing. Diversity of Operations

"Now concerning spiritual gifts, brethren, I do not want you to be ignorant:" (1 Corinthians 12:1 NKJV)

If you noticed the word gifts are italicized which means it was added by the translators for clarity. But in this case, it adds a slightly slanted perspective. It seems to limit the subject to just the gifts of the Spirit. This verse is communicating something on a much larger scope. God wants us to know about the things concerning the Holy Spirit and how He moves through each of us and that includes so much more than just the gifts of the Spirit. In 1 Corinthians 12:4-7, Paul speaks of different gifts, administrations, operations and manifestations of the Spirit. God wants us to understand how he moves and operates through us and others in all of these areas. He wants us to have information and understanding about spiritual things and how they work. Paul was trying to communicate to the Corinthian believers, and to us, too, that God doesn't want us uninformed of spiritual matters, things of and pertaining to the Holy Spirit. If you look up 1 Corinthians 12:4-6 in different translators you can see the different words used to convey the Greek meaning of diversity. Notice all the ways people chose to communicate these verses just to give us a clearer understanding of what God was trying to tell us. After all, He didn't want us to be uninformed of these spiritual things. They used terms like diversity, differences, varieties, various, distinctions just to keep us from putting God's spirit in a box, that goes for you, too.

You are just as unique and will use you as He pleases. He wants us to know so we can cooperate with Him and each other in all these different ways. So, whether it's a person called and equipped by God to stand in an office, like the office of the Apostle, or to be used to administer a gift, or operate in any diversity of the Spirit, like something that's apostolic, or pastoral, or prophetic. It can be expressed in a way as unique as God Himself. Unique because they are an expression of His loves and glory and grace. We can't possibly count the ways He will love people through us or use someone to touch our lives. Looking back on those inaugural events, those "First's" as He put it to me. I was surprised each time the leader told me that the Lord specifically told them to invite me, by name. It happened enough times that it got my attention. After a while I will admit I was a bit perplexed. Especially when we had great moves of the Spirit, yet I was rarely invited back. That's disheartening! I asked the Lord about it once and He said not to worry about it. It wasn't about me being invited back. My part was to break ground, and to help pioneer this spiritual land. I was beginning to understand an element of my ministry, but I had never seen it as being anything Apostolic in nature. As I look back on it now, through a new perspective, I have a greater insight into the role of things Apostolic. Apostles go in first. They are pioneers. They break ground. They plant. They blaze trails. I started seeing myself through different eyes and not thinking of myself as a failure. I was gaining understanding. It was never about me. It's about His Church, His Ecclesia, His Body. It was never about me growing "my" ministry, but God gaining the increase. Now I can embrace this with a new perspective and appreciation. I can see His diversity working through me and I really love this!

Last But Not Least – Women The Lord gave the word; great was the company of those who proclaimed it: "Kings of armies flee, they flee, and she who remains at home divides the spoil. Though you lie down among the sheepfolds, you will be like the wings of a dove covered with silver, and her feathers with yellow gold." (Psalms 68:11-13 NKJV)

This Company is specifically a female one! One of the only translations to bring this out is the Amplified Version, "The Lord gives the word [of power]; the women who bear and publish [the news] are a great host." Let's look at the word for company in this verse. It's the Hebrew word *tsaba'* and in the feminine form *tsbadah*. It means a mass of persons especially organized for war, like an army. But this is an army of women. It carries the implication of a campaign, and figuratively represents worship. I think of that Company of Women in Psalms 86. They were an advancing army of mighty warriors publishing the word of God. I can picture Deborah leading them and Miriam grabbing the tambourines as she leads them in a victory dance of praise. They were women of valor, *ishshah chayil*, right out of Proverbs 31. Whatever their part was, even if it was to stay by the stuff at home, they all shared together in the spoils of war.

There are seasons in our life when we are required to stay at home base even when we want to be out where the action is. Either way Jesus adorns us with wings of silver and feathers of gold. There are so many more examples in the Bible of women who partnered and worked together to accomplish the will of God. Brave women like Jocheved and Miriam, who defied Pharoah. They were an amazing mother daughter team who saved baby Moses, the future leader of the Nation. Ruth and Naomi partnered in a bond that provided the next link in the lineage of the Messiah. These stories of mothers and daughters really touch my heart because I'm so close with my daughter Anna and her girls. We share a bond of faith and love that is so strong and secure. We trust each other with all our hearts. Remember the two sisters, Mary and Martha? They had a special friendship with Jesus. When Jesus would come to Jerusalem they entertained Him in their home. Can you imagine sitting at His feet and hearing His words, and serving Him at your table? These sisters had very different personalities, perspectives and priorities. But Jesus helped them learn to complement each other instead of complaining. There are times it can be challenging to work with a sister in the Lord. Paul compelled Euodia and Syntyche to try and get along. They had all worked together and had been a powerful team. Paul even enlisted the help of the local body there to help them because their relationship was worth protecting.

Jesus had a company of women that followed him all the way to the cross and later were in the upper room at Pentecost. Some of them were women of wealth and influence that financed His earthly ministry, (Luke 8:1-3).Women, after all, was the first ones Jesus appeared to after His resurrection and the first to be sent to share the good news. He trusts us with some very important assignments.

Twenty years ago I began to devour biographies of women of God, especially Missionary women. I was so inspired by their courage and faithfulness. They became my hero's. I loved reading about the first person in 1901 to receive the baptism in the Spirit, a woman, Agnes Osman. Then one of the first at Azusa Street was another woman, Jennie Moore. There are many stories like that. They are a part of that great cloud of witnesses cheering us on. I wanted to help women with that kind of faith. The Lord began to connect me with women of my generation who were pioneering and making a difference, women including: Billey Brim, Marie-Hélène Moulin, Marie Brown, Liliana

Vernaud and recently Kitty Hamilton. I began to use seed faith to support my finances and my prayers. They were not well known by the masses but well known in my prayer closet. We make up a Prayer Force like Esther's maids. They were a part of dressing her in spiritual royalty before she went into the king. So many times we never even know their names. When I was researching Sacramento's Christian history I couldn't find the names of the women that came here with their husbands to bring the gospel. The most I could find out about these women was through their husbands, Mrs. Wheeler or Mrs. Owen. But these brave women left the comforts of their safe homes back east and traveled west over land and on ships under the tip of South America to make it to what was called the darkest place on earth. We won't know until we get to heaven all the mamas and grandmas who have prayed for their families. There are all the faithful women who covered their pastors and their missionaries for years.

I'm A Part of a Company

Around 1990 I started work with a small group of women. We began as a retreat among four local churches and it grew to include quite a number throughout the area. We had some 'over the top' experiences in God but things changed and it whittled down to just two churches. When we became an Assembly of 2 churches the Lord asked us to covenant with Him to contend for California. It was not a light thing. It was a true commitment to prayer. Most didn't understand it and paid little attention to us. Mighty things have come out of the birthing of this group. We are still contending and we won't quite till California comes back into the camp of the Lord. This Assembly is very precious to me. I have wonderful relationships with some amazing people around the globe. Many people I feel honored to know and be in relationship with, and that to me is more important than what I do individually. I love being a part of a team. I don't mind leading either. Whatever Jesus wants me to do. I just love to see plans and projects and dreams come together and bear fruit for the Kingdom of God. That is what thrills me! You see the most intriguing and thrilling part of being with 'A Company of Apostolic Women' is being a part. When Jesus is your Lord, and you are born again by his amazing grace through simple faith you have joined Jesus' Company of Women. You are a part of the company of women that follow Him, and still do. Jesus lifts us up with spiritual dignity and honor and we love Him for it. So no matter what your calling might be, you are chosen. Be faithful and trust in Him.

Pastor Corrine Cardoza

The Lord's Church

4427 Mather Blvd. Mather, CA 95655

tlc.mather@cfaith.com

www.tlcsac.net

Chapter 4

Elizabeth Hawker

Elizabeth Hawker / Sees Far White Eagle

"Faith will cause you to walk where reason
will not allow you to go"
-- Unknown

I read this quote somewhere in my study time and I do not recall who said it, but it has

stuck with me for years in my journey of faith in serving the Lord. Because the words are spirit words that have gone into my spirit. And I have found this to be true for my life.

I can remember to this day the first time I was talking with God as a young girl of six. I looked up at the sky and really felt what I know now as His hovering presence. It was a place where I had so much joy and knew I was not alone. I was outside in the front yard playing with a jug of water in the rose bushes. All of a sudden, my happy and safe place and talk with God was interrupted by two High School girls who looked huge to me. They were standing right in front of me and took my water jug from me. I was not afraid as they started to pull on my hair that mother had put into two beautiful braids with a ribbon tied to the end. They told me not to say anything or they would hurt me. They stood over me and called me names and spit on me. I was so afraid and could not cry out for my mother and did not have the strength to run. I was frozen, frightened and I lost my voice. The girls threatened me and said if I told anyone what they did to me or who they were they would come back and beat me up. The girls left and started to walk away. I was trembling in fear and finally I was able to run into the house and tell my mother through my tears. My mother ran out the door with me running after her. She found the girls and their mother and told them never to touch me again or she would call the police on them. This was a time of communion with God and the fear and trauma of that day broke it and scared my life and I lost my voice. My voice became silent.

I am the oldest of five children in the family. My parents both loved and taught us about the Lord. As a young child my mother or my grandmother would take us to the Catholic Church. As I look back I remember the amazing feeling of holiness and awe when I could attend. I remember always feeling this sadness. I would look at Jesus on the cross and just sit there on the hard wooden bench quietly and still. When I was in these services I felt that I was in this protective bubble and did not remember what was ever said. I can remember going up for communion and having this tremendous feeling of peace and honor and remember how amazing I felt after I partook of it. I believe this is where I received a healthy fear of the Lord that started a foundation in my life of a Holy God, a Holy reverence and fear of Him even though I had not known Him. I was very aware of Him in my experience of going to the Catholic Church. All of this would come together later in my life and I would find out what I was called to do.

From the time that I was born I lived in San Gabriel a suburb of Los Angeles, California till I was 12 years old. My father and mother decided it was time for us to move to the country to try and protect us from the drugs and gang life that was growing in the city. I remember one day clearly as my sister, brother and I were walking to school. There was this Hippy Bus Volkswagen van and it was all painted up with curtains that were closed. As we walked those in the Hippy van parked right in front of our yard on the street. They began to pile out and got sick all over the grass. It was a mess and one of us went back in to get my Father. He was very upset and told them to leave and go park somewhere else. He did not want his children to see them all drugged up. That was the last straw for my dad. He wanted to protect us from that life.

He moved the family after school was over, and we headed to a hidden place called Twin Oaks, California 3 hours from Los Angeles. When I say it is hidden it is among the rolling hills of the lower Sierra Nevada's. It was cattle country where there was still free range and everyone waved to you as they drove by. Everyone knew everyone back then. What a transition. We had lived in the city and now we had to learn what life was like living in the county.

Bears, Bobcats', rattle snakes, deer, as well as living an hour away from any doctor, market or shopping malls was a new way of living. We all learned to settle into our new life fast, especially that first summer as we were able to experience the intense dry heat of over 100 degrees for the first time. In this new place that we called home, l did not know that this would be the training and birthing place for the coming years of my call to ministry. It was a place in the backside of the desert. The Lord sovereignty hid me until the right time to bring me out with His mighty hand of deliverance.

It was here that my father and mother instilled more responsibility within me because I was the oldest of the 5 children. At times it was not fun, but I stepped up to the responsibility. I never wanted to be in trouble so I learned early that obedience carries a reward and disobedience has consequences. I learned through my parents to make right decisions and to do my best. It would help me as an adult. I was trained in all the areas regarding cleaning house, cooking, milking the cow and goat, doing chores, getting along with my siblings, babysitting; I learned how to serve others. I also learned a healthy respect and honor of my parents that has helped me in honoring others. I remember one time when I was 17 I told my mother no and she slapped me for the first time. I never told my mother no again, I was corrected and it was well deserved. My parents both came from broken homes and they wanted to raise us differently and give us all they never had. They wanted the very best for us. Our parents were not perfect but what they deposited into me and my siblings is priceless and has affected my life so much. I am so thankful for all the love, training, care and discipline that formed a solid foundation within me. Discipline is not pleasant at first but later it reaps fruit in our character if you allow it to train us and mold us.

It was in August of 1984 that I walked into a Non-Denominational church. I remember walking into a wall of love as the greeters welcomed me into the church. The woman who had invited me brought me to my seat and I sat there while the worship team was singing a song I will never forget. The power of anointed worship, it releases Holy Spirit to work in the hearts of the hearers. The song was *Emmanuel God Is With Us*. As I heard the words I could feel the incredible love that I longed for. It was so pure, compelling and healing. I began to cry uncontrollably and the woman who brought me saw what was happening to me. She asked me if I wanted to ask Jesus into my life to be saved. She told me that it was Holy Spirit touching me. All I could manage to say was "YES", and so right there she led me to Jesus and the service hadn't even started. I gave my life to Jesus during the playing of the song Emmanuel God is With Us, and now He was in me. The Void that was in my heart was now filled. No one could fill that void in my life. He filled me, healed my broken and lost heart, and delivered me and washed me clean. I could tangibly fill this all happening at one time. I was new. When I arrived home I was so filled with life and excited that I opened a Bible I was given and it fell open to the book of Luke and I heard audibly natural a loud voice say "Do not fear, little flock, for it is your Father's good pleasure to give you the kingdom", Luke 12:32. It was so big and stood out just like I heard that unknown voice say it to me. No one was in the house just me, I knew who was speaking. It was Holy Spirit saying not to fear and that He was well pleased to give me the kingdom. I would later learn what the kingdom was all about. As He spoke to me audibly I received it.

The Kingdom of God comes three ways, it comes nigh you, it comes upon you and it comes within you. Later as I grew I understood that the Kingdom of God was within me and that nothing could stop me, that I knew the Kingdom was within me and I became a threat to the enemy when I learned it.

Getting saved and giving my life to the Lord was the best "Yes" I ever said and I have never regretted it. It has been a process over the years of my saying "yes." " It has cost me to continue to keep my "Yes" and not compromise but stand fast in times of trials and brokenness.

At this time I was married and already had two small children. I had two abortions prior to my giving my life to the Lord. At this time in my life I was caring the guilt and shame of the abortions. Just before going into get my second abortion I wanted to die before doing that again. I was praying "God I want to die". I did not know how much power words carry. But this is what I wanted and truly felt at that time.

Since I was very young I always wanted to be a mother and a wife, because I wanted to be like my mother. Every time people came over to visit I was always taking the children and watching them, playing with school or something. I was going in for a second abortion because of fear and self hatred and at that time I was too afraid to walk out. When I went in for my procedure I was on the table, under anesthesia. I was in the upper corner of the room looking down at myself on the table and seeing the doctor and nurses' work on me and hearing them say "quick we are losing her". I remember feeling so light and feeling such peace and being surrounded by light and then the next thing I heard was this awful agonizing wailing of a woman and I wanted for someone to help the woman. I could hear as if it was far away and then I felt someone wake me and said to me to stop crying and be quiet as I was scaring all the other women. It was me that was wailing and crying because of what I had done. I had again allowed the doctor to take the very life from within my womb. I left that place sick not understanding why I could not speak up and say no. I had no strength to walk away. I was full of shame and guilt. My womb was created to give life and that is what I wanted and yet I killed it. How could I go on?

From that time for over a year I relived the abortion over and over every night and I could not tell anyone about the pain and shame I carried as they lived life each day. I believe that this was what led me to say yes to the invitation to go to church because I had no place to go. So the freedom from saying yes when He called was His grace and mercy and His endless boundless love He gives us when we ask for forgiveness and He washes us.

From that very day I never every had the nightmare of living the abortion again and I had an insatiable love and hunger for His Word. I had stepped into life and He was with me and I began to learn about Holy Spirit, Jesus and God my Father.

I was the first on both sides of my family to be born again and no one liked it. I was made fun of when I told them. The Family said "we are Catholic", and "oh now you're a holy roller?" I would say "I am born of the Spirit of God" and not justify my new life. I did not know at this time my "YES" to Jesus was a pivotal life change not only for my life but for generations to come. It was bigger than me.

What God has preordained in us and predestined in us is always bigger than us. He chose what family to put us in, and what year we are to be born, and what people group on the earth. His sovereign plan is amazing. He has a plan that we get to be a part of when we say yes to Him.

His Word says in Ephesians 1:5 NKJV- "having predestined us to adoption as sons by Jesus Christ to Himself, according to the good pleasure of His will." It is for His good pleasure and His will that we are here. How powerful is that?

In John 1:12, 13 Amplified – "But to as many as did receive and welcome Him, He gave the authority (power, privilege, right) to become the children of God, that is, to those who believe in (adhere to, trust in, and rely on) His name—Who owe their birth neither to blood nor to the will of the flesh [that of physical impulse] nor to the will of man [that of a natural father], but to God. [They are born of God!]"

God chose a woman with a womb and a man for a seed to form us all and yet it was by His Will that we are born into this world. God the Father knew what father and mother I needed and the DNA of both. In the Hidden place of that womb I would be created with everything that I would need. I came to Him to be transformed into His likeness and image to fulfill the calling in my life that I did not know I had. I was just so happy to be saved and learning about the new life and who was living in me.

I was put into the School of Holy Spirit daily once I took care of my mother in law who was bed ridden as well as my children and husband. I was in the word for hours and Holy Spirit was teaching me to hear and follow His voice. Hours were spent hours writing out scriptures and listening to teaching tapes of men and women of faith and writing every word down and every scripture. I was in every service and prayer meeting. I always made sure my family was being taken care of as I was growing and changing.

I saw my first miracle in my home when my oldest daughter Jennifer fell and hit the corner of the wood coffee table and slashed her head by her eyebrow. She was bleeding and crying. I grabbed a wet cold cloth and rushed to put it on her. The gash certainly needed stitches and all of a sudden I began to call on the Name of Jesus and pray healing over her. I lifted the wet cloth and I watched with my own eyes as the big gash closed up and stopped bleeding, and she stopped crying.

I had another time when my mother in law rang a bell for me in the middle of the night and I ran to the door but the door would not open. Something strong was holding the door closed. I tried to open and push it with all my might but it would not open. Finally I used the Name and authority of Jesus and the door opened. My mother in law was gasping for breath and I saw a black tangible cloud over her bed. I instantly knew it was the spirit of death. I knew to command it to go in Jesus name and it immediately left. She was able to breathe once it left. I prayed for her and released peace.

One night a friend called who had just given her life to the Lord. She told me that her husband was acting strange and growling in the bushes outside. She asked if I could come and help her. So I said ok not realizing what I was saying yes to. On the drive over I prayed in the spirit and covered myself with the blood of Jesus. When I arrived at their home I found the husband at the side of their home in a puddle of water in the bushes. When I tried to speak to him and ask him to come with me inside it was something that I had never experienced or witnessed before. The voice that spoke back to me was not my friend. It was a demon and it said "no 'to me and "I hate you. " I was praying in the spirit. It could not look at me. I only knew to speak the Blood of Jesus and the Name of Jesus. For a brief moment my friend got up and went into the house with me. It was there inside I thought "oh no help me". I did not have any idea what to do. I had the wife call the church and tell them what was happening and they helped me to pray for the husband. We were able to deal with some of the demons and he received some freedom until he got totally free the next day. I did not have a manual at that moment but I said yes and He was with me to bring the couple to freedom. He used my faith and obedience to train me.

It was two days later that this couple came over and we were reading the Word at 10:00 p.m. We were in the book of Acts, taking turns reading when all of a sudden about midnight the wife looked out the kitchen window and saw demons. She started getting sick. Once again I had no idea this is deliverance. Holy Spirit tells me to take her to the sink and have her declare the Blood of Jesus over herself. Then she is to use her Bible as the sword and cut them down and tell them to go.

With every moment of her obedience she was getting free. We then were directed to go outside, continuing to lift up the Word and declare the Name of Jesus. When we stepped outside everything changed. It was a hot summer's night in the city and dogs began to bark. I looked up and the sky was filled with thousands upon thousands of what I thought were shooting stars. Then the sound of wind came and the dogs were silent and no more demons were taunting my friend. She was free.

In the city you cannot see stars because of all the lights at that time of the morning. The Wind came around all three of us and with our natural ears was the whirling sound of the wind. We experienced peace and felt we could hear the sound of singing that was not of this earth. The words were not words you can describe. Then it was as if the moon was coming down to us. It got so close and it was so bright with all those shooting stars. They were flying at an increased rate that could be seen with the natural eyes. When the moon got very close I was able to see Jesus on the cross. I saw the crown of thrones He wore; I could feel the blood that was flowing from His head. I could feel the pain flowing from His side as well the nails in His hands and feet. The moon would go up and return with His heart torn to shreds and then he showed me His heart for the whole world; He showed me each one of my family members that would come to Him as I followed Him. He showed me my life was to be filled with joy and that I was to let my life shine with His light in me. He then showed me that moon that was so bright that lit up the whole back yard. He let me see that my life would start like a seed in the ground and it would grow and grow into a thornless red rose and the Holy Spirit as a dove landed on that beautiful red rose and put its beak in its midst of it.

That was my first ever open vision and encounter. I was seeking Him and it was He who called me and opened my eyes to the supernatural.

I walked with a childlike faith and passion to serve Him. The prophet Ezekiel experienced the hand of the Lord come upon Him and showed him great and amazing things. We must not move into mental assent or try to make a vision happen. I was just being when I experienced a visitation, a vision or saw into heaven. When these things happen to you, it is with a purpose and a gift. These supernatural things change you and bring the fear of the Lord. I have never taken these things lightly or for granted. They are precious to me and I am humbled that He has opened this realm to me.

Over the years I grew in the word as I learned to serve in the church. I am faithful to Him and let him work for me. I was not just being a hearer of the word I wanted the word to work within me. The first time I read Psalm 51:6-7 NKJV "Behold, you desire truth in the inward parts, and in the hidden part you will make me to know wisdom." It came alive in me. It was quickened in me and has always been my desire to align my life to truth. It has become one of the core values in my life that has kept me all these years.

Women began to ask me what was happening to me. I would just share a Bible verse or something that Holy Spirit was showing me. Soon I began to just meet a few women weekly at the local Denney's for coffee. I would open up and share the Word I was given and what Holy Spirit was speaking to me. I did not realize till years later I was teaching them, because I was just giving them what I was freely being given from Holy Spirit.

As I grew in Him I began to speak more. I became freer among people at church. I even began lifting my hands in worship and I found myself free to dance before the Lord in worship. I then began moving to the front row in the service because I was so hungry for Him and His word.

The Church I was in those early years brought in amazing men and women of faith and I knew by my spirit these were generals. I saw miracles, I saw faith, and I saw the manifestation of all the gifts of Holy Spirit in operation. I learned by Holy Spirit to pull on the anointing of ministers that were in the pulpit by praying quietly in the spirit and taking notes.

It was at one of these times that a guest minister, Prophet Dick Mills came to our church. He called me out and gave a word to me that I will never forget. The word of the Lord to me was that "God has called you and you are not just going to be a wife and mother at home clipping coupons. He has called you to something that is big and large and it will touch nations. The process that He will take you through many could not survive or be able to endure the process. He knows you will be able to go through it because He formed you in your mother's womb for this. " I was not looking for a Word of the Lord but it came and the Bible verses Dick Mills gave me were spot on.

There is a process that we must go through that is only for us. It will fashion us and form us to do His goodwill and pleasure. I did not fully understand the word at the time but I received it. There were other times that Dick Mills prophesied into my life and they have been fulfilled because it was the Word of the Lord. I had the choice to believe and receive it or reject it and not believe it. At the time the word was given to me I did not know what was awaiting me. Sometimes we think the word will come the way we want it to but it never does. I am thankful for true prophets of the Lord that carry the word of the Lord, for the word brings conformation of what He has spoken to us already. The Word also speaks to your past, your present and your future. Use that Word when the enemy comes to try and steal, kill and destroy it. We must stand on the word of the Lord and be unmovable knowing our identity in Christ. We must stay filled with the living word, full of the Spirit of God and ready for the battle that comes. We cannot wait until the battle comes or the crisis comes to get the word in us.

When I said "Yes" to Jesus as my Savior I said "Yes "to His Lordship. I also received Him as Master of every chamber in my heart. I could not be a master of my heart. He alone was seated on the throne of my heart. In that "Yes" I was not my own I was His, and I could not take my life back because I was His servant.

Not many days after that the enemy came. I was facing a battle because my husband left the children and me. I had the choice to follow Christ or let the circumstance crush me and stop me. On the third night of no sleep I was warring in my mind against all the why's, what if's and pain, crying in the night. I fell asleep for a few moments and suddenly I was awakened by a huge weight on my chest and something was choking me. I could not breathe and I could not move as I was waking up. I finally had enough of my voice and breath to get out the first syllables of the JESUS' name and I could see this vile demon on me. It let my throat go and fled immediately out my bedroom window. How powerful is the Name of Jesus. The enemy came to steal the word that was in me, but it had no power to take my life as I used His name. At His name demons tremble, at His name every knee will bow and tongue will confess that Jesus Christ is Lord.

So this is just a few key things that happened in my life before God revealed more of what I was called to and who I was.

I moved back home to Twin Oaks from Bakersfield, to the Hidden Place and upon moving back I started to get healing from Holy Spirit.

I was beginning to receive messages one after another. I wrote them down.

Within a couple of years I had remarried and was pregnant with another child. I was told that I had cervical cancer and the doctors wanted to take the baby but then they stepped out to get another opinion. While there alone in the room the peace of God came upon me and Holy Spirit said to me "They will do no procedure on you and they will not take this child from you. They will check you for cancer after the baby is born and they will find no cancer." As Holy Spirit spoke to me I left the doctor's office with my child in my womb and the word of the Lord. I gave birth to my son Jarred and when they checked me later for cancer they could not find any signs of it. God watches over His word to perform it and He is faithful to His word.

later an evangelical church came into the community. My family and I started to attend there instead of making the hour trip into Bakersfield. It was during this time I started getting visions and dreams of preaching the word to thousands in the nations and seeing miracles. I still had an insatiable hunger for the word. I was handwriting letters to over 100 pen pals in the US and other nations. I would write prayers to them and share what I was seeing. I prayed for women to have babies who were not able to conceive. Later they would write and send photos of the babies that were delivered. I prayed for a man to be restored to his right mind because he had a tormenting spirit trying to convince him to commit suicide. He was made whole. I did not realize that the Lord was teaching me the power of the written word and that there is no distance in the realm of the spirit. I just followed Holy Spirit, He was my teacher. I learned that everything I did for my family as a wife and mother was ministry unto Him. I allowed Him into every chamber of my heart even where there was insecurity, low self esteem, and anger, manipulation and control. These things could not stay in my life as Holy Spirit kept going deeper.

One night, after my family had gone to bed for the night the Lord spoke to me. By candle light Holy Spirit took me to Jeremiah 1 and He said "I have called you to be a Prophet to the Nations like Jeremiah" What me? How can this be, I just want to serve you, just be a mother and wife. It is enough you have granted my desire and have given me life. We make these excuses because we look at all the insecurities we have and we feel we are not enough. Like Gideon He chooses the least likely in the family, the lowly, But He knows what He is doing.

I tried to give excuses but then remembered I said "Yes" years earlier when I gave me life to Him. I said to Him "How can this be as I am like Moses, I cannot even speak or retain things, and no one knows me and I have no money how will I do this?" He said to me "I have called you. All you have to do is open your mouth and I will fill it with my words. All you have to do is let it rip! So all I could do was say "Yes" once again. It is such a little word with such implications. When the angel Gabriel sent of God came to Mary in Luke 1 spoke to Mary and her response was "YES" Be it unto me - Luke 1:38 Then Mary said, "Behold the maidservant of the Lord! Let it be to me according to your word." And the angel departed from her. When Mary gave her "YES" she did not realize the personal cost of pain, rejection and sorrow that she would go through to carry, give birth and see who was placed in her womb. But she said yes, because the Holy Seed that was placed within her womb was not just for her but for the world. Her womb was chosen for all mankind. She was called to birth the Savior of the World, Jesus the Messiah. What God has placed in our wombs to birth is bigger than us and we must not abort what He has already placed within our womb. We must give birth to it as the people who are held in darkness are waiting to be set free by what I carry and by what you carry. So once again I gave my total surrender and absolute "Yes" even though I did not fully understand what I said yes to.

It was soon after that that the others saw and recognized it and a woman named Mary, directed by Holy Spirit came to tell me that I was called to be a Prophet, like Jeremiah, to the Nations. She told Holy Spirit that he must be wrong because I could not speak. I lived in poverty and had all these children. She was looking at the outer woman, but God was looking at the inner woman. Finally she came and spoke to me and said "Elizabeth, God has called you to be a Prophet to the Nations". I just broke and cried because I had told no one what He told me, He just confirmed His word to me. So after that time I began to study about the Prophets and Holy Spirit. I read about a lot of the women of faith that were pioneers and ministered in nations, started churches, held healing crusades and lived by faith. While reading about these women I learned the personal cost they prayed to obey the call and the sacrifice and pain they went through and I knew this was the only path for me. He was preparing me, getting me strong before the tests.

The Pastors worked with me and began to disciple me and released me to prophesy and to teach the word. The very first time that I was released to minister behind the pulpit all I could do was weep, but when I opened my mouth He filled it and I knew that I knew that I was born for this. This was my calling. The Pastors would be leaving and they encouraged me to get my ministers license in the denomination we were attending. When I said "Yes" to the Lord in answering the call I knew the weight of responsibility that I would have, and also the accountability. I did not take it lightly. I told the Father that when I say "Yes" and accept the call in obedience to Him I would never open a door for myself; neither would I go through a door that He did not open. I told Him I would not go anywhere that He was not going, and I would go with Him anywhere He would lead. He put a hunger for the nations within me including heavy intercession for the nations. In obedience to Holy Spirit and my Pastors I took the ministers course and I received my minister's license through the denomination we were in at that time. That was a validation and very significant for me.

After I gave birth to a set of twins I became really sick and my body would not function well. My limbs had no strength and I was so tired it was hard to care for my newborn twins and my large family. I stayed in the word praying to the Father to give me a name of what was attacking my body. Holy Spirit said "Rheumatoid Arthritis. I had the name so I began to speak the Name of Jesus over the name of rheumatoid arthritis. Things got worse in my body and I finally had to tell my husband and family what was going on in my body. I needed their help but I did not want any unbelief spoken or prayed over me. I knew I would be totally healed because I had a call to the nations. I needed the word of faith prayers. I had to go to the doctor and was put on medication. They did diagnose me with Rheumatoid Arthritis. Every time I took the medication I spoke the living word into my body. I spoke the healing scriptures into my body. I looked into the future. I was not going to partner with the rheumatoid authorities and be full of pain and crippled. I looked that disease in the face and said no, you cannot have me. I am the temple of the Lord. You cannot stay here, I am an Ambassador of Christ, and He is my healer. After a couple of months of being on medication and speaking of healing and wholeness over my body, I started listening to Gloria Copeland's Healing School CDs. When my body was in pain I spoke to every rebellious cell in my body to be whole, to move as it was created to do. I spoke Psalm 103:1 over every part of my body out loud, "Bless the Lord oh my soul, and all that is within me bless His holy name." So blood you will bless the Lord, muscles you will bless the Lord and the pain will leave. After a few months Holy Spirit started to have me slowly get off the medication. You must learn to hear His voice so you can follow Him and do what He asks. We must KNOW HIS VOICE, and hear clearly walking in wisdom. I did not walk in foolishness. I was daily seeking Him, dependent upon Him and trusting Him to bring me through.

The Pastors had arranged a small church out in the desert for me to preach for. They knew I was ready and they were excited as me. But that morning I woke up with so much pain. I was trying to get ready. I kept worshiping the Lord and praying in the spirit. I never spoke about the pain or complained, I only spoke life. As I looked into the mirror while trying to curl my hair I saw the tears of pain falling and I said "Devil I will go and preach the Word of the Lord to those people today. This is the will of the Lord. I will not stop, I will go if they have to carry me, and I will go if I have to crawl and sit to preach, but I am going and I am healed. It was then that suddenly I felt a substance like hot thick honey fall on my head and fall all down my body and I was totally and instantly healed. No man touched me but Jesus Christ my Healer. I walked with so much joy. I had no more pain. I was the victor over rheumatoid arthritis; it could not stay in the body. I went and delivered the word standing fulfilling God's promise to me.

I began to lead prayer in my home, and hold monthly women's meetings. I also led and hosted women's conferences. I was a part of the new church that was being established and I served in different areas at different times. I served with joy as unto the Lord. I learned to follow the path of Jesus in Matthew 20:28 "just as the Son of Man did not come to be served, but to serve, and to give His life a ransom for many." I loved serving people and serving others in ministry. I count it a high honor to serve other leaders.

In 1999 I attended a meeting in Santa Maria where Prophets, Intercessors, leaders of California and Native Americans were coming together. My Pastor at that time wanted me to go. I tried to get out of it for several reasons. I did not know that this was an appointed time for me and a time for God to restore and heal me of my identity regarding being a Native American.

The meeting began with Native Americans walking into the church with their full regalia on and walking in to the music of Jonathon Miracle of Broken Walls, including Native American drums. Everyone stood up as this was the Grand Entry of the Host people representing different tribes. I will never forget that day and what I witnessed and experienced. It was so beautiful and it was so right. It was God's order and the beauty, honor and pride of who these Native American were in Christ Jesus. A man named Lou Silva from the Chumash tribe welcomed us into his tribal land. You could tangibly feel things moving in the spirit. People were weeping. A woman and Honorary Grand Chief Lynda Prince, of British Columbia stood up and led the protocol with the leaders and the gift exchange. There was repentance taking place that I had never witnessed before. I hung on every word and everything I saw. I was being awakened as a Native American woman. I was told that I could not be a born again believer and have your Native American culture. Even though I was not raised Native American, I still longed for my people and my culture. Being at this meeting I learned the truth. I saw and witnessed for myself God's proper order and call for Native Americans. He has a plan and purpose for us. Grand Chief Lynda Prince has 120 Drums that she travels with and uses for ministry. She had everyone come up to be anointed with oil. They then prayed for the drums to be released. When the drums were released it was with prophetic declarations over the state of California through worship. As the meeting was ending I went up to Grand Chief Lynda Prince sobbing and asked her to pray for me. She laid hands on my shoulders and called me back to my people and prayed that the Father would use me for my people. Her prayers rocked my life.

I am Gabrielino-Tongva, of the San Gabriel Mission Band of Indians of the Greater Los Angeles Basin and the Coastal Islands of California. It is on my father's side that I have my Native bloodline and inheritance. I was learning about my people and no longer carried the shame of being Native American. I was being restored. I was reconnecting with my own tribe and also learning from other Native Americans who were born again believers in Native American Contextual Cultural ministries.

As I write now I see that He wastes nothing. He uses all things for His glory to bring healing and restoration to our lives. I see that it was the Catholic Church that enslaved my people. They were robbed, killed, raped, beat and tortured. My ancestors were stopped from living the only way of life that they knew. The Catholic Church was used by the enemy to take our language and try to destroy who we were.

God always leaves a remnant in the earth and He has a plan. He brought me forth at the right time to be a voice for my people, to release His voice on the earth. It was in the Catholic Church that I felt His Presence and I learned the fear and holiness of Him that I later used later for the power of forgiveness. I was called to His Kingdom to bring healing to the land and the people.

I soon found myself at the World Indigenous Gathering in Australia and witnessed God through the Indigenous people of the Nations. It was a small glimpse of what heaven will be like when every tribe, every tongue and nation will be before Him on that day. I could see the different sides of God and hear the different sounds of nations and the redemptive gift of each nation that was represented there. It was there that I first met Dr Suuqiina and Quamaniq and we instantly became family. I was invited to attend their wedding. Dr Suuqiina and Quamaniq taught me about warfare by honor, and healing the land. They have been such a blessing to me as I learned so much through their revelations and truths. I have applied what I have learned to bring healing to my ancestral land. As I travel the nations I experience how Honor and Protocol opens the nations to you and you are given favor.

My tribe is not federally recognized. We are only state recognized. We do not have any land or a reservation like other tribes. This is why I was not raised traditionally. I was raised among Caucasians and Hispanic people. Sometimes I have been mistaken for Hispanic and when I say I am Native American they say speak your language, but I cannot because the language was lost.

In the hidden place of Twin Oaks in my prayer room at a Ranch Retreat I began to cry out for my native language, as well as crying out for my native name which is part of inheritance. I cried out for my people and for God to bless our people. I had the cry within me. My people had been robbed and plundered. Who will cry out Restore? Restoring my people became my cry. I looked out the window to the mountain range before me. It was called "the Sleeping Giant". Holy Spirit spoke to me one day saying, "I am sending over that mountain range one day to the Sleeping Giant as a Deliverer like Moses. You will not only deliver your people, but all the people of all tribes". He said "I have made you

Tongva and you will release my fire and when you say Tongva you are releasing tongues of fire".

I continued to serve my local church as I began to be called out to join with other Native American teams to go to other churches and reservations. I was also connecting with other Native Believers. I went to Many Nation One Voice Gatherings where Richard Twiss would lead the meetings in local churches. I was part of Honorary Grand Chief Lynda Prince's teams going to Israel and Ireland as well as different churches and reservations. I learned a lot from my Native brothers and sisters as I served them and served alongside them. How I would weep when I heard them pray in their own language, it was so anointed.

In 1994 I had a burden to Scotland and Ireland and with another couple. We started making plans to go, all by faith. We made our dates and purchased our flights, all by faith, having no connection just trusting the Lord as we went. It was two weeks before we were to fly out that my friend was given a contact in Ireland and the pastor in Scotland said "You all can stay at our home." They offered to host us and take us around to other churches and schools to minister.

A week before I was given a phone number to a Pastor in Scotland. When I called the Pastor answered the phone and it was hard at first to understand his heavy Scottish brogue. I explained who I was and wanted to come as Native Americans, to serve the church there. Pastor Crawford Kirkwood said to me, "We have been waiting for you, what has taken you so long. Come we will host you in our home even though we will be away on holiday. You can have our car and our people will look after you. You can minister and do what you need to do while you are here." We made the arrangement and gave him our flight information.

When I hung up the phone the Holy Spirit directed me to a book on my shelf. It fell open in my hands to a man named Hugh Reid, also known as Hugo Reid. Reid had left Scotland with a broken heart in the mid 1820's and came to Los Angeles when it was under Mexico. Later in life he married a Gabrielino Tongva woman by the name of Victoria and he adopted her children. Hugh began to be a voice for the Tongva people and wrote letters to the Los Angeles Star. They published the letters in the Star. He was not only a voice for my people but he helped my people. Holy Spirit said "Elizabeth I am sending you to be a voice to the Scottish people and call forth the remnant and the end time warrior worshipers, because one of their sons came to your land and was a voice for your people". I had no idea about this man till that moment Holy Spirit revealed it.

My first trip to Scotland and Ireland was amazing. God moved and we were well received. I felt that I had come home and I fell in love with the people and the Nation of Scotland. This call to Scotland and the Celtic nations was timely. I have had these nations in my heart since I was young. A year later I returned back to Scotland but this time I was alone. I finally got to meet and stay in the home of Pastors Crawford and Sheila Kirkwood. They released me to minister in their church and opened other doors for me to minister. Before leaving, Pastor Crawford said "our home is your home we will host you. This can be your base when you are here and we will take where you need to go. You never need to ask to come, just say I am coming," It was then I heard Holy Spirit say "You will not just come once or twice to this land, but I am sending you here every 3 to 4 months and you will stay 2-6 weeks at a time to serve in the trenches with these people." This was my mandate and I was there by faith as was spoken.

Scotland was another training ground in ministry. I left my family in the US and landed in Scotland to my new family each time. I went all over that nation and the Isles preaching and praying His word in homes, in churches, and conferences. I would also sing over the land everywhere I went. The song "Lord Raise up a Company of Prophets" by Robert Gay of Christian International was on my heart. I have prayed these lyrics and sung them in my own "key" everywhere I have traveled. I saw God move mightily in meetings, I saw healings and deliverance. I saw people get free as the fire of God was released I served the body of Christ all over that land. I have experienced so many supernatural things while staying and serving Pastor Crawford and Sheila Kirkwood. They have truly been a gift to me and are dear life time friends who not only opened the Nation of Scotland to me but opened their hearts to me and the call of God in my life.

When God puts a nation in you it is in you and you come to love that nation. You hear the sound of that nation and the cry of that nation. You cry out with the heart of God for that Nation. I would wake up in the morning and speak to the Nations, "Nations of the world I am coming." When people ask me if I have been to such a nation I will always answer "not yet, but I will in His time."

I was told by family and other believers that I needed to stay home and just be a pastor to native people that I needed to pastor a church. I was told by other pastors that as a woman I needed to sit my butt down and not preach, just be a wife and mother. There was a fire within me that I could not restrain. I knew that I knew He alone called me to go into the entire world and preach the good news. I knew He alone called me to be a Prophet to the Nations. I did not ask for the call or desire it. I just answered it. I also submitted and was released by my husband. I always made sure my family was taken care of before I left and while I was away. I knew that the safest place for my family was on the altar of the Lord.

He spoke to me, "as you minister to my family I will minister to your family. As you minister to my people I will minister to your people. As you minister to my nations I will minister to your nation." I have seen Him keep His word. There were times when it was hard to leave my family and I would try and stay home. My older children would tell me "no mom you must go for all of us, you must go. We will be ok" and they will help me to pack. The older children always helped with the younger ones and I made sure while on the road of ministry I always called and talked to them, usually daily. It was a sacrifice for me to go at times. I traveled to the nations by faith. I did not do any fundraising; people would hear I was going to Scotland or a nation and they would send a check or put money in my hand. I finally would tell family or those that told me to pastor, that I would be in disobedience and out of the will of God and I would end up damaging and hurting people because I was doing what people thought I should do. I was not called to be a Pastor. I promised I would honor Him and obey Him as He alone is my Judge. We must not compromise, but do what He has called us to and not walk in assignments or offices we are not called to. We cannot be self appointed either. God does the calling and appointing and He uses anointed men and women to confirm the call on their lives.

I have learned over the years to embrace the fire that comes and when I go through a trial to realize I am only going through and I am not camping out in the trial. I will come out stronger than before.

There came a time in my life Holy Spirit called me to declare the Kingdom alignment in all areas of my life and blast the shofar both morning and night till He told me to stop. This took courage and a real trust of the Lord. I started and everything in my life was shaken. It went on for a year. One day as I was doing my dishes I had no words to pray because the intensity of the battle was strong. I lifted my arms up in surrender as the tears fell. Holy Spirit spoke to me saying "it is done. Your arms of surrender are not a sign of giving up, but a total surrender to the plan and will of God." During that time there was such sanctifying work done for me.

Some people that had been friends were no longer friends. I was left again on my own, and my whole life changed because of Kingdom alignment. I am ever thankful that I have had both men and women pastors that I have been accountable to including male and female Prophets that I had a relationship with. I made myself accountable to them. When I went through these trials they helped me to stay the course and helped in my healing process. They loved me and supported me, and kept speaking life to me. During certain times they also brought corrections. We must be accountable and open to other leaders that we are submitted to. They have permission to speak into our lives and spur us on.

Apostle/prophet Candi MacAlpine- mama Candi has been one that I honor who has been in my life for years. She has walked with me through my growing and learning times. She has been there in the good times and the hard times. She has seen things in my life and has spoken truths into my life. She brought instruction and correction into my life as she saw things before they happened and helped me to stay the course. She has encouraged me to be obedient and faithful to my call. There is nothing that I have or cannot share with her. When she asked me to write my story I said okay to honor her. I knew I had to pull on what was within me and share what I have learned over the years serving my Father.

My life has so changed in the Kingdom Alignment. I had a prearranged courtship and then marriage to a Scottish man that I never saw coming. That is a story for another time perhaps a book of its own. It is one of God's redeeming love and call to purity and restoration.

My husband Ian and I started our new life 12 years ago in Oregon. Father said that our later years will be greater than our former years, and that we would enter into our promised land. I can truly say that the word of the Lord and His promises have been coming to pass in so many ways. I am living the dreams and the prophetic words that I was given through many years. I am still not done, and there is more. Ian and I are ordained with Christian International and have a home fellowship.

The nation of Brazil has opened up for me to go and minister and serve Apostle Geraldo Denardi and the body of Christ in that nation. I have ministered all over Brazil, from the very top of Brazil all the way in between down to Rio de Janeiro. I speak his word and release the fire of God as miracles and changes in regions happen wherever we go. The last time I was there before Covid hit I ministered in a church and the glory was so strong in the service I could barely stand and minister to the people. Many had come from far away to be in that meeting that night. I ministered prophetic words to some of the Apostles and Pastors that night. After the service was over I was in the back room for a meal and I sat at the table with my interrupter. I had male Apostles and Pastors sit down and began to ask me how I being a woman, a native woman, had a call to the nations as a prophet and how did I do healing of the Land. They had so many questions! I was trying to answer all of them. These men were really hungry and teachable. I say this humbly. It is by His grace that I have been called and minister for Him as He puts His word in my mouth. I know who I am and who I serve. I stay seated in heavenly places and rule as a female king in the Kingdom.

In my walk with the Lord I have been before Presidents, Governmental leaders of nations and cities. I have been before people in the movie industry and before people in the marketplace speak the Word of the Lord to them. He has sent me before tribal leaders on platforms where I stood in the gap as Native American to release His word and His name. There are so many things that have come to pass in my life.

I have learned over the years to call things into being that are not. "I have food you know not of" that I get when I feast at His table. My words are of a different kind. They are words of the spirit that are eternal. I speak Spirit Words that bring life. My mouth is my weapon because I have allowed Him to take the coal to my lips. These lips are His. "The Word of God says your servant is listening." The Lord has done so many things in my life and blessed me so much. There are too many to count or mention here and I know there is still more to come.

So all that I have written are things in my life that have laid a foundation in my life to my Apostolic Call as a Apostolic Woman to Birth Nations.

I will close with this story and then I want to release a charge to you that are reading this.

When I was ministering in a Church in another Nation I was told by the Pastor that I would only have thirty to 40 minutes to minister the Word. He wanted me done and everything wrapped up by 12 noon.

When I serve the local church in ministry I honor the Pastor and keep to what he has asked me. As service went with worship and then the Pastor got up. He kept going and I saw my time was getting less and I thought, help me Lord to deliver your word. You see the time I have left. When the Pastor finally and reluctantly called me up to minister I opened my mouth and I let Him fill it and I let the word come forth. Holy Spirit began to move. The people were on the edge of their seats as Holy Spirit was moving within them. I could see conviction falling and they began to pull on the anointing. I was able to relate a few words and then I had to stop as I only had 20 minutes. When the Pastor came and I handed the mic back he did not know what to say and then he said this "I want the fire she has".

Those words stuck with me for a long time. You cannot have someone else's fire. You have got to fan into flame the fire of God that is within you. You have to go through the fire to carry the fire. You have to desire the all consuming fire and give Him full access to your life. When you're in the fire you go in alone and you allow the fire to be turned up seven times hotter. The 4th Man will be in the fire with you. There is a price for the fire of God. I am not talking about feeling the fire when you go through a fire tunnel and you leave with just a feeling and there is no real fire on the inside of you. This fire will make you bold. It makes you strong and courageous in your walk of faith. The fire will burn away all dross and anything that does not reflect His image. The fire burns the flesh away, it purifies and refines. As He once spoke to me "How much of my fire do the people want? Do they want ankle deep fire or do they only want knee deep, or do they want waist deep fire? Do they only want the feeling of fire? He said that "my people do not want the all consuming fire because they do not want to give up control. They want to be in control, but when I can be the all consuming fire in their life I am in Control and not them. You can have my fire." I went through the fire because I wanted more of Him and I wanted purity. I also said no to a lot of things that sounded good but I could not do. If you want to carry the fire of God go through the fire. You will not come out burnt or smell like the fire, but you will burn for Him and you will cry for His will to be done in your life.

The fire and all the trials I have come through has given me the passion to serve Him and finish my course. I have stated many times you cannot give what you do not have. I want no part of a false fire; I want the all consuming fire.

To Him I give all the glory and honor of all that He has done in my life, I was the weakest and the least likely yet He chose me and I said yes. I stand in awe of Him every day and I am thankful for everything both the good and bad because he wastes nothing and He uses all the things that comes across in our life for His purpose.

As a Native American apostolic woman I charge you to press into Him. He has chosen and called you. You are unique and your calling is different. You do not have to fashion your life like someone else. Get rooted and grounded in the love of God. Be rooted and grounded in faith, be rooted and grounded in the truth. Walk in absolute obedience and yield to the Lord by submitting to Him when He speaks. Be filled with the Spirit and build yourself up. If you're not hungry for His word, pray for a holy hunger. Be faithful, learn to serve, live with a thankful heart, and give whenever there is an opportunity. Be submitted and accept the leaders you are serving. Learn to walk by faith and not by sight. Be found in Him. Start where you are now. Do not waste any more time. Know your identity in Christ Jesus and let Him lead and guide you and watch and see how He will transform you and bring you into the place that has predestined for you.

Elizabeth Hawker

Chapter 5

Jean Kristen-Blasi

Jesus came to me in 1972. He came into our living room as I sat in Norman's recliner crying to know Him. I kept trying to think how I could ask Him to come into my heart and didn't know what to say. Finally, I put my hands up and said, "Jesus help yourself to me" and I knew I was instantly born again. His Presence filled me and my whole living room. I called my spiritual mother and told her what had happened. She then said, "Did you ask for baptism of the Holy Spirit?" I said no that I didn't know there was a Holy Spirit.

The next day I was in my bedroom on my knees crying out to Jesus again asking for this Holy Spirit to baptize me. Here He came, the Holy Spirit came all through me and on me and my bedroom filled up with His presence. I have never been the same. He changed my life 180 degree. My husband Norman followed these steps soon after me and we both had the baptism of the Holy Spirit. We looked for a church that had the gifts of the Spirit moving and found very quickly there were nine. No one believed in the gifts. We were told to leave 'that stuff' alone. Well we didn't! Thank God! As we just kept ministering to people we found they too needed a place to fellowship so we opened our home and the next thing we knew we had a church fellowship operating. We realized we were called as pastors.

I have since pastored pastors all over the world. What a time of love. We were all so in love with Jesus and each other. We spent several years doing this and the Lord got me involved with ministry in *Aglow* and Norman in *Full Gospel Business Men's Fellowship*. We just kept obeying the Lord in whatever He would ask us to do. We were ministering full time and I didn't realize the Lord was training me for the road. My children were out of high school and I began to travel close to home a few days a week. Then the Lord sent me to California to minister. This exploded as I ministered nothing but Jesus and His Love for people. I did not have a religious spirit and never have been religious. I hate religion! Religion tells you everything you can't do and freedom in Christ lets you walk and talk with him and feel so loved. "Religion kills and Jesus heals"! I had met Jesus so that is what I gave. This is what the people liked as they got nothing but Jesus and love. The ministry grew and grew in California. My friend Penny Brill and I had been friends from the age of 11. She would travel throughout Northern California with me. What an incredible gift of God she was. I was a concert pianist in high school and out and there was a great need for worship leaders. I found myself leading worship everywhere I went then would begin to minister and set captives free. To this day I have the same ministry that Jesus did and that is to set captives free and heal them. Very few things are just a physical manifestation but hurt in the heart, and some demonic. I cast out the spirit of infirmity and other spirits at times and illness leaves.

The Lord had me training people everywhere He sent me to do the same thing He did. The Lord sent me to other Nations; about thirty-three, as I recall. So, I spent most of my time between California, Nations and home. I was on an airplane most of the time - more than once a week. You see, ministry to other Nations is no different than at home as all people have the same heart and that is to be set free. I would fly from Dallas to Northern California back to Dallas and to Europe then back to Dallas and spend a few days at home and then back to California. I kept in constant contact with my family. I would always talk to Norman about 12:00 midnight because he worked the night pharmacy shift as a Pharmacist and it would be 2:00 a.m. his time when business traffic would slow down. I would have just finished my meeting at midnight so we would talk and enjoy each other. What a guy! I called my children every day and we would talk about what was going on with them and I would tell them how much I loved them. My whole family has always backed me in ministry. They are the strength of my ministry. They have been great and I love them so dearly.

Well, the Lord just kept opening doors and it was awesome. The People, held captive, were set free, and then brought into ministry. Prophetic gifts were released to each one of them. I was a Prophet and an Apostle in training from rebirth. It takes years to develop these gifts into maturity. As to this day the ministry still sets captives free and always will.

I am leading an Intercessors group of five committed people in a time of critical Intercession. For two years we have been doing this. During this time has been a time to pray intently over our President and Nation and other Nations. We pray every day together over the phone. We are committed to this. You see commitment to the Lord is what counts. You start something He asks you to do and do it until He says stop. The Love of the Lord has grown deeper and deeper each year in me. Through the good times and the bad times His love and mine never failed. There were plenty of hard cities and people in my years of travel, but I was committed. How can there be bad times when you belong to Jesus and He has promised to use everything for our good. I have been walking with Jesus for 50 years and wouldn't change it for anything. God bless you and my charge to you is "Do whatever the Lord asks you to do and keep at it until He changes it! We don't have to do anything for Him, we get too, it is a privilege to obey and follow Him.

"Chernobyl"

A German evangelist had a dream about Chernobyl, which is in the Ukraine. In that dream the Lord told him to call a seasoned intercessor and myself, Jean Krisle in the United States and invite us to be part of the small team to go to the Ukraine with him. One of the requirements for this team was to be heavily covered by personal Intercessors. I got a hold of my personal intercessors, and they accepted the crucial responsibilities. We were told we might have to give our lives for this project because of the radiation still pouring out from the explosion. We flew into Germany and, after meeting with the rest of the team, went on to Chernobyl. The Lord told us to stop at a grocery store and buy a loaf of bread and a bottle of wine. Ukraine had been separated from Russia and was being starved out. We stopped at several places that the Ukrainians called grocery stores along the way only to be told they had not had any bread or wine in a long time. God always provides for what He says to do! We never doubted and never spoke a negative word. After many miles and stops, we finally found a store that had both the bread and the wine. We purchased the bread and wine and drove on to Chernobyl rejoicing!

After driving 5 hours in a cramped small car, we arrived at our destination and found homes emptied, no people, no cattle, and a dead river. We were told by our German leader to gather and make a circle. We then got on our knees to take communion. We set some bread and wine aside to give to the ground and to sanctify the ground. We prayed the scripture out of I Corinthians 10:16-17 and John 6 to the end, speaking about the meal that heals – the bread that brings life and the wine that cleanses – bringing remembrance to what Jesus has done. We took Jesus to the Ukraine with communion. Immediately after we finished communion a supernatural thing happened. 50 cows had gathered around us and were eating off the ground. Where the cows came from only the Lord knows! The Lord had said for us to find a large branch, a "live" branch, and throw it into the headwaters of the river. This was another impossible thing in the natural, as all the forests were dead or diseased. Well, we found one large, live branch in the forest along the way to the headwaters. We all believed strongly that the Lord had spoken to us out of Exodus 15:25 "Then he cried out to the LORD, and the LORD showed him a tree; and he threw it into the waters, and the waters became sweet". The leader of the team took the branch and ran from a long distance back, at a supernatural speed. Our mouths fell open because he was an older man and we knew he couldn't run that fast. He threw the branch into the water of the river. The branch caught twice on a portion of the river that stuck out. No one spoke a negative word but kept praying in the Spirit inside ourselves. The branch broke loose both times and finally went on to the headwaters.

As my friend and I were walking back across the pasture to the car, we suddenly saw three horses and they came running up to us, stopped, gave one 'nay' all in unison and then disappeared. We had such a supernatural move of God that day. Just like right out of the Bible. Jesus is still the same today, tomorrow and forever!

Sometime later our German leader and another man went back to the Ukraine to check it all out. God had truly cleansed everything! People had moved back into their homes, and they were using the water from the river. Cattle were grazing and drinking the water from the river. All was alive and growing again. What a result! What a team God put together for this project! Just like Elijah, this is just one of many supernatural stories that happened in my travels. I want to encourage you that if God speaks to you to do something, do it and God will do it. Everything works this way with God. Even if the Holy Spirit tells you to put a stick on the floor and have a person or people walk across it there will be a change and life will take place!

Jean Krisle

Chapter 6

Helena Hwang

Motherhood

As I sit here at a coffee shop looking at my life, I can tell I'm at another seven-year transition. My last season has been marked by my precious daughter, who started Kindergarten this week, August 2021.

I remember finishing up a board meeting for *Generals* in November of 2014, Cindy Jacobs was in the unfamiliar position of driving me to a restaurant. We were in her fun two-seater BMW in Oak Grove, TX, when I told her that I was looking into the IVF (in vitro fertilization) process to be a Mom. Shocked, she almost missed the exit of a familiar restaurant. Cindy's response was "you have always been a Vanguard".

To put it into context I had recently turned 50, was single, never married and had never had an "intimate" relationship. On November 13, 2014, after a crazy 50th year traveling all over the world for ministry, relationships and new ventures for Internet media and then concluding with a "frivolous lawsuit," my dad sat me down. He said, "you have always loved kids, you should have your own ". He saw how much I loved my nephew and niece, even taking them to Disneyland. He said, "Right now you have companionship with us (my parents), but who knows how much longer we will live."

A few days earlier my dad talked about a National Taiwan University alumni reunion lunch where he sat down next to a friend who showed pictures of their two-year old grandson. Their daughter was single, about my age and went through the Invitro Fertilization (IVF) process.

He strongly encouraged me to call their daughter to talk to her. I would never have considered it on my own, because I was single with no man in sight. In fact my last relationship was with a man who was significantly older and he did not want any more kids. He was ready for grandkids.

After that conversation, I allowed my lifelong dream of having kids to die. Ironic since one guy I almost went out with in high school reminded me when he got married that I wanted 14 kids and when was I going to get started. I even almost dropped out of college to work at an orphanage. Years ago, my dad had asked me about saving my eggs, but I was already over the age of 40 and at that time they wouldn't do it. Then in one moment that dream was reawakened.

That weekend I contacted the daughter of his college friend. She told me that it was the hardest, but best decision she had ever made. She actually did it before telling her parents because she was worried about the response of her Chinese parents. I was blessed; my dad had initiated the journey.

I immediately searched for a doctor on Google and found one, Dr. Saadat in Beverly Hills/West Hollywood, California. Dr. Saadat was voted as one of the most compassionate doctors and a leading doctor in IVF. As a confirmation the office was a few blocks from Radiance House of Prayer with Jonathan and Sharon Ngai. Their daughter Ellie is my Goddaughter and I was on their board.

I was 50 years old, and thought it was too late to have a child. Earlier in the year there were two occasions at *Harvest Rock* and in Singapore where Heidi Baker called for those who were barren and wanted children to stand for prayer. I grabbed onto those prayers, even though

I was still not married. At least Sarah and Hannah had a husband, but God. Dr. Saadat gave me options I had not even considered. As I met with him at that initial consultation my heart was rekindling with hope. I needed to go through some tests and procedures, but the opportunity was available for me to have my dream come true. I felt God's hand all the way.

Ten years earlier I was supposed to have surgery for fibroids in my uterus. My doctor fortunately canceled the surgery the day before because she knew I wanted to have kids, but the largest fibroid was 18 cm. She did not feel comfortable doing the myomectomy which would preserve my uterus, but there was a risk of me bleeding out and dying. Her recommendation was a hysterectomy. I searched and found a doctor who was able to shrink the fibroids to 10 cm and successfully removed them leaving my uterus whole but a bit scarred. Now, could my womb be filled by a living baby, instead of lifeless fibroids.

I left the appointment with Dr. Saadat, and cried tears of joy. I sat in the car and felt the grave clothes that covered my dream of having a child being removed. God took me through clips of my life, especially from 2007 on. Earlier that year, God had allowed me to bring closure with the man who did not want any more children. We had given it another go after five years of being apart, but this time I knew it wasn't what I wanted. He is still a friend, but we were in different seasons of life and had different expectations for a relationship. God impressed in my heart after the appointment with the doctor, "I know the desires of your heart, even though you were willing to give them up".

Wow, after being involved with ministry and work for about 30 years, I was thrust into the preparation for motherhood. I had to have my uterus cleaned out and then begin taking medication to restart my cycle, etc. I had to go through the legal process of "adoption". I spent a lot of time praying with my friend and intercessor, Christina Horn. We prayed through choices for donors and cleansing of any generational curses on the donors of the embryo. Then finally on June 1, 2015, the embryos were ready and on June 6th, two embryos were implanted in my womb. I was to be on complete bed rest for three days. Christina stayed with me and my parents prepared food. Things were going well until the end of the month when I began to have a rash and had to travel over an hour to see the doctor and I had to deal with the court case. I met up with a friend for breakfast, on June 27th, but when I got home, I found a bright red spot in my panty liner. I called Dr. Saadat, who said spotting is common, but he put me on bed rest. I was lying down and seemed to be getting better, but then I could feel blood coming out. My liner was all bloody and then a clot the size of half my fist came out. I felt I miscarried and began to cry. I called my Mom and Dr. Saadat. He said I had not necessarily miscarried. By the time my parents came I had settled down and had a supernatural peace.

Talking to Christina, she felt I was still pregnant. I thought so too. I did not have cramping and the bleeding pretty much stopped for that day. Mom and Dad were very sweet. I could tell they were stressed and sad. They asked me to go over to their house. Christina reminded me that she had felt I would be on a modified bed rest. Then she also said she saw a boy and a girl, but the girl was younger. She was not sure of age or maturity, heaven or on earth. I prayed and felt grace and comfort.

The weekend was quite scary. I stopped bleeding for a day, but then on Sunday another clump came out. I thought it was the second baby. I began to cry again. What could I have done differently? I had not done anything strenuous. There was nothing to do but to lean on my Abba Father. My mom and dad were worried. Mom said I could try again. Dad was really sweet to call me in the morning to tell me it's okay and that he loved me. Wow, so different from even a few short years ago.

I went to Dr. Saadat expecting to talk to him about the next time, but when he did the ultrasound, there were both of my babies. One had a strong heartbeat and the other was smaller and had not started having a heartbeat. He said they looked about the right size! He told me bleeding and clots happen. I just needed to stay on bed rest and continue with the meds.

Wow! What a relief! Thank you, Abba Father. You give life and You take it away. You know the number of days for every child. Psalm 139, especially verse 16. *"Your eyes saw my unformed substance, and in your book all the days of my life were written before ever they took shape, when as yet there was none of them."* Abba, I can rest in You, knowing that You have my babies' days numbered. They will not be taken early.

When I got back from the appointment, I stayed in bed at my parents' home. Wow, I didn't think that would happen. Thank you for providing my parents to take care of me as I take care of my little ones. Again let my womb be a warm, inviting, safe and nurturing place for my little babies. Keep them safe and healthy. Grow them up in your timing, in Your ordained way.

My time in bed reframed my life. No longer was I traveling the world often on a moment's notice. I was in bed which gave me lots of time to read and spend time with Abba to prepare me to be a Mom. I did lose one baby early on in the pregnancy, and went through a grieving process. The other little one that survived had a strong heartbeat from the very beginning at 1 month. As a high risk pregnancy, I had frequent appointments with doctors. I was so encouraged to discover that they were believers. They encouraged me as an older, single Mom. God was so gracious throughout the pregnancy. When I found out she was a girl, God prompted me to name her after my mom and dad, Anne became Anna and Li-san became Lisa. Annalisa, means Grace and Favor and God is bountiful or abundant. Graced with God's bounty! Her due date was February 22, 2016, but the day the doctor chose due to the former fibroids was February 8, 2016, which was Chinese New Year!

I have learned so much about God's love and priorities from giving me the honor to be Annalisa's mom. God has always talked to me about ministering as a family, but I thought it would be in the context of my husband. I had to readjust to Jesus being my husband and Abba Father being Annalisa's Daddy. The issue has come up at times, but Annalisa knows she is precious to God first and then I second.

God truly brings forth good out of what the enemy meant for evil. Annalisa had started part time preschool at a local church school at the age of three and one-half. Fortunately, when Covid hit I was home and could spend time with her. She hated zoom, but loved the preschool shows put on by our church, *Superbook* and other Christian shows. We went for walks in the neighborhood and to the beach. When many kids struggled with depression, Annalisa thrived with the time together. I was so blessed when on Good Friday 2020, in one of our talks before bed she accepted Jesus into her heart. I am so thankful for the extended time with her and the re-calibration in our lives.

Walking one day around our neighborhood, we saw a neighbor friend who I had not spent much time with in recent years. She was another single mom in a similar situation as me, with a son about a year younger than Annalisa. God's perfect timing again because he was just at the age to start playing with others. We ended up informally forming a pod with them and have continued to do many activities together. As moms, we began to pray for our kids, as well as generational and inheritance issues and our neighborhood.

As Isaiah 55:9 says God's ways are higher than our ways and His thoughts are higher than my thoughts. Another example during Covid was that God moved me down to Laguna Beach to be a block away from my parents in 2004. At the height of ministry with *TheCall* and an invitation to be ordained in 2003, I had a dream to focus on my family, especially my dad, which I will share more about later. Since I lived around the corner we had almost daily visits over to my parent's home. I could do all the shopping and errands while my daughter stayed with my parents in the midst of the quarantine. We could also provide interaction for my parents especially as my dad's decline with Alzheimer's.

A third source of community care blossomed organically. Some of my neighbors pulled out chairs so that we could chat in a socially distanced way. My daughter and I lovingly called it Courtyard Thursday's. If Covid had not happened then I would not have recalibrated to focus so intentionally on my family, neighbors or oikos. Previously, I was focused on things nationally and globally, but I was shifted to my family and neighborhood. One of my single mother's friends chose to quit a top medical director position to stay with her young daughter. After the year she said, "Doctors are replaceable, but moms aren't."

God also recalibrated me to make Annalisa my priority. She knows that she is second only to Jesus, while I am unmarried. I had to reevaluate my commitments including the wonderful boards I was privileged to serve on. I began seeing what Paul said in 1 Corinthians 4:15 "For though you might have ten thousand instructors in Christ, yet you do not have many fathers (mothers)".

Through Annalisa, I learned about God's love even if I couldn't do anything for Him. My need to prove myself to my parents and in extension to God was finally given a death blow. I saw my imperfect love for this little one who in the world's eyes, did so little for me. How much more does our Heavenly Father love us?

Beginnings

I am now going to go back to the beginning of my life and into my family history which will give more context into the significance of my journey as a woman vanguard. As I am transitioning into this next season, I will elaborate how I am coming full circle in many ways.

God has been unpacking what He meant by legacy and inheritance that was spoken and prophesied to me years ago. One of the main messages of my life has to do with dealing with the Curses of three-four generations so that the blessings can flow down 1,000 generations from Exodus 34:7 and Deuteronomy 7:9. I knew very little about my family history until my Masters in Social Work class 1986, where we were to do and write about our family's genogram. When I asked my Mom, she told me to make it up. I had to talk with my grandmother in broken Mandarin Chinese, since her main languages were Taiwanese, Japanese and some Mandarin Chinese and mine was English with some Mandarin. I had heard that my maternal grandfather had died while my mom was two or three years old but knew very little about my extended family. The genogram stirred up lots of unresolved issues for my Mom that she did not want to tell me about. It wasn't until 2013 when I talked with my uncle (my Mom's half brother) and then went on a journey to visit my "roots" in Taiwan that I got a fuller understanding of my mom's side of the family. I felt God was leading me to go according to Exodus 20:5-6 to break the curses off our generational line of three and four generations so that the blessings could flow down 1000 generations. I saw patterns in my generation and my mom's generation that I did not want to reap or pass down. God orchestrated every step of my impromptu trip. I was able to go to the family home and office my Mom lived in ReiFang when she was very young, the HouTong coal mine, the marker at YamingShan National Park, and the schools she went to. I was able to make an album for my Mom which included pictures when she was growing up as well as the pictures from my trip.

The most amazing thing was that after the first week of going around to places with my relatives, I prayed and said it would be great if I could connect with two amazing intercessors that were from Taiwan, but living in Israel and Beijing, China, Mei Ching Liu, and Rebecca Lin. I asked my relatives to go to a meeting at ELIM Christian bookstore that has a Tabernacle of David (TOD) Prayer Room run by Miriam Chang. In the midst of a typhoon I saw them there. Both were not supposed to still be in Taiwan but had extended their stay that week. During the meeting I thought it would be really good to go through deliverance with Taiwanese Chinese people who understood the spirits that are in my family line. One of the women there knew of a deliverance minister who came and walked all of us through deliverance before embarking on the journey. They felt led to go with me to the key places connected to my family. We had a powerful time praying at each location.

My mom was born in 1938 in Taiwan during a tumultuous time. The island had been controlled by the Japanese since the first Sino-

Japanese war in 1895 until 1945 during WWII when it was given to the Republic of China (ROC) by the Allied forces. My mom is from a Taiwanese Chinese family that has lived for seven-nine generations in Taiwan. During the Japanese occupation of Taiwan, my grandfather and his older brother worked for the Japanese managing a coal mine. At that time coal was considered black gold. Later the Japanese gave up the coal mine thinking that there wasn't any more. My grandfather and his older brother bought the coal mine and found a new vein, which eventually made it the largest coal mine in Taiwan. The coal from the mine powered the north part of the island and the railroads. Later, part of the YangMingSan National Park was "given" to Chiang Kai Shek as well as a home and hot spring to the Vice President by my mom's family when the Nationalist army escaped from China to Taiwan.

During the turmoil in Taiwan in the early 1940's suspicion raged. My grandfather and his brothers involved in the coal mine were questioned, beaten and imprisoned because someone in the company told the Japanese that my family had connections to China. My grandfather had visited Hangzhou, China once in his early 20s for vacation, but had no ties. Nevertheless, he was beaten to death. My mom recounted that at two or three years of age, she looked up and told my grandmother that she saw an image of her dad and said goodbye. My great grandfather died shortly after because of the stress of my grandfather being beaten to death.

From 1945 when Taiwan was returned to the ROC by the Allied forces there were many conflicts between the "Wai Shen Ren" (Mainland China born) and "Ben Shen Ren" (Taiwan Born). Many Taiwanese were massacred starting from February 28, 1947, with estimates between 18,000-28,000. My Mom recounts coming to their home where her older brothers were hiding. Some people were hung in the streets as examples. She shared recently about a classmate's father, a nice doctor. He was being taken and killed. I can't imagine the trauma that my mom experienced and yet survived even thrived through this experience.

My maternal grandmother was the second wife. The first wife died in childbirth. The first wife had three boys and four girls, but the third boy and youngest two girls were given to another family member when she died. My mom was the older of two girls from my grandmother. Later there was a lot of vying for my grandmother's shares of the family company and coal mine by the oldest two brothers. Girls in the culture were not thought of to receive shares. In listening to some of my cousins, I could see a pattern of stolen inheritances continuing and causing major breeches in families.

My mom recently recounted how my grandmother was quite entrepreneurial and resourceful as a single mother of two young kids and older stepchildren, despite all that she had been through. She moved the family from the coal mining town and bought and built a number of properties in Taipei. My mom also shared that her dad's mother who had bound feet was also quite resourceful, running the home, building a house, and also selling things.

My mom was very studious and was accepted at top schools, Taipei's First Girls School (BeiYi Nyu) and Taiwan National University (TaiDa). My mom still keeps in touch with her high school and college friends that are both in Taiwan and America.

In 1999, God led me to take a four-month Sabbatical from ministry, (pioneering and running ALPHA at *Harvest Rock Church*) running and working as a Licensed Clinical Social Worker at the *Maternal Child*

Immunology Clinic (MCIC), the pediatric prenatal HIV clinic at UCLA. I remember in a time of worship and drumming, I felt God tell me to do Chinese brush painting in China. I was wondering how I could find out about any classes since Google was not around yet and I did not read Chinese. At the beginning of my sabbatical, God led me to a two-week intensive on inner healing training through *Elijah House* in San Diego, California. I stayed with my friend Monique at her aunt's house, Jean Shen. God orchestrated my time there because she was a Prophetic Chinese Brush Painter. She invited me to sit in on her class, where I overheard a couple of her students saying that they were going to go on a month intensive Chinese Brush Painting course in China. It was after my commitments in Malaysia and Singapore and before I had to go back to work. Equally amazing was that of all places in China it was in my Dad's home town of Hangzhou. Later I found out it was during the 50th anniversary of the establishment of the PRC. I could not have arranged for anything more perfect if I tried. I arranged to stay in my own room which gave me flexibility to meet with my relatives on my dad's side that were still in China. During the day I went to the Chinese brush painting classes, which were translated into English. Then in the evening, after all my classmates who were over the age of 65 went to sleep, I would go visit my relatives who would share stories about my paternal grandmother.

My dad, Li-San Hwang was born in 1935, in a family village, Hwang-Di, near Hangzhou, China prior to the Second Sino-Japanese war of 1937-1945. In context it was the Chinese theater of the Pacific theater of WWII. A significant event in the war between China and Japan was the Nanjing Massacre of December 13, 1937- January 1938. He grew up amid air raids which burned villages and left people in fear of their life. My father recounts that after the raids, even though they were rather well off by the village standards, there were times all they had to eat was burned rice.

His father, my grandfather, was a military leader, rising to major general in the Chinese National Army of the Kuomintang (KMT - Chinese Nationalist Party) under Chiang Kai-shek. He was often away for long periods of time during periods of war with the Japanese and later with the Communist.

My dad's mother, my grandmother, Yu Xiang Jun was the first wife from the next village nearby, Yu-Di. She had three boys, my dad being the third. The oldest, was quite a bit older, died when my dad was young. He remembers that he had to go with his mom and brother to stay at a "temple" which was really cold, instead of going to a hospital or medical facility. He believes that if he received proper medical care he would have survived. His second brother died very young so he does not know anything about him.

My great grandfather and grandmother lived with them as well. My dad remembers when he was really young, he would stand on his tippy toes and his grandfather would give him a little wine or something to eat. When my dad was a boy, my grandfather brought a city "wife" to live in the same home. My grandfather and the city wife had one daughter in China and later several children in Taiwan. My dad grew up with his mom being mistreated and would at times save rice so his mom could eat. Since he was from the village wife, many times he was cold and slept with one of the servants.

The home my dad grew up in is still standing and has recently been refurbished and turned into a community center with funds contributed by my dad.

After the Sino-Japanese War my grandfather had been in charge of Shanghai port in China. My dad recounts that a gold shipper had been thankful that my grandfather had not extorted him. He offered to help my grandfather's family escape out of China during Mao and the Communists takeover of China in 1949. My dad was the only boy at the time. The village wife was given the choice to stay with his mom in China or escape with his father, the city wife, and their daughter. In tears he gave my dad the handkerchief that he had saved up to give to his mom. She told him to go because there was nothing for him in China.

His mom was left in China to care for her in-laws who did not treat her well amid the Communist takeover. Her former husband was a military leader of the opposing army. My dad, at age 14, never saw his mother again. She died in 1964, the year of my birth. China would not open up until after Mao died in 1976 and Deng Xiaoping, launched the Open Door Policy in 1978.

He was allowed to come back because the city wife had not had a boy yet. Only recently has my Dad recounted the harrowing journey from ZhouShan, an island near Ningbo where the Nationalist army retreated from to go on a small boat to Taiwan. He recounts the large waves which caused most to be sick and the putrid smells. Then upon arriving in Taiwan his immigration records state that his stepmother was his mom. My dad's family lost almost everything in the escape. His father who had been a military leader was unfortunately aligned to the son of Chiang Kai Shek that did not come into power.

Dad worked hard while in Taiwan hoping to be able to help his mother. At 14 he had to not only raise himself, but later on help financially because his father and the rest of the family were in Taiwan. He excelled in school and went to the prestigious *TaiDa University* in Taipei, Taiwan studying Civil Engineering. He wanted to build bridges.

During his senior year, he met a scared freshman on a bus going to the University during finals week on January 22, 1958. The young woman was panicked because she forgot her student ID, which she needed to take the exams. Dad overheard her discussing this with her friend, and responded casually to have the friend vouch for her and she would be fine. Neither knowing the name of the other, my dad was smitten. When class started up again, my dad who rode a bike would go around her bus stop to try to meet her again. Finally, when he saw her, he rode his bike over and blurted out "my name is Li-San, what's yours?"

My mom, a real pioneer, excelled in school and was able to go to the top girls' high school in Taiwan, BeiYi Nyu (Taipei First Girls School) and then Tai Da University (National Taiwan University). When she met my dad, they began a "politically and socially" incorrect relationship in Taiwan. Dad was known as a "WaiShen Ren" foreign born from China, while Mom was considered a "BenShen Ren" local person having been in Taiwan for seven or eight generations. Financially, my father's family had lost everything after the escape from China, while my Mom's family was one of the wealthiest families in Taiwan. To put it in context the division was worse than black and white in America during the civil rights time. Thankfully my mom's mom felt like he was a good man and let them get engaged and even helped Dad with his plane ticket to America, so he did not have to take a ship.

My parents were engaged on February 22, 1960, in Taiwan, before my dad left for America. He was going to study at Michigan State for his

Masters degree in September of 1960. For two years they communicated with hundreds of letters across the ocean, until my mom graduated and was able to join my dad in America in September 1962. Amazingly, my dad was able to solve a project that the University had been working on for 10 years and was now due. His professor wanted him to stay at Michigan State for his PhD, but when my dad said he wanted to go to Caltech in Pasadena, CA he fully supported him. In fact, my dad's English was poor, so his professor wrote to a top professor at Caltech and said, "I would take him if I were you." Dad got into Caltech without really applying!

My Dad, who had recently learned to drive, drove across the country to pick up my Mom who was flying from Taiwan to LAX airport in Los Angeles, CA. My mom and dad were married in a small chapel in Pasadena on 12/22/1962 with people my parents had recently met in CA. The person that gave my mom away at the wedding was a Chinese professor at Caltech that my dad had just met. They were the first of their family and friends to pioneer in the new land of America. Years later I found out about the Chinese Exclusionary Act of 1882 which prohibited the immigration and naturalization of Chinese immigrants. It was lifted in name only in the 1940s during WWII because they wanted the Chinese as allies against the Japanese. It was fully lifted in 1968 with the Immigration Naturalization Act. When I learned about this I was struck that I was a citizen being born in 1964, before my parents could be citizens. Not only that I was born in the bridge year between the generation of the Boomers and Busters.

I was born in Pasadena, CA as a Caltech baby. My dad was in the throes of his PhD Comprehensive exams as I was coming into this world. My early years were centered on Caltech. One of my earliest memories was around the age of five, when I was being evacuated from our apartment, because a neighbor accidentally fell asleep with a cigarette that lit her mattress on fire. Not long after we moved to a new home at the base of the mountains of Pasadena, which my parents kept for 40 years.

Growing up in the 60's and 70's, Pasadena had very few families of Asian descent. The schools I went to were also almost exclusively white. Our secluded neighborhood in the mountain/canyon area of Pasadena had one Hispanic family with two girls, Liz and Susan, one Black family with one girl, Gina, and my family which was Chinese American. I remember walking down the sloped street with Liz, Susan, Gina and a white friend Casey and thinking we were a rainbow coalition. This was part of the foundation for my passion to see the bridge between ethnic groups.

My parents were always very kind and respectful to all races and looked to the content of their character. One time the professor who gave my mom away at their wedding came over to our home in the morning, when they were supposed to come over in the evening. The couple had come over to see if my parents wanted to disinvite them because their daughter was going to marry a black man. My parents advised their friends that if their daughter and the man love each other, that they should support the marriage. I believe this came from what my parents went through in their own relationship even though they were both of Chinese descent.

In high school I began to volunteer at an organization called Villa Esperanza. They worked with kids and adults who were developmentally delayed either with Down syndrome or less common autism. This experience made a tremendous impact on my life because education was "god" in my family, but these kids who would not even make it to first grade, were so sweet and loving. These Down syndrome kids taught me the value of each person; this opened my heart up to Jesus because I realized that education couldn't be God and that there must be more. I believe this realization that every person is valuable opened my heart to give my life to Jesus as savior when I was a freshman in high school. Later on in high school, my best friend, Karen and I worked together to develop the Community Service program at our high school. As Heads of Community service, we researched and interviewed many of the places in Pasadena that students could volunteer at and made a manual with opportunities and commitments.

Going into Pomona College in 1982, I was conflicted by my desire to change the world and my families focus on math and sciences. I started college as a physics/engineering major, but ended up graduating in cultural anthropology and public policy. I was very involved in the InterVarsity Christian Fellowship and as a relatively new Christian was a small group leader, then on the Executive team as Communications Coordinator. During the summer after my junior year, I was a short-term missionary in Taiwan at the *Mustard Seed Orphanage* near Taipei where my Mom grew up and where my dad went to University. I was so impacted there that I considered full time missions work. As part of my time in Taiwan, we were able to see some of the other Mustard Seed ministries, like the nurses training school for the aboriginal people and a leper colony. The most impacting part of my time was when a white South African OMF missionary took the short termers to the leper colony in Taiwan. I had read about lepers in Taiwan, but did not realize leprosy still existed. We went to visit the residents who had leprosy and then went to their chapel service. To this day I am so impacted by the black South African who was preaching about the Good Samaritan and sharing how Jesus healed his hatred towards whites, by the white South African missionary reaching out and serving him in of all places Taiwan at a leper colony. Jesus is truly a healer of the racial divide and the human heart.

Returning to college I wanted to be a part of a community that could bring transformation. I wrote up a whole plan on setting up community centers in underserved areas, where older people could mentor and provide apprenticeships for those who may not have as many opportunities as I had. I also applied for a Masters in Social Work program at UCLA, because I figured if I was going to impact policies I needed hands-on work. On the surface my parents were not happy about this, but it was better than becoming a missionary. Looking back, I realize that my dad was worried about how I would support myself and especially with all that happened to his mom. My Mom on the other hand had always been interested in helping the underserved especially with education.

When I went to graduate school at UCLA in 1986, I thought I would learn tools to change people's lives and the world, but I was quickly awakened. I read about the Settlement Houses, which were community centers at the turn of the century, but that was long gone. Simultaneously, I started going to a new, small, mostly Asian American Vineyard type church in Alhambra, CA. Many of the people attending were current or former young leaders of college ministries like *Asian American Christian Fellowship* and College ministries at Chinese churches in the area. The church was led by a couple who were gifted prophetically and apostolically. In fact we heard stories of the parents of the wife, Jean Liang, who were blacklisted by name and had to leave China. They were the leaders of a Christian campus movement like *Inter Varsity* in China. They saw people healed and deliverance and other great signs and wonders. I remember one story where her

Mom was given the gift of tongues in a Chinese dialect that she didn't know and kept it. They were located right next to the high school and had developed a hang out place in the basement of the church for students. They were a referral source for *Young Life* and *Youth For Christ* as well as *Focus on the Family*. I was seeing lives transformed, people who had been abused as children getting healed and broken marriages restored. In contrast to Social Work School I got a glimpse of how a community could bring transformation in lives and society. It seemed like a dream come true.

I began to devote more time at the church and by the summer after watching a video of food being multiplied in the poor town of Juarez, Mexico. Four of us who were in graduate programs at UCLA, USC, Fuller, and *Rosemead School of Psychology* all dropped out and moved into the Training Center. It was to be a summer training center to equip us to impact communities locally and globally, but ended up becoming an ongoing community.

Unfortunately, because of brokenness in the leaders, the community became a cult in terms of control. It was also in the midst of the "shepherding movement" where there was so much control. Discipleship was taken into an abusive extreme. Coming from a social work background and my gut sense, I questioned inside what was going on, but because I was a relatively new Christian and they had come from a multigenerational Christian family, I assumed they were right. I believe that since Jean Liang's parents were so busy traveling around China doing ministry, that Jean and her siblings had wounds in their heart that came out on us. Her parents had put ministry above family, where from scripture God worked through the family to do ministry.

Though painful, going through the time in the "community" helped establish that God's order was God first, family and then ministry. I was so touched when I asked my five year old daughter if she knew why I loved her so much. Her response was "because God loves you first". Such wisdom, if we don't know God's love and have Him first, then it is difficult to try to have other things try to satisfy us.

On a trip with the community to Yosemite, I was wrestling with God. I went away to a secluded area and God showed me a picture of a nice little house. He then tilted the house up and showed me the foundation. It had cracks in it. Then He said that I could leave it as is and I would be okay, or He could deal with the cracks. Not knowing what it would entail, I asked Him to deal with the cracks. It has been a journey over the last 30 years for God to restore those cracks.

I remember my parents coming to see me during that time while I was working in a print shop at the *U.S. Center for World Missions*. They were devastated. Here, their daughter who had graduated from Pomona College was working at a print shop. I did not want them to think that the community wanted to take all my money; I gave my parents back everything, my trust fund, car, computer, credit card and checking account. I was also briefly disowned by my parents. They didn't know what else to do with me.

One of the days I was doing my weekly shopping for the community, I had a little boy from China going with me. Since I was doing lots of errands, I thought I would drop by Victory Park, near where I grew up, a place I often rode my bike to. As he was sliding I noticed a few other Asian kids. I asked them what school they were attending. They told me they were homeschooled, so I asked them to introduce me to their mom, since the community was interested in homeschooling. I began to talk with their mom, Sue Ann. She told me they had moved from Maryland a few years earlier and had planted a church. She gave me a tract of her husband, Che Ahn, with a picture of a Korean man with long hair. Little did I know that was a divine appointment for a relationship that continues to this day.

I went back to the community and told Jean that I had met a pastor's wife that was homeschooling. There were so many amazing things going on, but at the same time I was often sent away to a balcony, a different house and eventually to a motel to repent for days. The final incident happened Labor Day weekend 1988, when I heard a cousin of a friend of mine who was taken out of the community by her family had died in a freak pool accident. I was later accused of manipulating for attention. I was sent to a motel to repent, but did not know what I was repenting for. I was then brought before the community for public confession. I did not believe I had done anything wrong and God had not shown me anything. They sent me home to my parents and basically said I had a seared conscience. Later, I would understand that if I had a seared conscience I wouldn't even have cared.

When I went to my parents' home, they did not know what to do with me. They did not want me to go back. They sent me to my brother in Berkeley, where I had a friend, Suzanne Jue (Shimanuki), a friend from summer classes at CAL Berkeley. She had been IVCF exec at Berkeley, while I was IVCF Exec at Pomona College and we had kept in touch throughout college calling every other week on landlines. She took me in. I slept and slept. In the community, we were up for early morning and late night prayer meetings, except while I was sent to repent. Physically I was exhausted with sleep deprivation. Emotionally, I was clinically depressed. Relationally, all my relationships had been severed. Spiritually, I was told I had walked away from God and had a seared conscience.

My mom then met me in Berkeley, and we went to Yosemite. I remember very little of it, except for a point of familiarity. God knew I needed to go back to the place where He had spoken to me.

Months earlier I had been with the community and God had given me the vision of my life as a house and its foundation. I did not know what I was in for. God was true to His word; he was taking down my house and relaying my foundation. He did not want my foundation to be what I could do for Him or to work for Him. He wanted me to solidly be founded as His daughter and to know His love. It wasn't until I had my daughter that I really had it established in my heart.

Going back to my parents home the first month I slept and watched TV almost every day. I remember looking out the window one day in October and seeing a butterfly fly right to the window. I felt God speak to me and say that he was transforming me into that butterfly. The transformation was not based on what I could do, but what He did in me and created me for. The same week, my friend from Berkeley called me up and asked me what I needed; she had a few thousand dollars extra. What was crazy was that she was preparing to go as a missionary to Kenya and she was asking me if I needed money and not $20. I didn't know what to say. I said maybe I could use it for a car. She said she would get back to me. She talked with her fiancé and dad, and then called me back. She said why I didn't borrow her car while she was gone for her two-year assignment. I was floored, she was letting me borrow her brand new car and I had nothing to give in return.

During this time Jean sent a four-page single spaced letter saying that I could come back if I repented. I called to arrange to pick up my few remaining things. I went there and repented for what I knew was sin. Jean said when you repent you can come back. I left there and went to the nearby park that I was often sent to. There God spoke to me and said I had repented and did not have to go back again. I cried and felt released.

I had also been visiting a Vineyard church in Arcadia and this little church was pastored by the Dad of the kids I had met in the park months before. I would go to church after it started and leave before it ended because I didn't want to taint anybody, thinking I had a seared conscience and was an immoral believer. Not only that, the church was at the US Center for World Mission Campus, where I had ridden my bike as a kid, worked at the Institute for Chinese Studies as an internship in College, and worked at Panda Prints, the print and t-shirt shop while at the Community. God knew I needed a stake of familiarity as he was relaying my foundation. That Sunday in October 1988, I actually allowed someone to sit next to me at service and rededicated my life to Jesus. It was also the Sunday that Pastor Che spoke about a church plant to the Philippines that did not go well. I was so impacted that he took full responsibility of going ahead of God as a new church trying to plant a church. I cried seeing a pastor take ownership of the blame instead of putting it on others. That Sunday was the first time I allowed someone to sit next to me. A black woman, Michelle Sorey sat down next to me and we talked after the service. She invited me to a small group that was led by a pastor named Lou Engle and his wife Terese at the home of Ellen Napoleon, soon to be Flores. I remember the first small group I went to. They had an ice breaker question saying where we were from. People went around and said, Kenya, Burma,

Philippines … then many different states, but when they got to me, I responded "Pasadena", Terese said "no where are you from, I said Pasadena", then she said "where were you born," I responded "Pasadena". Then she asked where my parents were from, I joked "Pasadena, but then said Taiwan and China". I loved being in a multicultural church environment.

I went to the new members' class the following week and Pastor Che talked about the church and its core values. At the end he asked if we had any questions. People asked about children's ministry and other "safe questions". God spoke to me and told me to ask about women in ministry. I did not want to ask the question because I knew the answer and after being in the community I never wanted to lead again. I wrote down the question and thought I would ask afterwards. God said ask now, or it will be a stumbling block for you. I argued internally because I also did not like speaking up in groups after what had happened in the community. When I was in kindergarten I would get in trouble for answering too much. I finally raised my hand and tried to couch it as gently as possible. I said "I noticed all the pictures of the apostolic team and the pastors are all men, what is your view of women in ministry". Pastor Che answered, "we believe women can teach the children's ministry and women's ministry, but do not believe that women can lead men. No one will agree with everything and it is whether you are called to this church or not". I was so relieved, because I never wanted to lead again. I continued to get more and more connected to the church, Abundant Life and small groups as well as babysitting Pastor Che and Lou's kids.

Right after the Tiananmen Square Incident, a family returned from Asia. I was introduced to them in the small group and quickly built a friendship. They had been leaders in IVCF as I had been, during their college years. They were mission minded and wanted to see friendship evangelism, discipleship and transformation as missions. They were sent out quickly to lead a group which I joined. As part of the cell group model, groups were being planted. One of the single guys, Stephan and I were sent out to lead the first group with a single woman as a co leader. Complications arose when he felt like I was the one for him. After a period of time I ended up as the leader of a group with men and women. The question that I was prompted to ask at the new members class became prophetic and again I was a "Vanguard".

Pastors Che and Lou were rocked by a gathering in Argentina with Che's mentor Professor C. Peter Wagner, Cindy Jacobs and Ed Silvoso. I remember Pastor Che coming back and repenting for sectarianism with the fruit of repentance. He raised an offering and then called pastors of churches in the area of different sizes, denominations, and ethnic groups to meet for lunch, share and repent and give them a check. I believe that was the seeds for his invitation to be part of *Love LA*, *March for Jesus* and eventually *TheCall.*

Within that same week I found an ad for an after school and preschool director at a YWCA in North Hollywood, CA. After looking for weeks at jobs working with abused children, God had said the week before not to take that type of job since I had been abused. This job was to play with the kids. I went and was offered the job. I was to be director, van driver, teacher, counselor for this small program. Wow, how healing!

I loved it, because I was given the freedom to create. I raised interns who had friends or relatives killed in gang incidents. I had written about community centers in college. I also saw orphanages and training schools during my Taiwan mission's trip. I wanted to give the kids experiences that the kids would not normally have. I was the van driver also so I brought the kids weekly to care for them and ride ponies at a nearby stable and ice skating rink. The summer program was my highlight. I set up a weekly themed curriculum that alternated between culture (Native American, Hispanic, African American, Asian American and Caucasian) and nature (Air, Water/Sea, Land, Animals). We went to the beach weekly as well as horseback riding and ice skating. Then I added museums, zoos, aquariums, Hollywood Bowl and other fun learning experiences. Many of the kids and youth volunteers had never even been to the beach. We incorporated food, dance, arts and crafts, stories and music from different cultures. I could have continued there, but my Masters program at UCLA was waiting.

When I left I was broken. I was back in my parents' home after having briefly been disowned. I did not have a car, computer, credit card, or checking account. I had given back everything to my parents. Grad school was starting up, but I had dropped out a year earlier. The Dean of Admissions, Terrance Roberts, one of the Little Rock Nine, told me that if I waited a year, he would get me a scholarship. Praise God for his wisdom.

God orchestrated everything. Right before I returned to the second year of my social work program, I "divinely" bumped into a person from my small high school (40 people in my class), who was going into the same 2nd year of the Social Work program at UCLA. She was also a Christian, so on my first day back at UCLA she introduced me to eight other active Christians out of our cohort of 80 who were strong Christians. This was quite a contrast from my first year where I was the only active Christian. One of the people she introduced me to was Terri Watanabe (later Sayama). She had been involved with the *Asian*

American Christian Fellowship in college and knew some of the leaders who were in the community.

Once again God was giving me a stake of familiarity. She and I became fast friends and thesis partners. We wrote the first report on Unaccompanied Minors from Taiwan or informally known as Parachute Kids. We arranged to talk with teachers, pastors, police officers, counselors and any other people interfacing with this population of kids as well as the former minors who were now at least 18. These under 14 year old kids were dropped off by their parents because of the political situation between Taiwan and China in the 80's and 90's. Terri and I would pray before and after each interview. We even won an award from the Taiwanese newspaper for our thesis.

After graduation in 1990, I was hired at the Chinese Service Center to see if I could pioneer a program to work with the "Parachute children". I did a lot of networking, but could not get a grant before the finances ran out. Terri started working as a Social Worker for LA County, Department of Health Service. She called me up and told me there was a position open as a Social Worker in the HIV Test Site. This was at the height of the HIV/AIDS epidemic. Rumors were still going around that it could be transmitted in the air.

Here I was in 1990, a Christian, Chinese American, single, never had sex, woman being offered to work at a CDC HIV Counseling and Testing site. My initial response was how about if we switched positions. My focus had been dealing with child abuse, but I didn't think I was ready to deal with the AIDS crisis. Not wanting to work there I put out a "fleece". I was going to talk to 3 people that I knew about it, and knew the third, my parents, would say no, so I would be safe. First, my cell group leader said yes, and then pastor Che said yes and finally when I asked my Mom, her response was "you should do it, and then you can help the families". Oh no, God was confirming for me to go. God also reminded me of when I went to the leper colony in Taiwan during college and said AIDS is the leprosy of today. I need Christians to touch those who no one else wants to touch to bring My Light into the darkness.

I began to read everything on HIV/AIDS, homosexuality, IV drug use and anything related. I remember reading the book "How Will I Tell My Mother", co authored by Steve Arterburn. It was the story of his brother who was a Christian, went into the homosexual lifestyle, came out and then was in the hospital with a full blown AIDS diagnosis and had only a few months to live. His first thought was how I will tell my mother! The amazing thing was that his family and church did not reject him, but came around him and walked him through until he died. He died right after finishing the book with his brother. I also read the book, *And the Band Played On,* which journeyed from patient 0 through the initial stages of the AIDS epidemic. God asked me to be His Light (my name means Light).

As a Social Worker, I was able to be a pioneer or vanguard in HIV. Pastor Che asked me for information and actually preached about HIV/AIDS at church. Then he referred people to me for testing and counseling. Working in HIV, God showed me how the enemy would use HIV to enter and take over our own T cells that fight off foreign invaders to become HIV copy machines. What an analogy of what the enemy does to enter and invade our minds, emotions, relationship and churches. Is that what we are dealing with now with this 2019 Virus?

God put me in the test site to educate, reach out and support those who were fearful and even those infected by HIV. I learned so much from my patients, like Sarah who forgave everyone even the person who gave her HIV and "friends" who betrayed her and told her high profile employer she was HIV. She told me she didn't want anything to keep her from the kingdom of God. There was Norma whose family I supported from testing at the county to treatment. The family came to ALPHA and I had the privilege of baptizing the kids. One of them recently reached out to me on Facebook. Tracy was one who impacted so many and was profiled in a photo book on the faces of AIDS.

I believed that out of that place UCLA where AIDS was first diagnosed that my patients would be healed or raised from the dead. I remember one evening during my prayer watch in the 24/7 house of prayer at Harvest Rock Church I was praying for my patients, especially one little girl who had just died of AIDS. Every organ shut down that day. I felt impressed to walk out to the main sanctuary at Mott Auditorium. Right when I walked out an African woman I have never seen before or since began recounting how she was in her home country and a woman was carried into her home on her death bed with AIDS. The woman died in her home. She prayed and nothing happened. She prayed again, nothing happened. She began telling the Lord if He doesn't, she is quitting. She told God "You have to resurrect this woman because it will not look good if reports come out that a woman dies in a praying woman's house." As a Social Worker I was to see the girl's mother the next day. She was a Jehovah Witness and was at the cemetery. With this testimony, I was emboldened to pray for resurrection. I had a couple of friends come with me; one even brought a sandwich and banana. I shared a little bit of the story with the girl's mother and asked if it would be okay for me to pray for her. In a little room at the cemetery with the little girl's brother watching we prayed for life to come back to her. She was going to be taken back to UCLA for an autopsy. We prayed for 20-30 minutes until the ambulance arrived. We left and went back to church where the first Harvest International Ministries conference was taking place and Mahesh Chauvda was speaking. He had been talking about raising people from the dead and right when we walked in he said that one day you will be going to morgues and cemeteries and praying for people who have just died. My friends and I began laughing because it was not one day but that day.

I learned a lot about infectious diseases during my 11 years working in HIV/AIDS for the County of LA, Department of Health Services and UCLA Medical Center. In fact when I worked for the Dept of Health Services (DHS), we were a CDC test site focusing on epidemiology for HIV. I also worked with the Medical Director and Nursing Director to help train nurses and set up test sites all over the North county of LA. Then I worked as a trainer on HIV testing for the LA County Office of HIV/AIDS.

At the beginning of *Harvest Rock Church* in 1994, I was very active in the renewal meetings and then the cell groups. When I returned from an impromptu short term mission trip with a group called Champions in Taiwan, Brent Johnston and the worship leader John Lee asked if I would pray about co-leading a cell group with them. It started off with a bang and often had 50-60 people attending. We began with many leaders, some who had much more experience than I did. One day God said that I was one of four of the women generals. I was a bit intimidated, because they had far more experience. I then had a dream of my co leader, Brett Johnson and I equally leading in preparation for a battle. I stepped back to defer to Brett, thinking that I should do that because of what was taught about male headship. He had to step over into my place and then a whole section of our troop was slaughtered.

The Lord said this time it is practice, but in the future in a real battle, the troop would really be slaughtered. I repented to the Lord for my wrong deferral and abdication of my place in leadership.

Our group was amazing and after a few months we began planting groups. I ended up leading a group that changed almost quarterly as we sent out more groups. God impressed me with three words, that we were a "Showcase, a Diamond, and a Launching pad". I learned a lot about how to allow each group sent out to have its own identity depending on who was in the group. It also included those remaining.

After a few years of cell leading, I was asked to head up ALPHA for new and non-believers, a new program from *Holy Trinity Brampton* in England. During that time Pastor Che announced from the pulpit in the New Year's message that I was going to be ordained. I would have been the first woman at *Harvest Rock Church* ordained. After a while nothing was said of it, and then I heard through a leader that the pastors' wives were not in agreement with me being the first woman. While running ALPHA, God told me to step down or He would make me step down. I told the pastor over me, but he did not tell the rest of the pastors. I finally wrote a letter to all of the pastors saying that I was resigning and taking a 4 month sabbatical from work at UCLA and ministry. All I was doing was volunteering, but one of the pastors' wives thought I was on full time paid staff. In actuality I had a full time job at UCLA. I am thankful that God had me step down when He did because he wanted to further clean out and heal areas of my life and the cracks in my foundation. Not only on a personal level but the church went through a major sifting where about 50 of the middle layer of leadership and almost 200 people left for one reason or another. Many of them were friends of mine. If I had not stepped down and gone on sabbatical to Asia, I may not have been able to step back in when I was asked to answer the call to *TheCall* the following year.

Wow, today is September 2, 2021; 21 years after *TheCall DC* on September 2, 2000. I had been on Sabbatical from work at UCLA and from ministry. God told me to go to TheCall DC and He would show me why later. Pastor Pam Wright asked me if I wanted to room with her family. ABBA Father knew that I needed to be part of a family at this historic gathering.

In October 2000 after *TheCall DC*, while I was still on sabbatical from ministry, and still working at *UCLA Medical Center*, I was asked to coordinate a conference for *Harvest Rock Church.* The conference was in a month and most of the leaders were exhausted from *TheCall.* Only the speakers were finalized, everything else was up in the air and it was projected to be the largest conference with about 5000 attendees. When I prayed God said to do it. One of the first nights God downloaded a structure and manual for the organization and volunteers. I felt the Lord based things from the interaction between Jethro and Moses in Exodus 18 and especially in 18:25 "And Moses chose able men out of all Israel, and made them heads over the people: rulers of Thousands, rulers of hundreds, rulers of fifties and ruler of tens." He showed me to find established leaders and since as a church we already had cell groups, I got approval to talk with all the cell leaders to volunteer as a group over sections of what needed to be done. They already knew the people and I already knew the cell leaders. Quickly we were able to staff all the positions and had a master list of leaders over each section. I felt blessed to hear from the pastors that it was the most well organized conference they had.

Then in December when I went to drop off a Christmas gift to Lou, he said "Helena, will you help me with *TheCall*". What was going to be one gathering was about to become a movement. My thought was no, since I knew the people who worked on *TheCall DC* and I also knew they were wiped out. However, I responded I would pray about it. I was still working at *UCLA Medical Center* as a social worker in HIV.

The next week Lou asked me what I had heard. I told him I had not really heard much except when I was on AOL I saw an article on the contrast between the leadership styles of President Clinton and President Bush. In brief they said that President Clinton was charismatic and brought a team where he was the best, but President Bush was not as charismatic but he was bringing people who were much stronger than him and he was just bringing them together. Lou said between Che and he, we have too much charisma; we just need someone to bring it together. I still couldn't give him an answer.

Then I receive a call from Pastor Che's assistant that he wants me to meet him for an interview on Christmas Eve. When I met with Pastor Che, it wasn't an interview, but a job offer with a written job description. I told him I had not heard from God yet.

That same week I found out about a week-long Vertical Leap (business entrepreneurial skills) Training the Trainer camp with Al and Hattie Hollingsworth between Christmas and New Years Day at their retreat center AlHatties. I felt led to go to pray about my decision, but it was already December 22 and I was scheduled to work. As a long shot I mentioned it to my supervisor at the medical center, who never gave people off at that time if it had not been scheduled way in advance. Her response was yes and why don't I take it as an educational leave, so I was even paid to go. I was going to an all-black training so the first person I saw there was Fred Berry, who headed up mobilizing prayer in the African American community for *TheCall DC*. He then looks at me, not another person who had worked for TheCall, and says when is the next *TheCall*. Later in the week a woman I had never met who was a radio talk show host from Alabama said to me what large project are you working on? I tell her, I'm not working on any, but I am praying about one. She says "Good, take it and pray about everyone on it."

I went down from the mountain retreat center and met up with a college friend from Delaware to watch *Crouching Tiger, Hidden Dragon*. She asks me if her brother can come. Over dinner I found out he helped mobilize the Asian American community for prayer for *TheCall DC* and his wife was a controller for the *National Association of Evangelicals* (NAE). In less than one week, I felt like I received 3 confirmations to take the job. When I mentioned what happened to one of the other *Harvest Rock* Pastors, he said then you know that pastor Che is not your boss, pastor Lou is not your boss, but God is your boss.

On New Year's Eve, I went to *Harvest Rock's* New Year's Eve midnight prayer and wept before the Lord because many of my friends had left the church earlier in the year. I felt like I was making a choice to leave the friendships and step in *TheCall*. Right when the New Year struck, I went to wish pastor Che a Happy New Year. He asked me if I had an answer. I said "yes, I had an answer, and the answer was 'Yes'." So, on January 1, 2001, I started on *TheCall Hollywood*, which switched soon after to *TheCall Boston*. What was supposed to be one *TheCall* gathering morphed into 12 around the world, with seven in the U.S. in three years.

I worked two part time jobs, which were both full time jobs up until September 10, 2010. I was still contending for miracles with my patients at UCLA. Right before the first board meeting, Cindy Jacobs came with me to pray for a little girl with AIDS in the ICU. I learned a great lesson that day. When we finished praying she said the Lord wanted to take her home and heal her in heaven, because there was too much trauma here on earth. Her Mom had died of AIDS and the family had a history of gang violence and IV drug use.

I juggled between the two jobs, traveling each month to the East Coast preparing for *TheCall Boston* on September 22, 2001, and initiating mobilization for *TheCall NYC* the following year. I remember the Brazilians prophesied that it would look like it wouldn't happen, but it would. None of us knew what that would mean.

Signs were becoming clearer that I would be working on more than one *TheCall* gathering. We began scouting NYC after clear indication that we were to do a gathering in NYC, the financial center of America. I knew I would not be able to continue working in both jobs. I gave UCLA over a month's notice, with my last day being September 10, 2001. They gave me an incredible going away party and gave me a Waterford crystal clock.

From September 7-9, 2001, we had a key international board meeting with leaders to give guidance for TheCall Boston and future *TheCalls*. One of the prophets that I didn't know, Mickey Robinson came to me and said to me "you are leaving civilian duty and going into the military". He had no idea that I was leaving UCLA the next day, and had no idea what would transpire on the 11th.

As my assistant, Rochelle Burright and I drove pastor Che to the airport to go to the Marriott at the base of the Twin Towers in NYC for the kickoff of meetings with pastors across NYC we received a phone call from the pastor flying from DC to meet Che in NYC. He said have you heard that the tower was hit by a plane?" No, we were having a meeting on the way to the airport so the radio was off. We turned on the radio and heard the initial reports. Che, being very pragmatic, said well it's a good thing I'm flying into New Jersey. We arrive at the airport to be waved off and told that all air travel is grounded. It was surreal. When we got back we saw the planes hitting the towers and the towers collapsing. Praise God for pastor Che's commitment to take a Sabbath on Monday which postponed his flight to Tuesday morning, September 11, or he would have been in the towers.

TheCall Boston was now truly a solemn assembly. We began getting calls that bus loads of people were no longer going to go. In fact, it was unclear whether we were going to have the gathering since it was to be in the Boston City Hall Plaza, next to all the governmental buildings and where the first plane took off. What looked like we weren't going to have it was coming to pass. Praise God Attorney General Ashcroft, a Christian allowed us to continue.

Pastor Che, Lou and I as well as our team were some of the first to get back onto planes. In fact we were asked to spread out so that the plane would be balanced. What an historic day praying for 12-hours in a true solemn assembly.

As soon as Boston was over, I remember going into NYC where they said that ministries were eaten alive when outside ministries tried to do gatherings. The first gathering of pastors was supposed to be on September 11, 2001, at the Empire State Building, but it was postponed. With all that transpired with 9/11 things were shifted. Pastors of different streams who would normally not work together joined together for a week of blessing culminating with *TheCall NYC* on September 22, 2002, exactly nine months and 11 days from 9/11.

At our delayed first meeting of key networks of leaders in NYC at the *Empire State Building*, it was all male pastors and leaders except our *TheCall* team that included Rodlyn Park from Eagles Wings, Dixie Galloway from New York City Relief, and me. Women leaders were clearly needed to be a bridge between ministries.

As a woman leader in ministry at that time it was definitely a pioneering work. I was holding the balance between making a way for women, and also not coming at it as a feminist. We need men and women walking together to have a whole and healthy body. I was reminded of the dream God had given me when I was co leading a small group at the beginning of *Harvest Rock Church* in 1995. I had wrongly abdicated to male leadership.

Now in this larger situation I knew I needed to step up and not defer. Even though I was the National Director and eventually the Vice President of Operations, many male leaders would assume that I was Pastor Che or Lou's assistant. If I had stepped back and only been the assistant then what I was called to do would not be done. Many parts would have been bottlenecked with them.

Our first international *TheCall* gathering was in the Philippines with Jerome Ocampo of *Jesus Rev*. In October 2001. Cindy Jacobs had given a prophetic word with a number of specific words with fulfillments that ended up in national newspapers. In fact, the Philippines office of *Jesus Rev* was contacted by a major in the Philippines army on behalf of the generals because they had heard a copy of the recording. The gathering for me was significant because

Pastor Che asked to wash my feet as a spiritual daughter. I wept and wept when he did that.

In 2003 during my time at *TheCall*, I was offered again to become a pastor at *Harvest Rock Church*. This was about seven years after the first time when Pastor Che talked about ordaining me as the first woman pastor at *Harvest Rock*.

God gave me another dream. This time I was walking out of a building which I would later realize was the administrative building next to Ambassador Auditorium. This was a year before *Harvest Rock Church* was looking to buy the property. I was walking out of the building when my Dad was walking towards me. I went to hug him, which was not common at the time; he almost fainted in my arms. A former assistant of Lou's was coming out and I asked him to get Pastors Che or Lou, thinking they could pray for my Dad. I realize Pastor Che representing evangelism and Lou representing prayer were busy talking with each other. God impressed on me that I needed to pray and share with my Dad and not depend on others to do that. I could tell my Dad was close to coming to the Lord and had the sense that his heart was soft and something to do with Microsoft. I got the strong sense that I needed to focus on my Dad and family. I told Pastor Che the next day that I needed to decline and focus on my family. After *TheCall* ended it was very strange to be at *Harvest Rock* and not be so active since I had also become the conference coordinator.

During the last year of my time at *TheCall*, God gave me several prophetic words and impressions about taking back the air waves. He was showing me boardrooms and broadcast rooms with monitors all around. I had no idea how that would happen. *TheCall* went into hibernation at the end of 2003 with my last day being September 4,

2004. Again I was on sabbatical. What a journey, pioneering with God and *TheCall* team. There are so many more stories, but for a later time.

After *TheCall* and the dream I had about my dad, I began to spend much more time with my parents. I ended up moving down to Laguna where they had built a house. We worked through many of the unresolved issues from my growing up years through some hard incidences. God was going even deeper in dealing with my foundation in relation to my family of origin so that I could see ABBA Father correctly. He dealt with and healed my orphan issues in ways that only He could. In healing those old wounds and words that were said like "get out and don't come back", He healed my rejection and abandonment issues. I was now able to see the abandonment and rejection issues that my parents had to deal with in their lives. As I healed I was able to learn about my parents' lives and pray for healing and ending of the patterns and curses that were passed down. I was able to make photo albums and collect letters from their friends, family and colleagues to make an album of letters. My Dad even learned to say I love you and to hug me when I was 40 years old.

I also began to spend time once a week with my Dad going over stocks. This has given me a foundation for my own investments and time with my Dad in an area of his expertise.

I ended up going back for my Executive MBA at UC Irvine 2005-2007 to learn what I was doing at *TheCall* as Vice President of Operations. God also showed me it was important not to just give people fish like in Social Work, but to train people to fish, to give them access to the fishing holes and to own them. During my time there I began to do things in the marketplace. God was showing me a diamond that the media was the new ministry and marketplace was the new missions with miracles powering all of it. I had the opportunity to speak to marketplace leaders in Singapore, go to the Beijing International book fair as a board member of *Gospel Light Worldwide*. I would then go to Beijing and Shanghai to learn about businesses there with the EMBA program at UCI. In 2007 I was also invited to head up mobilization for the Cultural Festival Square for the Beijing Olympics in 2008 through a startup group; however it blew up because of leadership issues.

In 2008 I was drafted again, this time by people my brother had worked with at MGM. My brother (not a believer yet) started working with a startup company with a former VP from MGM and a former International President from Warner Brothers and Tele-pictures. None of them were believers but they figured there was lots of money among Christians after the *Passion of The Christ* movie. They wanted to build a platform for Christians working with an Israeli Internet TV platform (RAYV). My brother asked me to meet with the CEO because I was a Christian. In January 2008 while at the Starting the Year off Right conference at *Glory of Zion*, I was offered to be VP of Corporate Development at this new media company. Wow, the prophetic words about my involvement in media in the broadcast and board rooms were beginning to be fulfilled in unexpected ways.

With the confirmation from the words during *TheCall* and a word from Chuck Pierce that I would be a wedge opening the way for others to go through, I joined. Nine months later the companies began to fall apart since they blew through the startup money and were trying to go around me with my personal ministry contacts. By November 1, 2008, the day we were able to live stream *TheCall* San Diego using a mobile broadcaster and RayV was launching the Internet TV platform for the NBA globally, the company fell apart.

I continued briefly with my brother with the Israeli company, but by March of 2009 it became clear then that it would not work. RayV took me in and incubated my company. I was invited to have an office in their offices. I was able to sit in some of their meetings and learn about media and Israeli business operations on a level that far exceeded me. I got to visit their operations in Israel, and meet their team. The Israeli/Hebraic way is to work together even with companies that could be seen as competitors. They would have summits where top Financiers, Startup and established media and tech companies would come together, present and do deals. I got to meet leadership and hear about Waze, LiveU, Livestream and numerous other companies. It reminded me of how my Dad ran his company. He would allow each company that was bought to still operate independently, but would streamline legal, finances, technical operations. The whole is greater than the sum of the parts.

I started my company, VAV media on May 5, 2009 (*Vision and Voices* - also VAV is a Hebrew letter which means connector - Heaven "VAV" Earth (Genesis 1:1) and Alpha VAV Omega (Revelations 1:8 and 22:13). Unfortunately, it was right after the crash in 2008 so ministries/Christians were pulling back and not stepping forward. I pivoted to do international deals and working as an affiliate, even connecting RayV to a Korean media company.

I also began learning from my dad about stock and investments.

In 2011, I was connected to Dalen Harrison, from *Impact/Ole Media*. He was looking at doing at a much larger scale what God had shown me about taking back the airwaves. I believe he is one of the ones who I was being a wedge for. Dalen's company broadcast live the World Cup over the Internet and mobile in Mexico. He was in high level due diligence with a mega retailer but after a year it fell through because of unrelated issues with the retailer. Then as Impact Media inked a deal with RayV, a week later RayV said they had to stop because they sold to an undisclosed company. Later I found out it was Yahoo and then Verizon.

In 2014 an opportunity opened up to potentially broadcast the Manny Pacquiao fight and build an Internet TV platform for the country of Philippines and beyond with the 2nd largest mobile company. Things moved forward and then fell apart because of another party that said they had rights but didn't. God impressed on me that they were Sanballat and Tobiah, like in the book of Nehemiah. Then He said "Are you willing to allow me to use the money I gave you to expose things?" What could I say? This situation put brakes on all that I was doing, but I thank God for it because otherwise I would never have had the time to have my daughter.

I have continued to connect with Dalen and the platform that he pivoted to. When we were in the Philippines one of the mayors of an island said that it is great that you can increase our TV channels from two to 150, but can you bring a teacher. He began researching and realized that the Educational platforms were antiquated and not available for the less developed countries that may only have 2G capability. He and his team have been able to develop a platform that currently the country of Ethiopia is about to use for their whole country. They already have approvals from the Prime Minister and the Ministers of Education and Finance. If that is finally completed then they will be a model/showcase for the rest of Africa. It is also being considered for parts of India, Indonesia and the Philippines. I have continued as their intercessor and investor. It frees me up to be a VAV/connector that God has made me to be.

I believe that the time is ripe for Kingdom Distribution and Education platforms with Kingdom Content, Kingdom Financiers and Marketers to come together.

Helena Hwang
Helena@VAVmedia.com

Chapter 7

Valerie K Jackson

Apostle – "Sent One"

It was two days before Halloween, and I was at work at the Post Office. I was getting ready to leave for lunch. (Yes, there are Christians in the Postal Service,) As a postal clerk, I always took lunch from 2-4 pm. This was a schedule I picked so I could be home when my children got off the school bus. My husband would then get home about 3:30 pm, just when I would leave to go back to work. This routine suited us well. But on this day, I turned to the left instead of to the right, and parked across from a house near the Post Office. I sat there wondering why I needed to go to that house, although I felt that the Spirit led me there. In my mind I was thinking this is crazy! I need to go home to my kids. But I did have an overwhelming feeling that I must be at this house. I started to pray, as I learned a long time ago, (the hard way, mind you) that I do not always have to understand what the Lord is doing. I just must obey. Still feeling that I needed to turn around and go home to my children, but also feeling so strong that I needed to be across the street from this house, I prayed. I asked the Lord," Why am I here, and what is it you want me to do? Please take care of my kids as they are getting off the bus and I am not there." Suddenly, as I was finishing this prayer, I saw darkness in the Spirit, over the house.

Now, I am not going to debate theology with you about this, I am just telling you what happened. This black darkness was covering the house and it was like gossamer. It was like looking through a veil. It covered the whole house and I only saw it for a couple of seconds, but long enough to send my spirit into travail. I had no idea what I was praying about, but I knew it was serious and I HAD TO PRAY! Let me backup and tell you why I KNEW that I had to pray. Approximately a year before being in front of the house, I had another experience where I saw darkness and it didn't end well. My brother-in-law and his wife were camping with my husband and me. They had everything the world says is valuable: money, good careers, a beautiful home, they were a lovely couple. We, on the other hand, were struggling financially, as middle-class people do. We had a good life, but mainly we struggled because we were raising children. As my brother-in-law and I were sitting across from each other at a picnic table, he was talking to me. Suddenly I saw this gossamer like black darkness on him. Of course, he was completely unaware of the blackness and kept talking to me. But it freaked me out! It was like, for a split second, I saw into the spiritual realm beyond the veil. I got up from the table and was trying to figure out what I had just seen. I went to my husband and tried to tell him that something was wrong with his brother. Well, my husband, who did not have spiritual discernment, told me," He is fine. He has nothing in this world to be upset about and you are wrong." He also added, "Don't start getting weird on me like some of the people you know." He was referring to the fact that I had gone to a retreat and learned about the Holy Spirit and it changed my life for the good. I loved the Holy Spirit and it caused me to read the Bible, go to church, and be filled with joy.

We had been married about eight years and I went from a normal woman to an on fire Jesus' lover, filled with the Spirit. My poor husband wasn't sure what to do with his new wife. So, I constantly reminded myself that he hadn't changed, but I had. Grace was what the Lord required me to give him. (God is faithful because my husband later, before he died, got saved and filled with the spirit. He said to me," I now know what you have been trying to tell me." But that is another story.) Shortly after the experience of seeing the darkness on my husband's brother on the camping trip, my brother-in-law killed himself. At the funeral everyone was crying. My husband kept telling me that he should have listened to me. I was also crying, but more about what I saw in the spirit and trying to understand it. I told the Lord if I ever saw that darkness again, I would pray even if I didn't understand.

So now you know the backstory and why I was determined to pray when I saw the darkness over that house. I sat across from that house and prayed through my two-hour lunch break. I went back to work, still unaware of why I prayed. But the Spirit was still on high alert in my spirit to pray. The next day when I returned to work, there were people everywhere. News- broadcasters, investigators, and police swarmed that house. I asked what was happening and a co-worker told me that a man broke into the little girl's bedroom and attempted to kidnap her. He tripped and dropped the child on his way out of the house, and her father heard the noise. Her father went after the man and the man dropped the girl again on the front lawn. She was rescued. I was so excited because I knew the Lord saved that child. I was the SENT- ONE that God used to pray for that little girl. Apparently, the man went on down to another town and attempted to kidnap a second little girl, but was unsuccessful again. When he was arrested, he told the police he had been paid to find a girl around 9-10 years old for a Halloween ceremony that they would use the child for. Both girls were safe and the man went to prison for attempted kidnapping. How he got caught is also amazing. He went to a town where my sister was a dispatcher for the Sheriff's Office. He was caught by the Sheriff. Both my sister and the Sheriff are Christians. It is amazing to me how the Lord used all of us to save that child. I tried to tell the girl's parents about what the Lord did to save their daughter.

I don't know if they believed me or not. It is not easy to be used by God at times as people will not understand you. Sometimes you won't understand yourself. But when God speaks to your spirit, you know, that you know, THAT YOU KNOW! The Lord has used me in many different situations that have all proved to me that I am a SENTONE. Apostle means," Sent one", it also means, as Paul said, "Is one who doesn't build on anyone else's foundation." Romans 15:20. It means to preach the gospel where people do not know it. So, I reach out to those who do not know, but I also will be used by the Lord in the prophetic. God will use you to be what the Holy Spirit has ordained you to be when he gives you His gifts.

When I was a child, I was not raised in a Christian home and so I never really learned about the Lord. The only time the Lord's name was used in my home was when my dad was mad at my mom. Then Jesus' name was used very loudly and with anger. My Dad also got saved before he died. Praise the Lord. My mom was a well-educated woman and thought she didn't need God. She said, "She was too intelligent for that crutch." My grandmother died when my mother was about 14 years old and she never quite recovered from her mother's death. She blamed the very God she didn't really believe in. She also was saved and served the Lord later in life. Our mother loved my three sisters and me very much, but she was a melancholy person, and was frequently depressed. This was hard on me since I am a very upbeat and happy person and was always trying to make my mother happy. All four of us would try to please our mother. My mother got interested in books on self-help and the power of the mind, mainly books that were written for the educated mind to encourage pride in one's intellect, with no dependence on God. She was interested in Dianetics, (1) written by the founder of the church of Scientology, and Psycho Cybernetics, (2). I thank the Lord she didn't go deeper into these teachings as we already had a lot of occult in our family. Being 100% disabled from World War II and the Korean War, my father was drugged by the doctor's continually for PTSD, (Post Traumatic Stress Disorder). It was so disturbing to him; he used alcohol to escape the nightmares, and depression. Despite his struggles, he was a kind, fun loving man who tried to make us very joyful, even though he wasn't. Today we are just beginning to understand the damage done to a person by Trauma.

When I was four years old, a neighbor took three of us girls to Vacation Bible School. I am sure my mother was glad to get 3 of her 4 girls out of the house. At VBS I accepted the Lord and to this day I know that God honored the prayer of a four-year-old and I thank him for His love and care. My testimony is that the Lord was always taking care and protecting me, even though I didn't know it. At VBS we learned "Bringing in the Sheaves", (didn't know what the sheaves were but, I did know we were bringing them in), and "Onward Christian Soldiers." I still remember both songs. Many times, in my life when I was afraid, I would sing "Onward Christian Soldiers." I also got a little plaque that said, "The Family That Prays Together Stays Together." It had hands in prayer on the plaque. This was in my bedroom for years and I would pray and hold it in my arms as my parents were fighting over money, my father's obsessive drinking and many other issues my mother lived with. Thankfully, they were never abusive to us. I give my mother a lot of credit because a lesser woman would have left. But she stayed for the sake of her girls, or as she referred to us as her, "Little Women." I am sure that the Lord gave her strength to keep us all together as family. Our family was very important to my mother. I guess you could say we were a dysfunctional family, but I say we had a lot of love. We didn't know anything else, so dysfunctional or not we made it through and the Lord was faithful to us.

As I got older, I always knew I was a Christian, but I went to church when it was convenient or if I needed to pray. It wasn't important to me if my husband was a Christian or not. I met a man who was very kind and we were married for 38 years before he died of cancer. We had two beautiful children and a good life. We raced snowmobiles in the early 80's and we went all over to race the sleds. At a meet in New Meadows Idaho, one of the guys from my husband's team came over as I was unpacking our suitcases, and he saw my Bible. I took it with me everywhere I went, but I never read it. He asked me if I was a Christian and I said "Yes." So, he invited me to go to church. At that time in my life, I would have probably gone to any church that I thought was Christian, someone invited me to because I did not know the difference. I still go to that church today, forty years later. Carrying the Bible with me, even though I didn't read it, was a blessing. God honored that as He always protected me and my family. God meets you where you are. A great example is, as I was racing the snowmobiles, my goggles got fogged up, and I couldn't see. I went off the track and ended up about 30 feet in the air and went out about 50 feet. I remembered my training to stay on the sled and pull the tether cord. My sled landed in a powder of soft snow and I was completely fine. That was a miracle, as I could have been killed. My sister -in-law was mad because the announcer kept saying," We have a man off the track." And she kept yelling, "It's a girl!" When the trophies were presented at a ceremony, I was awarded a trophy that said, "The Long Jump Award, presented to "Bonzi- Mama". I won the Long Jump award, and there wasn't any long jump award in the race. It was a joke. I know God protected me. Why did He always protect me? He wasn't finished with my assignment in this life.

Another time God's hand of protection was on me, when we were sledding up in the mountains, and my husband and his friends got their sleds stuck in the snow. Riders must go for a ride in the early morning while the snow is hard, or else when the sun comes up and the snow gets soft, you can get stuck. I told the guys that it was too warm, but they didn't listen to me. So, they went over the side of the hill and rode for a while and then they got stuck when they tried to come back up the mountain.

As I waited for them to return, I got tired and laid down on my sled to rest and fell asleep. Suddenly my husband was standing over me yelling "Are you alright?' I woke up and said," Yes, why? What is wrong?" He said, "Look", and I looked on the ground and in the snow were tracks of a mountain lion that had encircled my sled. The size of the tracks was huge, so it was a big cat. The tracks were so close to me that he probably smelled me as I slept right through the whole situation. I thank God that He had me go to sleep or that cat would have given me a heart attack if I had seen him coming. I used to think this was a funny story but since then, I have heard of several people who have been eaten. Now, I think. Thank -you- Thank- you Lord.

There are many other times that I know God protected me and I know I am here today and my children, because of Him. What is my assignment in life was always my question and what did the Lord have planned for me to do? I now know it is to be a SENT-ONE. Well one assignment as a SENT-ONE was when my niece was having her baby. The baby was born looking like rubber. He wasn't moving or crying, and was almost a pale, milky white color. As this baby was a little Half white and half Hispanic, he should have had more olive coloring. The Spirit inside of me rose and I said, "This is not happening!" I knew he wasn't breathing and he looked like all the color was gone in his little body. The Lord rose inside of me and I ran over to where the baby was lying, and I put my hand on him and started to pray loudly in the Spirit. The nurses told me to move back. I kept praying and suddenly he started to cry and life came back into his little body. He was starting to turn the color he was supposed to be. Then I heard my niece moaning and looked over at her. The doctor was trying to save her from hemorrhaging. There was lots of blood and so I started to pray for her.

This baby should never have been born as my niece was going to have a hysterectomy when they discovered she was pregnant. It was a very difficult delivery, but she and the baby both lived. Today he is 23 years old and a healthy handsome young man. My other niece who at the time was around fifteen years, and was in rebellion, saw all this and she became a Christian. As she saw the power of God, bring life to that little baby. She is a strong Christian today twenty-three years later. Being a SENT-ONE for God is very exciting as you never know when God is going to use you and thrilling when you see what He will do through your obedience.

I used to think everyone in the body of Christ had these experiences and it was normal for Christians. But as I shared my experiences with people, I would get such strange responses; I soon realized my experiences weren't normal.

I thought everyone heard God, not audibly, but in your spirit. I again found out that not only do a lot of people not hear they don't like you to say you do. I worked in the Post Office with two other Christians and they did not believe me. When I shared some of these situations, they tried to discourage me. The only person in my office who I thought understood me was the cleaning lady and she was very New-Age. I didn't know much about the New Age. I learned very quickly that she did not believe in only ONE Christ.

It was a very hard time for me, as the two Christians were telling me the gifts of the spirit didn't operate today, while, the one person who not only believed in the gifts, but she would affirm them, as spiritual. Yet, she wasn't a Christian, as I understood Christianity. She would say she was Christian. I later found out that she had totally different beliefs than I did. This lady believed in many Christ's. She told me she herself was becoming Christ. My thought was, "You aren't Christ and if you are, we are all in trouble, because you couldn't possibly forgive me of sins."

This is the problem for people who are Christ or think they are. They are not able to forgive my sins as they have as many as the rest of us. I started to study the New Age to understand the difference. She confronted me one day very sweetly and asked me," Can't you believe there is more than one Christ." I said, "No, because John 3:16 says that God so loved the world that He gave His only begotten son." One means singular, which means there is only one.

Soon, that sweet harmonious woman became very hostile and all her harmony went right out the window. I felt like I was being attacked in the spirit. I called my friend for prayer after I got home from work. So, the Christians didn't believe me and the New Ager was not what I thought she was. This was the beginning of the Lord teaching me about the New Age. I needed to be taught. Soon after that experience, we had many New Agers come to our Post Office daily, dropping their children off at the school that had just opened across from my Post Office. I also started to learn about all the witchcraft that was in our town. I called it, on the job instruction, and I got a crash course. It is funny, because I could have been just like them if I hadn't gone to Vacation Bible School and gotten saved. Thank you, Lord.

How did I deal with all this? Well, the Lord knew I needed to have help, so He directed me to a group of about 10 Aglow International women who got together every Monday night for two-three hours of prayer. This was from the early eighties until around the middle of the nineties. This group of ladies became a lifeline for me many times. We covered our families, churches, ministries, Aglow and our town. We were baby Christians, just trying to get stronger in the Lord. Many times, I got confused or attacked by people, or by dark spirits.

There were many times I was confronted by the new age or the occult, since our town was very prevalent in both. We would pray for each other. We prayed together for about 14 years. During that time, we had many encounters and they are amazing stories in themselves.

I am just going to say if you start praying and searching for the Lord with all your heart, He will help you to find Him. Aglow international was my mother and teacher and I thank God for that ministry. In 1982, I worked at the Post Office, and was invited to an Aglow meeting. I went for the first time. I thought they were crazy. They were all praying and falling and the woman who was speaking was praying about demons and I could not wait to leave. I heard people in another room yelling out loud and I asked the lady who invited me to the meeting, "Are they having an auction in the other room, since it sounded like they were yelling out calls." And she laughed and said "No, they are praying." Well then, I knew they were crazy and I made a very polite excuse to leave as soon as possible. As I was making my way to the door to leave, a very sweet woman with a lovely smile said, "are you leaving?' I said, yes." She gave me a warm loving hug and said" Here, God wants you to have this." I looked down and it was a track on the game of Dungeon and Dragons, and now I really thought they were crazy. So, I put the track in my purse and left, resolving to never go back. Watch what you say! Within a week's time, a neighbor boy came to my house to play with my son who was about seven years old at the time. The neighbor boy had a game of Dungeons and Dragons with him. I did not know what the game was, but I remembered the track. I still thought the Aglow ladies were crazy, but how did that woman know I needed that track? I got the track out of my purse and read it. Then I told the boy that my son could not play that game with him.

I went back to Aglow after that because I wanted to understand how the lady knew that the boy would be at my house with that game. It brought back a memory of my childhood, when a neighbor of ours stopped my mother from allowing a man to teach me how to tap into my spiritual gifts. He told my mom that He could see I had a gift and he wanted to bring out my gift. He said it would increase my gift by connecting it to the spirit realm. The same neighbor who took us to Vacation Bible School told my mother not to let Richard, who was her brother, try to tap me into the realm of the spirit. She showed my mother scriptures about witchcraft and warned my mother about how dangerous it was to tap into the occult.

My mother did not like Barbara telling her this, as my mother was into spiritual things. My mother told Barbara," Your welcome here anytime Barbara, but don't bring your Bible." My mother was a little scared of what Barbara told her so she told Richard he could not teach me how to tap into the spirit realm. Praise The Lord.

My mother was raised by a father who was deep into the Masonic Lodge and she was a Rainbow girl. My great grandmother was a physic healer. She was very well paid for her gift. It was interesting since my grandmother was always quite sickly and died when my mother was 14 years old. The occult had been operating through my lineage. When I was a child, I had a great spirit of fear. This happens when the doors to the enemy are opened. Thank God I got deliverance from the Spirit of fear, and now I want to help others get set free. On the other side, in my lineage were many Christians. God prevailed. Keep praying for your children as God is greater than anything they are into. My testimony is that God has always been there to protect and provide for me. He is a God that is so worthy of praise.

I went back to Aglow, because I didn't understand how that lady knew I would need to know about the Dungeons and Dragons game. I kept going because I felt drawn by their love. They taught me much of the spirit and I grew in my understanding.

After I returned to Aglow, I grew in their great discipleship. I started to serve. I served on the local Lighthouse Team, and then became President of the Lighthouse; I eventually became the Area Board President and then eventually the Regional Coordinator for Church - Aglow over California and Hawaii. I would have continued to serve but God opened another door for me.

I am now the National Director for the *Prayer Council* of the United States. God took the prayers of a four-year-old and directed my life and I have been so blessed. It hasn't been easy but God is always with me. He not only saved me; He uses me as a sent one.

A sent one is also known as Apostolic which simply means God uses you and works in your life in exciting ways even if you don't understand. You will be on a journey, and at times it will make you cry and feel afraid to go forward, but filled with great joy. As God directs your path, sit down, and hold on because you are on a ride of your life. Another time I woke up and was praying in tongues out loud, fervently praying without knowing why I was praying, but I knew it was serious. After about an hour, I felt calmer and went back to sleep, but still woke up off and on to pray. The next morning, still not knowing what I was praying about, my son came home from a trip he had taken with his friends. They had gone camping to celebrate their graduation from high school. They were camping on the beach and they were robbed by a gang of six young men. The men told them they were going to shoot them and put their bodies in the ocean, so no one would ever find them. I learned to note the date and time when God uses me in prayer as I often find out later that it is confirmed by circumstances in the natural world. I am so glad that God didn't allow me to know it was my own son I was praying for as I would have probably just panicked. But, as soon as my son walked through the door, I realized it was him that I was praying for the night before. I asked him what happened and that is when I learned they had been robbed. It was another time I was the sent one that the Lord used to save all those boys, not just my own son.

Many times, as a sent one I have not understood what God was doing but simply walked in obedience. Just like the followers of Jesus in the Bible who went where God sent them. They did whatever the Spirit led them to do and said what the Spirit led them to say. Why is this important? 1Cortinthians 6:19-20 says, "You are not your own, you were bought with a price; therefore, glorify God in your body, in your spirit, which is God's." I don't tell you these stories, to make it look as though I am special, but you too can be used by the Lord. Not all gifts are apostolic, and not all people are prophets, but all of us have gifts that the Holy Spirit can use and we all are called to walk by the Spirit. Don't allow fear to keep you from allowing the Holy Spirit to use you. Accept whatever your gift is and move forward with the knowledge that there is a great calling on you and the journey is exciting and joyful. You never know how the Lord will use you next!

Valerie K Jackson

Chapter 8

Jan Anderson

Pick me Pick Me! My heart was pounding inside my chest, but I was trying so hard for my face to say: 'I don't care'! Most likely you have been there, teams are being chosen, two captains taking turns picking from the group who they want. They want the best players for their team. At times I was not last, but always 'at the end' of the chosen.

I desperately wanted to be picked, to be chosen. I did not want to be that person; you know that person "you have to take her'. This summarized my inner identity. I am sharing the aerial view of the key markers, or memorial stones in my life's journey. Opening marker, I am number five of six children with Christian parents.

My earliest recollection is sitting on a church pew when I was three years old. It was when my dad decided to divorce my mother. My mother in my eyes was a solid rock. She trusted Jesus in everything. My dad disappeared from my life. Oh, he would show up every few years for a visit and would send me a yearly birthday card, but he was basically absent. My dad definitely didn't pick me!

Marker #1

At nine years old I raised my hand in church to accept Jesus as my savior, but it was in my sophomore year in high school that I made a dramatic commitment to Jesus. I picked Jesus. My choices locked in on biblical standards which resulted in the battle over relationships in my life. Who would I give close proximity to my heart and mind?

Marker #2

Later that same year I met this guy. His name was Zane who was radically in love with Jesus and was called to become a pastor. I knew I was definitely not qualified to be a pastor's wife because I did not play the piano or organ or sing. When our relationship moved towards marriage it thrust me into a face to face encounter with God. Little did I know I would go into a 2 Cor. 3:18 season

Marker #3

God began uncovering my unforgiveness towards my dad but God gave me grace to face the specific pain. I had generally forgiven my dad, but I had prayed "I want to be whole; I want to be completely free". God replayed the specific hurts, and the pain of abandonment and rejection in my life. The more I faced the pain and the more I chose to forgive, the freer I became. The process of layers of pain resulted in layers of forgiveness.

Marker #4

Amid my healing journey, I married Zane. It was the best decision I ever made second to Christ. We had our first son Deron, then our daughter Danae, and our last son Taylor. My children are the greatest joys of my life. They brought me to the deepest healing possible. What I wouldn't do for myself I did for my children. I realized I was subtly communicating to my children that God was distant, not tenderhearted, but God loved us because we are a result of His creation. It was my love for my children that caused me to cry out to God on a deeper level. It felt like my biological dad was blocking me, keeping me from an intimate relationship with God.

Marker #5

Face to face. It was a Thursday night. My husband and I had an explosive argument, and I blew up. The argument didn't merit the level of anger. I said to Zane, "I've got to go and pray, something is very wrong". I went upstairs to our room and instead of praying I exploded in anger at God. "God why didn't you stop my dad from the affairs, stop my dad from divorcing my mom. I believe you are sovereign, all powerful and you could have stopped my dad, but you didn't, I hate you". There it was my deepest pain; deepest hurt, greatest anger was at God. I began to feel fearful over what I had just said to God when I felt the strong arms of God wrap around me and pull me close to him. God was not offended, intimated or angry at me. He understood that I didn't understand how the divorce happened. At that divine moment, face to face with God He now became Abba Daddy. Father God brought the deepest healing and greatest freedom to my life. My identity now was in my Abba Daddy and not my earthly dad. I could now love God as His daughter, love my husband, my children, love others from a secure and stable place of wholeness and liberty.

Marker #6

Throughout my life there were significant spiritual fathers and mothers that believed in me (picked me) and mentored me. They built upon the foundation of my identity. God brought divine friendships into my life. Candi was a comrade in the kingdom who walked through life with me. She challenged me in my gifting and introduced me to the company of women. These women: Cindy, Michelle, Kay, Karen, Sonya, Kathy and Carol were the company of Proverbs 27:17. They brought incredible joy as a part of my spiritual lineage. It is from my true identity in Christ that I have called women to their God ordained place, mobilized the young and the older in prayer, brought transformation into our city, slayed giants, experienced signs, wonders and miracles. They sharpened and strengthened my calling.

Closing Marker

Why do I exist? Because God picked me before conception he will prevail. Life and choices of others contradicted His choice of me. Through Gold's perfect love, truth, forgiveness, repentance and healing I became a beloved daughter. It is from my place as a daughter I became a spiritual mother.

I am now mothering some spiritual daughters and calling some spiritual daughters into being spiritual mothers and that is great news. God continues to pick me, pick us Haggai 2:9. "The glory of the latter shall be greater than the former". My translation.

Final Thought

Business was my greatest obstacle to finding my identity. Life is a constant balancing act. Too often the scales tip the wrong way. The most important thing, God-Family-Good Health is sometimes outweighed by the proverbial tyranny of the urgent. The American dream, your God given ministry can turn into a nightmare. Martha at heart, but life forces me into Martha mode (Luke 10:38-42 busyness can drag you through life. Busyness can be a harsh yoke. Resist the rush. Move into your created worth in Christ alone.

Jan Anderson

Chapter 9

Jeannie Lein

From Hell to Heaven

I was born in a small city in the Interior of the State of Goiás, in Brazil. Although predominantly Roman Catholic in name, most of the people practice a combination of spiritualistic rituals (witchcraft) and Catholicism. I knew that my traditions were Catholic, yet I hardly attended a regular Sunday Mass. My memories about the church were related to events, weddings, and baptisms. At one time, my father decided that we should start going to mass and we did it for a period of one month, only to end in the same thing: indifference, apathy, and boredom. While being fed by my father with the Catholic concept, my mother had been instructed in her life by the principles of the gospel of Allan Kardec, which many recognize as the founder of Kardecism, a form of spiritism in Brazil. The concepts of reincarnation and that sin does not exist were injected into my mind from an incredibly young age. So I was raised with great spiritual confusion. Because of this spiritual chaos, I wanted from the bottom of my heart to know the true God. When I was ten years old, we moved to the State's Capital.

Little did I know that God had a unique plan for my life that would begin in this new place. I grew up loving music and dance, especially ballet and jazz, and dedicated myself to it. I was never attracted to drugs, alcohol, or illicit sex. I considered myself a good girl with a strong interest in spiritual things. I longed to discover what I thought of as the true religion, whatever that was. Although in a certain way, I was involved in everything in my mother's religion, they could never convince me to go through with the initiation ceremonies.

Then in 1986 I met Jesus Christ and was born again. I know that God delivered me from the power of Satan. I knew, even then, that the Lord had a spectacular plan to fulfill in my life. A goodbye to the past. My boyfriend, Henry Lein, and I were born spiritually during the greatest revival of all times in South America. A revival had started in the mid-1980s in Argentina, and then quickly spread to Brazil, Colombia, and other parts of the continent. We witnessed supernatural miracles and spectacular liberations. We literally began our Christian lives knowing the supernatural workings of God. We were so amazed at what we experienced in each meeting that our greatest pleasure was being in the House of God. We went to church every day and joyfully participated in each of the seven weekly services. In the afternoons we attended campaigns and special events. It was incredible! The sound of the church in prayer broke the heavens. It was powerful! It made our faith radical. There was no return. We knew we were going to serve our Lord forever. We witnessed with our own eyes the opening of blind eyes. We watched paralyzed people stand up from their wheelchairs to walk again. Demon possessed people were set free from their bondage right in front of us. The impact of God's work in lives reached out to the plazas and squares, soon filling them with believers worshiping God. The churches overflowed. Spiritually hungry hearts were baptized in the fire of the Holy Ghost. More important than these simple manifestations of the Glory of God, peoples were radically transformed forever. We were a part of them! We lived days of glory and power, which will forever be engraved in our memory.

The Sunday Morning That Changed Our Lives Forever

I will try to relate an experience that was not mine personally but impacted my life forever. On a certain Sunday morning, 17-year-old Henry Lein was lying on his bed praying, waiting for the time to go to church. It was still early but the desire to be in the house of God made him ready long before the hour. Suddenly, Henry realized that he was suspended in the air and everything he saw was perceived in a third dimension. He clearly knew that he was having a supernatural experience with God. A flaming sword appeared in the air and moved toward his forehead. When the sword touched his head, a remarkable voice began to speak saying, "Because it is not man who takes you to distant lands, but I am the One Who takes you there." The voice declared specific things that would become of our lives, and what would happen in the United States of America, including our ministry. The voice spoke for a long time revealing the perfect plan that God had for that 17-year-old boy and his 16- year-old girlfriend who would eventually become his wife. A story of love, miracles, and supernatural manifestations began to unfold. The lives of two young people who decided to give everything to the service of the Lord were changed forever. When that incredible experience ended, Henry was in tears. From that moment, Henry lived with singular determination to walk in obedience to the Lord's instructions. Within minutes, Henry came to take me to the morning service. He was still crying. I listened in awe as he told me of his incredible experience. We arrived at church while it was still early. The building was empty; only the janitorial team was present, quietly working. We had our heads lowered and were both crying. Someone came and placed his hands on our heads and began to prophesy the same words that Henry had heard in his room. Now it was my turn to listen and understand God's call upon our lives. Amazing! To this day we do not know who prayed for us - we never raised our heads to see his face. From that day everything changed. We were at a new beginning. We still needed to see God's confirmation to move forward, including receiving confirmation and the blessing of our parents and pastors. We were obviously amazed when they said, "yes." It was God! It was evident that God had called us to serve Him in a distant land, with a different language and people. He was the One who prepared every miracle along the way. He was the One who taught us how to deny ourselves, to find Him in His many facets, and to know Him as the true God of the Bible. If I were to tell every detail and every miracle that happened from that Sunday morning until the moment we departed for the United States, I would lack pages to describe it.

Amidst that powerful revival, the Lord called us to the ministry at the young ages of 18 and 19. We were married in Brazil, May 23, 1987, at 10 o'clock in morning. Our pastor included a commissioning into ministry in the wedding ceremony. We embarked to the United States of America that very evening, to serve as missionaries to the multicultural Hispanic people of America.

> *"The Spirit of the Lord GOD is upon me, because the LORD has anointed me to bring good tidings to the afflicted; he has sent me to bind up the brokenhearted, to proclaim liberty to the captives, and the opening of the prison to those who are bound; to proclaim the year of the LORD's favor, and the day of vengeance of our God; to comfort all who mourn; to grant to those who mourn in Zion--to give them a garland instead of ashes, the oil of gladness instead of mourning, the mantle of praise instead of a faint spirit; that they may be called oaks of righteousness, the planting of the LORD, that he may be glorified. They shall build up the ancient*

ruins, they shall raise up the former devastations; they shall repair the ruined cities, the devastations of many generations." (Isaiah 61:1-4 RSV)

A Man Called "Sent" -- Our arrival in America was quite confusing.

In 1987, the internet was not available to the average person; the communication system was complicated. With so much technology now, it's difficult to realize that communication was so precarious at that time. The person who should have notified my aunt of our arrival never contacted her to let her know that two newlywed kids were landing in the United States. Consequently, there was no one to pick us up at Los Angeles International Airport - LAX. We were literally two teenagers who had never left our home nation, did not speak English, arriving in a strange place, depending only on a word from God and a supernatural experience. We didn't even speak Spanish, a language spoken by many Southern Californians. We finally managed to get someone to help us make a phone call.

Today, we laugh at the situation, but we were greatly scared. Finally, we managed to find the auntie who should have taken care of us when we arrived. Not knowing of our arrival, she did not take any responsibility and left us in a filthy motel, with red lights, red blankets, and a crude cement bathroom in the city of Hollywood. Very scary indeed. Nor did my auntie offer us food. We were so exhausted and confused that we fell asleep without having a bite to eat. We awoke at noon to auntie knocking on the door. She had brought us something to eat, which our unaccustomed stomachs rejected, and we quickly vomited. The next day, I felt terribly ill. Auntie reappeared to take us to another hotel. She left us there because she would travel to another nation that same day. Our faith was being tested. Our arrival on this mission field left us feeling abandoned; there had been a word from the Lord…but everything seemed very dark.

Once settled in the second hotel, we tried to contact the pastor who would officially receive us, to help in his church, as necessary. We called him and left a message. Again, it seemed that the enemy wanted to foil the plans; this pastor thought that we were a different couple and did not return our call. It is incredible the oppositions we may face even when we are in the perfect plan and will of God. This is where we must never give up, but rather persevering. So, we did. We faced many difficult situations in our new land. We were very hungry; nothing stayed in our stomachs. We were so sick! All that day, we had had nothing to eat; and so we prayed, "Lord Jesus, we are hungry. Amen!" At the conclusion of our short but genuine prayer, someone knocked on the door of our room. We opened it to a small, elderly man who said to us in Portuguese, "Hello, you do not know me, but someone told me that there is a Brazilian couple here at the hotel and I imagine that you could be hungry. Do you want to eat?" We were surprised and stunned!

The surprise was so great that we did not even ask him his name; we merely got into his car. He took us to a supermarket, and we were able to buy food; we cooked it on the small stove in our hotel room. We had a real meal for the first time in America. At the end of the evening, when we realized we did not know his name, we said: "What is your name?" "Messiah." He answered smiling! The small old man hugged us and left, and we never saw him again.

Uncertain Days

The following days were very uncertain. Our money was almost gone, and we needed to find the purpose for which we had come to the States.

With someone's help, I went to a doctor, as I was still feeling sick. This person also told us about someone who was renting a room, since we were out of money and had to leave the hotel the next day. We were in a hurry to find a new place and went to see her. The house was filled with black candles and candles of many colors. The owner of the house was a professional witch; the devil had set a trap for us. Obviously, we discerned his schemes and were not interested in staying there.

We came back to the hotel in need of a miracle. We could only stay one more night in that hotel. As we knelt to pray, we held hands and said another prayer with all our hearts: "Lord, why are we here? Why did you tell us to come? What is your purpose with all this? Now we do not have a place to stay. What do we do?" As we got up from saying that prayer the phone rang. It was 11 o'clock at night and the words were these: "I would like to speak to Henry. This is Marcio, and maybe you won't understand what I'm going to tell you. I was about to go to work, and I was praying as I always do. The Holy Spirit told me that the couple of Brazilians which my pastor had told me about were in Hollywood. That you had been brought by God to America and I was supposed to call you, and take you to Santa Ana." Can you imagine our reaction? Can you for a moment perceive God's constant care in fulfilling His plans with us? Of course, the next morning as we looked outside, we saw a blue car approaching to take us to the purpose for which God had brought us to this country. We were finally leaving the hotel that had witnessed our cries of desperation. That was the moment where everything began to make sense.

Today in our hearts, there is only gratitude towards those two crucial people that God used to fulfill our destiny. The next few years were not easy, but God used every circumstance and situation to shape our lives and prepare us for what He had ahead.

Scorpion and Snake, or Land of Milk and Honey?

We served the Lord for many years in Santa Ana until the day He clearly sent us to open a church in the City of Riverside, California. The Year was 1997. We knew that the territory was known to be a difficult one spiritually. We were greeted by church leaders in the area who warned us of how hard it was going to be. They also told us that new churches were closing in the city and that Riverside was a land of spiritual scorpions and snakes. Of course, we were in awe, but very certain of God's calling and were in no way intimidated by fear and negative words spoken to us; but obviously we were aware that this was a journey of intense spiritual warfare.

We surely understand that when we embark on whatever mission Jesus delegates to us, it will not be an easy one. There will be human and spiritual opposition. Unfortunately, there will also be voices of discouragement which will speak loudly to make us give up and believe that this is not for us. Along with these human voices, spiritual voices will whisper, trying to cause depression, and apathy. The purpose is to make us give up on God's idea for our lives forever. Have you ever experienced it at some point? We have, again and again!

Within days of our arrival in the City of Riverside, the Lord impressed us with the need to begin a seven-day fast. Henry was fasting on water alone and on the day before ending his fast, the Lord indicated that he should climb one of the hills in Riverside, to anoint it, to bless it, and to consecrate the city to God, making decrees and declarations over the people of the Imperial Valley. At around 5:00 pm, Henry took his bottle of oil and his Bible and began to climb the hill. As he walked, he could see from afar the figure of a man with raised hands on the top of the hill, speaking loudly; he seemed to be praying. Henry was happy

160

to think that he might find a Christian man, a prayer partner. As he approached, he was surprised by the demanding voice of the man who asked him, "What are you doing here?" The guy did not seem friendly at all, quite the opposite. Henry kindly replied, "I am a pastor and I have come to pray and bless the city." Again, in a tone of anger and bitterness, he replied, "Well, you were late. I already cursed it." Shocked by this response, Henry realized he was facing a territorial spirit who already knew of our arrival to establish the kingdom of God in Riverside. This spirit wanted to advance in the spiritual world, make evil decrees and cast curses on the people. Now Henry understood the reason the Lord had instructed him to climb the hill and pray over the city. It was spiritual warfare that lasted for five hours. The evil spirit in the mouth of the man affirmed that our enemy had the church of Christ captive in his hands and asked, "Has any Christian ever knocked on your door to tell you about Christ? See, I have them in my hands, so they don't preach the gospel." At that moment, Henry pointed his finger in the man's face and replied, "But I want you to know that the church that is being founded in this city will be known for the strength of its evangelism." As he continued to rebuke the spirit of darkness, the man was thrown by the demons to the ground and wriggled between some branches.

A Real Spiritual Fight

Amid all the war that was going on, the Holy Spirit reminded Henry of the purpose for which He had sent him. He learned that we should always focus on doing what is commanded by God and never get distracted in the process. Henry gave the order in the Name of Jesus for the man to get off the highest rock where he was sitting and for him to be still and not to move. He obediently did so and sat silently on the ground. Henry climbed onto the highest rock, poured anointing oil on it, and fervently prayed in Jesus' name to reverse every word the enemy had said about the city. He blessed the city, each person, each family, the churches, the mayor, the city departments, police officers, etc.

When it was all over, the man looked at him with defeated eyes and said: "I will never be able to return to this rock again." Henry asked him why and he replied, "Because you have anointed the high place." It was an impressive victory of God over darkness. Henry then spoke to the human part of the man, not the spirit. As they talked, he learned that the young man was the son of a pastor, a backslidden Christian who no longer walked in his faith. That day as the young man had climbed that hill, he had only one intention: to curse the city and then commit suicide. Amazing! There in the darkness under the stars, the Holy Spirit spoke clearly to Henry: "Show him God's love and embrace him!" As he did, the young man cried profusely, a cry of liberation.

Henry had never heard anyone cry in this way. What followed was miraculous. The man rededicated his life to Jesus and decided to return to his parents' home and make peace with his family and church. What a wonderful divine intervention. Anything is possible when we decide to obey the smallest instructions from God.

The River and The Fishes

The next day Henry would finish his seven-day water fast. He woke up early to pray and consecrate this time of fasting to God, while I prepared our breakfast. While praying Henry had a clear vision and an image opened before his eyes which he describes as having been like in the third dimension. In this vision, he saw himself crouching down planting a river. As he explained later, we all know that you cannot plant a river. Seeds, flowers, vegetables, etc. are planted, but the reality of planting a river does not exist. But in this vision, it was exactly what he was doing: He was planting a river. While planting it, Henry tried to make the river grow, opening its banks, fixing its flow, but he did not achieve much. As he observed it, he realized that the waters were not sparkling, but rather cloudy, opaque, and two little fish were swimming very slowly. Suddenly, an intense light came from behind, and Henry clearly felt that God was in the room and His presence was extraordinarily strong. He knew that he was having a supernatural experience with the Lord.

This powerful light passed through his body and crossed him. The fear of God filled his entire being. He quickly removed his hands from what he was doing because he knew that the light was going in the direction of the river. When the light touched the river it came to life and began to expand greatly in all directions, becoming a huge river, to the point that the end could no longer be seen.

The water seemed to have a soul, and it was crystal clear. The two fish that previously moved so slowly now swam rapidly from one side to the other, and they began to multiply. Seeing this, Henry had the ability to count the multiplication in his head and the fish went from two to four...from four to eight...from eight to 16...and they continued to multiply until they filled the entire room, leaving no empty space. The fish were happy, full of life, energy. In the blink of an eye, the vision disappeared while Henry stood there amazed at what had just happened. When he came into the kitchen and shared the vision with me, we cried together. We knew that God grew the ministry that was barely begun, and He would multiply it in a great way. Our understanding: The River is symbolic of the ministry and the fish represents Christians.

When we have our hands in the ministry, everything is done with great difficulty, sacrifice and it does not grow as we wish. But when we remove our hands from the river and let God do what He wants, everything flows, and the growth and multiplication are a result of letting God guide it. In times of pressure, crisis, difficult circumstances, where we think that we are the ones who can solve the situation, we must remove our hands and let God do His work. Together on that day, we agreed that the Holy Spirit would be the Pastor of *Evermore Church* and we would be His collaborators – co-laborers. God has been faithful, guiding to this day.

The Holy Spirit is the Lord of our lives and ministry, and He always will be. After so many experiences, confirmations, and proofs of God's love, the work was finally established in the City of Riverside and to our joy; it grew rapidly, becoming an influence in the city, in the nation and even outside of it. Truly God has been too good to us. Throughout our history to this day, we have passed through valleys, mountains, great challenges, trials, conquests, losses, victories, and more.

Many years have proved the goodness and faithfulness of our God. But the Lord has brought us here. Now through the years the church has grown tremendously. We have seen God's hand the whole way. We now have three services each Sunday, including one in English. We've been able to influence many pastors and leaders from across the country through monthly meetings and mentoring one-on-one. Evermore Church is still focused on Encounters, our weekends at retreat centers focused on salvation, emotional healing, and deliverance. Folks are transformed by the power of the Holy Spirit in miraculous ways. Our annual conventions, including Braveheart for women, are means of extending God's Kingdom. Braveheart is a bilingual movement that grew out of a need to minister to women in a world where females have been subjected to indignities. We come with healing, deliverance, and restoration directed specifically to women. It's a two-day event focusing not only on our spiritual lives, but also on physical health and beauty. Our intention is to transform every broken, damaged, and bruised heart, into brave hearts, through God's healing power.

Since *Braveheart* began in 2015. Over 15,000 women have encountered Jesus in a new way. We fight for a better world, where every woman is respected and loved. Henry and I are now grandparents to three beautiful children who will continue the work we have begun. None of this could have been done without the help and guidance of the Holy Spirit. He has been so faithful. To God be the glory! *"From him and through him and for him are all things. To him be the glory forever! Amen."* Romans 11:36

Jeannie Lein

Chapter 10

Judy Ball

Judy Ball is a renowned intercessor and international speaker. Along with her husband, Jerry, they lead groups of powerful intercessors, praying at events, in cities, for congregations and many people worldwide. Since 1995, responding to God's special call to Israel, they have taken over 20 teams to strategically intercede for this nation: as well as annually partnering with the International Christian Embassy of Jerusalem (ICEJ) for the sole purpose of interceding for the 7,000 people and 60 different nations during the Feast of Tabernacles.

In 2011, after realizing that half of our world leaders are educated at eight U.S. Ivy League Colleges - with only 4% having a Judeo-Christian worldview, "Ignite Ivy" & "Ignite America" was founded. These events are specifically designed to attract student leaders from around the country who desire a deeper relationship with Jesus, purposely to ignite God's fire within them, resulting in transformed college campuses back to their Godly foundations. Jerry & Judy are long standing members of *America's National Prayer Committee* – NPC, working closely with the leaders for the *National Day of Prayer*. They have lasting relationships with other like-minded ministries such as *Promise Keepers*, Aglow, *End-Time Handmaidens*, Dutch Sheets, Bob and Rose Weiner - *Youth Now*, Lou Engle - *TheCall*, and Dave Warn - *Collegiate Action*.

Father, I Will to Do Your Will Now at the age of 80 I know that I was born to be an apostolic woman. An apostle is a sent one. John 3:34 *"For he whom God hath sent speaketh the words of God: for God giveth not the Spirit by measure unto him."* John 4:34: *"My meat is to do the will of Him that sent me and to finish His work."* This chapter is about a lady who believed God would send her to do what He created her to do to fulfill His call on her life for her generation. When I am weak and trembling in the flesh, when I hear His instructions, I say I am being sent as Jesus was sent, with the Holy Spirit without measure and my meat is to finish what He has sent me to do. I learned early as a teenager to ask the Lord questions and listen to receive His instructions. If the answers that I heard were not much, much bigger than something that I could do by myself it probably wasn't from Him.

It was during the early teenage years that a foundation for my faith in God was developed. The truth is that the God who made the universe answers prayers. Prayers were answered when three ladies – one in particular, Wilma Brown – came to our home to pray for my mother and brother during critical illnesses. When I was thirteen my mother was diagnosed with cervical cancer. At that time cancer could only be treated with an insertion of radioactive cobalt. This process made her very sick. My little brother was diagnosed with polio and doctors told us he would eventually be in an iron lung. Ladies from the ARP (*Associate Reformed Presbyterian*) church where our family attended came during those illnesses. I heard one lady, Wilma Brown, pray simple prayers that reached God and there were answers. My brother, Billy, came home from the hospital and never had to be put in an iron lung. My mother came home from the hospital. She suffered from scar tissue in her digestive system from the strong treatment, but she lived until I was thirty-three years of age.

The scripture *"This is the confidence we have in approaching God: that if we ask anything according to His will, He hears us"* (1 John 5:14) became a reality to me. My cousin, Leonard Cone, took a year off from seminary to help my daddy and our family during a time when my mother and brother were very sick. He worked for Daddy during the day and came home to comfort the family at night. He built us swings and took us on hayrides. He was truly our Mary Poppins. When he came home from work in the afternoons, the first thing he would do is take his Bible and walk down in the woods. One day I followed to see what he was doing. He was propped up against a tree reading his Bible and talking out loud to God. This so impressed me that when he left to return to seminary, I decided to do the same thing each afternoon when I came home from school. I went to a beautiful place in the woods below our home that was thick with green moss. This place became my thinking spot. I read all the parts of the Bible that were written in red and talked to God.

Mother lived supernaturally for years to see her request to God fulfilled – to live until all three of her children finished college and had a family. During the last week of her life I was with her. I heard the Lord ask, "Judy, what do you believe?" I answered, "Lord, I believe you can raise Mother up and heal her." Then I heard, "But, what does she believe?" "She believes that she will be with you forever," I answered. Then I heard, "What is greater, that for temporal or eternal?" I rushed into Mother's room and bowed down at her bed and told her what I had heard. She patted my head and looked into my eyes with so much love and relief. She said, "I am so glad you know." She went to be with her Father in Heaven the next week. The fear of death was removed from me. For as much as the children are partakers of flesh and blood, he also himself likewise took part of the same; that through death he might destroy him that had the power of death, that is, the devil. And deliver them who through fear of death were all their lifetime subject to bondage – Hebrews 2:14-15 the truth is that we can talk about everything to God, that reading the Bible develops an intimate relationship with God and that He cares about us and will direct our path to fulfill the call of God on our life.

It was while I was sitting on the moss bed one afternoon that I asked the Lord about a football player named Jerry that passed me in the school hallway and picked on me. At first, I was offended but then I began to look forward to seeing him. I asked the Lord about Jerry Ball, the football hero in our school and one of the most respected young men by his peers and in our community. I was a little surprised when I heard from the Lord that Jerry would be my husband. I was very young at that time but little by little I knew that this would happen. Jerry received a full football scholarship at Wake Forest University (he was on the dean's list and recognized in Who's Who Among Students his senior year) and I also attend Wake Forest as an education major.

Our courtship had three loves – (1) the love you have for me, (2) the love I have for you, and (3) the love we have for God. We were married after college. We just celebrated our 60th anniversary with Jesus leading and guiding our lives. We have two daughters who have given us two loving sons-in-law, eight wonderful grandchildren, fifteen great grandchildren with one more on the way. We lived in Robbins, North Carolina for the first five years of our marriage. Jerry taught and coached, and I taught eighth grade. There were many miracles in our lives during that time, two being the births of our daughters, Talica Lee and Tara Virginia. I had learned to hear God's voice and knew that He is love but I had not seen in the Bible about confessing our sins, baptism in water, and baptism of the Holy Spirit or the blood of Jesus that defeated the devil. I felt that love works would change people, so I worked day and night doing love works from my flesh and was totally exhausted. Jerry felt the Lord was leading us to leave Robbins. I was not ready to go but I wanted to follow my husband's guidance. He resigned from his job. We decided to take our girls to Six Flags over Georgia and stay with my first cousin, Tricia, who I had not seen in years. In our younger years Tricia and I had shared every Thanksgiving together at our home in the country and our fathers and brothers would go hunting.

We would have a big Thanksgiving dinner together. She was very dignified. I was a tomboy, country girl. As we entered Tricia's home we found an incredibly happy marriage, great children (two boys and a girl) and a loving hospitality that was beyond normal. Jerry believed in a new job and told Buck, Tricia's husband. Buck went upstairs to pray for the exact conditions that Jerry requested and the next day Jerry received a call with a job offer to move to Spring Hope, NC and coach at Southern Nash High School. Wow - instant answer. I asked Tricia, "what is different here with you and Buck?" She said, "We have been filled with the Holy Spirit. We were baptized with the Holy Spirit of God, and we speak in tongues. We know that the power of the shed blood of Jesus erases all of our sins when we repent, and we have power over the devil who seeks to destroy us and send us to hell instead of Heaven." I was so excited and told Tricia that I wanted this and asked her to pray for me.

The next day Jerry and I took our girls to Six Flags over Georgia. I asked Jerry to take the girls for a little while and let me sit by myself. I was so astounded because all of my life I felt that I knew all about God. He had been so good to me, and He had answered my prayer requests from my moss bed. This was something so amazing. I begged, "Please, Father, teach me, fill me with that same Holy Spirit that Tricia and Buck have."

We moved to Spring Hope and bought a farmhouse that was old but near the elementary school. I missed our beautiful English tutor home with chandeliers. I had one light bulb hanging down in every room in this farmhouse. We had been there two or three weeks when we returned to visit our former city, Robbins. We spent the night with good friends who lived near the Presbyterian Church that we had attended. I had directed the choir and planned beautiful Christmas programs. Kindergarten was not a part of the education system at that time, but I had turned the three rooms upstairs in our home into a kindergarten so that our two girls could have a great start in school. Our girls went to Sunday school. They saw us and the Big Brother Big Sisters program redo poor children's homes and bring them to church. It was a good life, but it was by our love of might and power, not by the Holy Spirit. One rainy Sunday morning on our return visit Jerry decided to stay with our friends with the girls. I walked down to the church in the rain, took a seat and tears came into my eyes as the choir came out. The guest speaker was playing a clarinet at the beginning of the service. I had played a clarinet when I was in the band but mine never sounded like that. In a moment as he began to speak, I knew that he had that baptism in the Holy Spirit that I so wanted. After the service was over, I walked to the front of the church and asked him if he had the baptism of the Holy Spirit. He said yes, so I asked him to pray for me. We went into the pastor's study. He touched the top of my head and asked Jesus to fill me with His Holy Spirit and I began to speak in tongues. That was the beginning of life in the dimension of the Spirit that I had not even dreamed of until our visit to my Cousin Tricia's home.

Miracles in Spring Hope

The first year in Spring Hope I started a kindergarten at the Methodist Church. Tara was five and had been in my kindergarten in Robbins since she was three. Talica was in my kindergarten one year before she went to first grade in Robbins. They were both very smart. Talica, so sensitive to Jesus, was very exact in all that she did in school. Tara was very smart but precision in everything was not her nature.

They were so precious, and they loved Jesus. Talica attended the graded school within walking distance of our home and the church was around the corner. Mrs. Bass, Talica's first grade teacher, was blown away with Talica's ability and her loving personality. Tara loved her new friends in kindergarten and loved it when we talked about Jesus and prayed. Both girls looked forward to Jerry reading to them and tucking them in every night. Coaching took up a lot of Jerry's time but he never neglected his girls, including me. Sometimes the girls would ask me, "Mama, is daddy playing with the pointed ball or the round ball tonight?" We attended the Methodist Church in Spring Hope. We had attended a Lutheran church and also a Baptist church in our earlier years.

We moved several times for Jerry to help build football programs. He was a highly respected coach, and we attended the churches where most of the boys who played for him attended because we believed in Jesus and the churches we attended believed in the Bible. The second year we were in Spring Hope I was the Education and Christian Counselor at the Freewill Baptist Children's Home. I loved the chance to lead 72 children on their walk with Jesus. I prayed every day for the Lord to send me to the one that needed me most that day.

Many miracles happened during our time at Spring Hope. Here are a few: Goldfish returns to life. We had a neighbor come over to watch the girls for a few minutes each weekday after school. One day during that time Talica wanted to change the water in her fishbowl. She put her little fish in the sink in hot water thinking the water would be more comfortable than cold. About that time I walked into the house, the goldfish was dead and Talica was crying, "Mama, please pray for my fish." I put the dead fish in another bowl with Tara's fish and I asked both girls to kneel down and I would pray. Before I prayed, I told both girls we were going to ask Jesus to come and give life back to the little fish, but we had to remember no matter what happened we are going to thank Jesus. Both girls agreed. It was Talica's faith, not mine, that gave life back to that fish. I spoke the words and our loving Father gave life. I tested that fish by putting my hand in the bowl. Tara's fish would dart away and Talica's fish, the one that had died, would come and touch my hand. Amazing is the love of Jesus.

Talica is 58 years old now and she says that fish has given her faith throughout her life. Pastor's heart is healed. Peter Marshall, Jr. was coming to a nearby town, and we went to hear him. When he called for people to come up for prayer I rushed up. There was a gentleman standing next to me and when Peter came to me, he instructed me to put my hands on the front of this man's chest and on his back and say, "In Jesus' name be healed." The man fell to the ground. I went quickly back to my seat thinking that he might be dead. The next time I saw him was at the Children's Home. He was the Chairman of the Board of Directors. He saw me and said you were the one who prayed for me. He had been scheduled to have open heart surgery the next week, but his heart was completely healed. He invited me to preach where he was pastor of a Goodwill Baptist Church. The Holy Spirit came that day with signs and wonders following the preaching of the gospel.

There was a little boy hit by a car that God healed. I was on my way to school when I came upon a car wreck. The car had hit a little boy and he was lying near the front tire. I stopped and someone asked if I was his mom. I said no but I am his guardian and I bent over him and prayed. I stayed very close as they put him in the ambulance. He was unconscious. I told the paramedics that I had to be with him in the ambulance, so they let me climb in and sit near him with my hand on him. I stayed with him until they rolled him into the emergency room. I was assured that he would live and recover. I never knew the little boy's name.

A few weeks later I was at the elementary school to meet with one of my children and a little boy came up and put his arms around me and said, "Thank you, I love you. You were the lady with me when I was hit by a car." Wow what an amazing God.

A Teenage girl was healed of trauma at Children's Home. At the Children's Home I had a treasure box with visits to the circus, airplane rides, a weekend with a family to do fun things and many more prizes. I checked the children's grades and if they had really improved, they could choose a reward. There was a high school student, Brenda, who just could not improve no matter how hard she tried. I felt bad for her so one day I asked her to come to my office. I told her we were going to ask our Father to show us what to do. We sat there in silence after we prayed. During the silence I asked the Lord to reveal to me something so I could help Brenda. He did. "Did you see your father shoot and kill your mother?" I asked. She began to cry. I told her Jesus had been there, but no one called on him, so I was going to ask him to go back there with her and take this horror out of her heart and mind and heal her.

174

We asked, Jesus answered our prayers and she graduated with honors. Jeff with cystic fibrosis improves. One Sunday we sat behind Jeff and his parents at church. I could see that Jeff had surgery on his eyes and was very thin, but he was full of personality as he greeted people. I asked the Lord if there was anything that we could do to help this family. I really do not remember how it all came about but Jeff's mom and dad became our best friends and Jeff was Jerry's football manager. Jeff had cystic fibrosis and had to sleep under a breathing tent.

His parents would beat on his back every morning to get his lungs cleared. Jerry and I, as well as many more, prayed for him and his family. Jeff was able to come out from under the tent for the time we were there. Jesus became his breath, and he was with Jerry on the football field as his manager in all kinds of weather. Jeff was able to drive his own truck and was so happy. He lived years in great joy, and he arranged some community youth meetings for Jerry and me to lead.

The Miracle Football Win

The second year that we were in Spring Hope our football team had only won two games. That night we were playing the team in the conference that was undefeated. I was in my orange chair where I talked to God. I prayed, "Dear Father, your word says in 3 John 1:2, Beloved, I wish above all things that you may prosper and be in health, even as your soul prospers. Father, Jerry's soul is prospering and for his day-to-day life to prosper he needs to win football games." I heard a whisper,"Go buy some refreshments for a celebration. Tonight is the night that his team will also prosper as their soul prospers. Jerry is a witness to these amazing young men." That night I went up in the stands to sit and watch this victory that the Lord had told me would happen. I usually ran up and down the sidelines encouraging the players. I had heard and believed the word and was confident of the victory. With eight minutes left in the game we were behind three touchdowns. Quietly I prayed, "Father I believe your word." I heard his reply. "Judy, what is faith?" I remembered that it is the substance of things hoped for, the evidence of things not seen. I looked at the scoreboard and thought to myself that I must see the score differently. I heard Jesus say your thoughts are correct, but you must praise me for everything that happens from now on. Suddenly the other team had a 15-yard penalty. I walked back and forth. Thank you. Jesus. Thank you, Jesus. Then, a ten-yard penalty happened. Thank you, Jesus. Thank you, Jesus. Suddenly as the clock was quickly counting down, our boys intercepted the ball and ran for a touchdown. They were able to score four touchdowns in four minutes - a miracle. Many of the players were from the Children's Home. This miracle changed their lives and mine. I thought that I had an answer for all games but found out quickly that every situation is different. We ask and hear and believe what the Lord says and then praise until it comes to pass.

Visited by Two Angels

A few weeks after we were in Spring Hope a very dignified man knocked at our front door. I opened the door and greeted him. He said to me, "I have a message for you. The Lord said for you to do his will." I have remembered that word every day of my life. We had been in Spring Hope a little over two years when I received the message that my mother's cancer was back, and the doctor had given her only a short time to live. I ran out the door running up and down the sidewalk crying when I met a beautiful black lady. She said to me, "Honey, you are just made of dirt, you can't carry this. Call on Jesus, cast this burden on Him and He will help you." Those two statements from the man at the door and the lady on the sidewalk are so from the heart and truth of a life lived with Jesus in us the hope of glory. Col.1:27

A Life of Intercession

From the moss bed of prayer and Earth to Heaven intercession with Jesus, Heaven is coming down all around us. Hebrews 10:19. We enter into the Holy of Holies by the blood of Jesus to join Jesus who ever makes intercession. In 1997 Jerry and I were given the ministry of Breaker of Dawn. It has been an apostolic intercession ministry. Our teams have led intercession for 24 years for the Feast of Tabernacles in Jerusalem. We led intercession for Promise Keepers gatherings, Rick Joyner conferences, Lou Engle's the first *TheCall* on the Mall in Washington, DC and national and international Aglow conferences. The Lord gives us protection from backlash and needless casualties. Jerry always prays Psalm 91, and he breaks curses, hexes, incantations, mind binding and mind controlling actions taken against us, and he binds all iniquity and infirmities. He releases a blessing on each intercessor. We anoint each intercessor with the fire of intercession. We eat the last supper together to believe that we are one in the Spirit and are one body with one voice of intercession with Jesus. We declare that we are all sent as Jesus was with the Holy Spirit without measure (John 3:34) and our meat is to finish what we are sent to do. John 4:34 We always say go out believing. I am thankful for a life of personal intercession with Jesus. 1 John 3:8, *"For this purpose was the Son of God manifest to destroy the works of the devil."*

Transformed Nations - Fiji

The Fiji Rugby 7's sang and praised Jesus as the Son of God right after they won the Gold Medal at the 2021 Olympics. Jerry and I, along with two of our grandchildren, Megan age 22 and Marshall age 20, visited

Fiji. Once in the city of Suva and the second time we visited three transformed villages: one on the coast, one in the mountains and one on the inner island. The places we stayed had no beds or tables. We slept and ate on the floor when we were there. The towns were being set on fire and young people were committing suicide, both in the cities and the villages. There was witchcraft and worship of demons and smoking pipes filled with drugs.

The beginning of the revival and the healing of the land started when the president of Fiji called the pastors in the cities and the villages together to repent and call on God to heal their land. The young people on the base where we began our trip were up at sunrise worshiping with all of their hearts. They prayed fervently for the transformation of villages. The pastors went to the villages and preached the gospel. Whole villages on the coast and in the mountains came to the Lord. They burned the totem poles, pipes and all witchcraft paraphernalia. The people came to Christ in the evangelistic meetings where the simple gospel was preached. People were healed and so was the land.

Our granddaughter interviewed the Fijian people and Scott, who was now her husband, filmed the testimonies. Two of those interviewed were women at the ocean catching fish. They had seen a huge light come from above and touch the ocean. The fish that they caught were big, whereas before they had been very small. There were many miracles throughout the land. Young people became dedicated to Jesus and suicide was turned into hope and life.

I visited Almolonga, Guatamala with a team that was studying transformed villages. We were there after 88% of the villagers, who were once lost, became Christians. The bars became places of worship and the vegetables that they grew were three times larger than before.

I saw this firsthand. We were there for a celebration with the small in stature Indians who were dressed in clothes that they had woven. They were the most beautiful people praising the Lord after being transformed by the preaching of the word of God. Buenos Aires, Argentina Buenos Aires was in revival.

I was asked to be one of three intercessors for a leadership conference hosted by Peter Wagner for a hundred leaders from all over the world. The three of us spent hours ministering to these delegates. We witnessed them being filled with the Holy Spirit. There was a deliverance tent where hundreds were being delivered. We were there when the revival was moving in hundreds as the gospel was being preached and where the manifest presence of the Holy Spirit was demonstrated. We, as well as the leaders, were being transformed as we witnessed this revival. While in Buenos Aires Carol and John Arnott came to our room and the three of us - Bobbye Byerly, Bunny Warlen, and I, prayed for them. We asked for them to be baptized with the Holy fire of the Holy Spirit for revival.

They went back to Canada and that is when the Toronto Revival began. A young man from England, Roger Mitchell, asked me to pray that he would not cry when he repented for the British destroying ships in the Falkland Island where many Argentine young men were killed. I told him that I would pray that he would shed tears of repentance. I had been given Revelations 22:2 - In the midst of the street of it, and on either side of the river, was there the tree of life, which bare twelve manners of fruits, and yielded her fruit every month: and the leaves of the tree were for the healing of the nations. Roger did repent with many tears and great love and repentance broke out.

I was part of an intercession team in Korea where there was a global consultation of leaders coming together to ask the Lord to pour out His presence all over the world the same way that He was pouring His Holy Spirit out in Korea. One day our team of intercessors was standing at the back of the auditorium interceding for a breakthrough for the 4,000 world leaders. I felt led to go down front and stand by a large organ. Roger Mitchell, the young man I had prayed for in Argentina, was there at the organ. He asked me where the intercession room was, and we went. He fell on his face and began weeping and that started a river of tears from all of the intercessors. Without any announcements the leaders from all nations began to come into the room to repent on their knees to each other. This went on two nations at a time until well into the night. The Druze came into the room to repent to the Armenians. The Druze had murdered many of the Armenians. There was weeping and the love of the Holy Spirit was so good.

Grandson raised from the dead - Trip to Nigeria –

Ordination by Bensen Idahosa in Benin City, Nigeria

These events happened in my life between 1987 and 1994. It was a Saturday morning in 1987 that I attended an Aglow meeting in Statesville, North Carolina. I was the Aglow State Prayer Coordinator for N.C. and loved the Aglow ministry. Looking back, life would have been so different if I had not attended that meeting. It is so important that we go each day, each hour where we are led to be, to meet those who are ordained to be strategic in our lives. That day I met Bernita Conway, a renowned Bible teacher, known for simple faith in Jesus with miracles following her. At the Aglow meeting she shared a testimony of a missionary who had gone to Africa and had seen a baby raised from the dead. That missionary had seen the dead raised by declaring Ezekiel 18:32: *"The Lord does not take pleasure in death, turn and live."* He also bound the gates of Heaven and hell and continued to speak that scripture. Hearing that I turned to the front of my Bible where the words King James was, and I wrote over the top of the whole page I believe this.

The next day I was keeping two of our grandchildren, Megan - four years old and Marshall - 18 months old, for our daughter and her husband to go to church. Megan had sniffles so I happily stayed home with both of them. I was rocking Marshall. He fell asleep and suddenly I realized that he was not breathing. I shook him. He did not breathe. I shouted out loud that I had to call 911 but suddenly a peace came upon me, and I heard the words, "Judy, you know what to do." I remembered Ezekiel 18:32. I did not think of time and there was no fear, no panic. I walked around the kitchen, living room and bedroom. I would put Marshall from my shoulder to my lap and he was not breathing. I kept saying, "Marshall, the Lord does not take pleasure in the death of you. You turn and live." I don't know how many times I did this or how long it was, but I looked over my shoulder and his little fingers started to wiggle. In a few minutes Marshall was fully back. I called the church and asked that Tara and Gary (Marshall's parents) and Jerry come home. When they arrived Marshall was running around with no ill effects of what had just happened.

I had a brain tumor removed in 1994 and after surgery I had to be quiet with short visits from my family. Marshall and I had two very special visits during that time. One of the fun things that I would do with all of the grandchildren was to give them a basket and go on nature walks in the woods to collect bark, moss, rocks, etc. That day I asked Marshall what he would like to find, and he said an arrowhead. I told him we would bow our heads and ask Jesus to help him find one since I could not go with him. Later that afternoon after his hunt he came running to show me what he had found. He had a string, a piece of leather, a small ball but then he said I found something that I can't give to you. He pulled out two perfect arrowheads. He had found them in a little patch of dirt in a very grassy field. To this day he still has those arrowheads.

We had more time to talk on our next visit. I was in a big chair and Marshall was in a small one next to me. We talked for a while, and it came to my mind about the time he had stopped breathing. I asked him if he remembered going to Heaven. His little face glowed all over as he smiled really big and got very excited. "Oh, Mema, He told me that I could tell you all about it." I was in shock. Marshall said, "Ask me some questions." So I did. I asked about flowers, and he said there were beautiful flowers and that I would really love them. He said they stand straight up, and they are gold. Then he continued to say there was a swimming pool and it had no bottom, and guess what? You don't have to speak out loud in Heaven, you just think, and He hears you.

He told of seeing Jerry's daddy and that he had blue eyes. Jerry's father was blind and only Jerry's mom knew what color his eyes were. Marshall had been a quiet little boy but after this encounter he became quite the talker. I will go back in my story to the Aglow meeting and Bernita Conway. I made it a point to get to know Bernita and share Marshall's miracle. She invited Jerry and me to some meetings where she was preparing a team to go to Nigeria, Africa. I felt because of her teaching and the miracle of Marshall's life that I was called to go to Nigeria with her. Jerry agreed with this decision. We finished all of our preparations for the trip. After arriving in Africa our team divided up and we preached daily in different churches. One day we were all together at the compound of Bensen Idahosa. I loved the place and the people. We did not meet Archbishop Idahosa, but I picked up a book, Fire in My Bones.

I found out that this book was the life story of Benson Idahosa and this book changed my life and destiny. This book was about a young man who was thrown away on a garbage heap and was saved by his mother, raised as a slave by his uncle and at 18 years of age met a preacher who taught him about Jesus, the miracle worker. He rode his bicycle and looked for someone to raise from the dead. He found a little girl at Dr. Margaret, his future wife's, home. The little girl was raised from the dead. Many more miracles followed this man. All of Nigeria was touched by his life. On the flight home from Nigeria I whispered to my Father in Heaven, "If anyone ever ordains me, I want it to be Bensen Idahosa." I never mentioned this request to anyone, and I only told Jerry years later.

The brain tumor surgery that saved my life was in 1994. One week after a surgery that was prayed for around the world, I received a call from a friend who I had met several years earlier. Her name was Deborah. She asked if she could visit Jerry and me and spend the night because she was going to Charlotte, NC to hear Bensen Idahosa. We, of course, invited her to stay. When she came, I told Jerry I had to go with her to hear this man. On the way to Charlotte, Deborah told me that she had completed all of the work to go to Nigeria to be ordained by Bensen Idahosa. I just listened, but whispered in the spirit, "When she goes Lord, you know I must go with her." Eight weeks from my surgery and after many immunity vaccines, I was packed, and Jerry was sending me off to Nigeria. He alone knew that I had asked the Lord to be ordained by Bensen Idahosa. I had also asked God to let me meet his wife, his driver, his cook and anyone that interacted with him before I was ordained by him.

Well, here's what happened. Deborah and I were housed in a nearby hotel. Every morning for three days they brought us to the home for breakfast. We sat at the table with Bensen and his family. We met his driver, his cook and most importantly, Dr. Margaret, his wife. The ordination service was to be on Saturday. It was Friday morning and I had to fly home on Saturday morning to intercede for a national Aglow meeting so I would not be able to attend the service. The driver came to pick us up from the hotel on Friday morning for breakfast. I whispered to Deborah to go on out to the car. She left and I knelt down by the bed and said, "Father, you heard my request years ago and you arranged for me to be here now. You must do something to let him know that I am here."

I went out to the car to make the trip for breakfast. As we entered the home, Dr. Margaret told me that Bensen was in the garden and wanted to see me. I began to shake all over. I entered the garden and saw him sitting at a school desk with his arms reaching over the front. I supposed he had been meeting with God. In a deep voice he said, "What do you want?" I told him my whole story and he replied, "Let the will of the Lord be done tonight. Be on the stage and I will call you forth." That night Dr. Margaret seated me on a stage with no one I knew, and I was looking out over a sea of beautiful black people who I did not know. I sat there through worship and the opening prayer. Then Bensen called out, "Let the woman from America come forth." He did not even know my name! He said to me, "Do you want to bear fruit that remains?" I answered yes and he said, "Bow the knee." He and his elders poured oil all over me and my new white suit. I literally crawled to the corner of the stage and stayed there until Dr. Margaret came for me to go back to the hotel. The anointing for fire in my bones has been with me since that time in 1994.

The Call to Israel

In January 1995 a few months after the life changing brain tumor surgery a friend of mine who I had prayed with in Washington, DC asked me to join her and other intercessors to pray for Ed McAteer's breakfast where Christians would honor the Jews. I had not been called to Israel at that time and knew very little about how to intercede. This breakfast was in a large hotel in Nashville, Tennessee. The intercessors had a room for intercession. We gathered there the night before breakfast. I had been in intercession for leaders and other conferences but never just for Israel.

I sat in a corner seeing intercessors wearing talits, and blowing shofars as they prayed. I prayed in tongues. The morning of the breakfast we intercessors had a table right in front of the speakers. The first speaker was a Jewish woman who survived the Holocaust. Hearing her story I began to cry. Then beautiful banners made by Kay and Pete Williams came in with a speaker saying rise and shine Levi for your light has come and the Glory of the Lord has risen upon you. They went through the 12 tribes of Israel, and I was on the floor sobbing by the 12th tribe. I looked up and a woman was kneeling down over me and asked if she could help me. I blubbered through tears as to why I was so upset about the 12 tribes of Israel. She said, "Judy, you have been called to Israel." I asked her what that meant. That lady was Shirley Ellis, and she and her husband spent the next few months visiting us, bringing books to us and going through scriptures to show us why Biblical Israel is a call for all believers to understand while they pray for the peace of Jerusalem.

She flew Jerry and me to New York to meet Susan Michael, the ICEJ director for America. Susan was a founder of the International Christian Embassy in Jerusalem when other embassies left. We also met the international director, Juhan Iucoff. Shirley knew that we led intercession for Promise Keepers meetings and for Rick Joyner. She suggested that our ministry, Breaker of Dawn, would bring intercessors to pray for the Feast of Tabernacles each fall in Israel. We have been intercessors for the Feast of Tabernacles for 23 years.

We have taken 240 students to Israel from the Ivy League campuses and other universities with Covenant Journey and Passages. We have been intercessors for many leaders in Israel for all of the 23 years such as Chris Mitchell, CBN Israel anchor. They are our family.

The Call to The Ivy League Campuses

Jerry and I took Megan, our granddaughter, and Marshall, our grandson, on a prayer journey to the Ivy campuses with Lou Engle and son, Jessie, and Dutch Sheet and daughter, Sarah, and Will Ford. Megan, Marshall, Jessie and Sarah were teenagers. We learned that in years past slaves would gather in the barn with an old wash pot. They would turn the wash pot over and pray under it so their prayers could not be heard by outside people because they would be beaten for their prayer life. Will had a black wash pot that we carried with us to every chapel of the eight Ivy campuses. We prayed under that washpot that the prayers of the slave generation would touch this generation and set them free from the slavery of the power of sin.

Breaker of Dawn Ministries had a Holy Convocation at the Lion of Judah Church in Boston. We gathered with prayer leaders who wanted to pray for the Ivy League campuses. Jerry and I have been intercessors for Bob and Rose Weiner for over 20 years. Bob and Rose were ministering on Harvard Square in a rented penthouse overlooking Harvard. Jerry and I would come there to pray for them and minister to students.

One night a student from Harvard said to me, "Mama Judy, did you know that 50% of the world's leaders go to the eight Ivy League campuses and only 4% have a Judeo Christian faith?" That night after the students left, we asked the Lord what we should do? We heard "Ignite Ivy." We set a date and gathered a few believing students from each of the Ivy League campuses, plus MIT. We met on the campus at Northfield, Massachusetts where D.L. Moody is buried. That was the beginning of ten years of Ignite Ivy.

Our last year in Boston was 2020. Over a three day span our sessions were filled with worship lead by Joe Salzano, Clarion and Nancy McQueen and Mark Bristow. They had musical worship, complete with many instruments, and Holy Spirit worship. There were extended times of intercession for the campuses. There were teachings on the Holy Spirit as taught by Jesus in Mark 16 and students were filled with the Holy Spirit and they spoke in tongues. We saw lives transformed by the teaching of the written word of God. We had leaders from Israel to speak on the Biblical history of Israel.

We were asked by the Museum of the Bible to take Ignite Ivy students to Israel through the Passages Program. We took 240 students to Israel. Many of these students, who are sold out to Jesus, are now world leaders. Over the ten-year period we also had Ignite America conferences with students from campuses all over America. We were in Colorado Springs, Colorado, Oklahoma City, Oklahoma, Shreveport, Louisiana and Campbellsville, Kentucky. Hundreds of students were in outpourings of the Holy Spirit for three days as they heard Christian lawyers, doctors, leaders from Israel and young evangelists as they witnessed miracles after the preaching of the gospel. They were blessed with a father's blessing and shared communion. We anointed them and sent them out in power and love and hope.

Jerry and I celebrated 60 years of growing in oneness this year, 2021. True love is about looking forward, together, into eternity. We have two books: a blue one for him and a pink one for me. We write love letters to each other on special occasions or just at any random time during the year. The love letters we have written always have 1-2-3 the love you have for me, the love I have for you and the love we have for God. We would like to share a few portions of these letters.

We will continue to be strong knowing the light and joy of the Lord will get brighter and brighter as the Breaker goes before us to shatter darkness whenever the Lord sends us.

From Jerry on our 50th anniversary – we were at the beach: My Judy, I love you, the one who for so many years has supported me in all endeavors to become what God created me to become. You have supported my successes and my failures. You have always been there for me. You have modeled to our girls and granddaughters what a woman of God can be. You have not only shown what it was like, but you have lived a lifestyle of it. As I sit here thinking back over our years together, I am amazed and so thankful for you and for God who chose me to share this life with you. To have and to hold in sickness, in health, for richer, for poorer, for better, for worse until death we do part. We are one with each other and one with Him.

You have made our life together so wonderful by giving time and giving yourself to me to have peace and joy, love and security in each other and in Christ. We are 50 years into our marriage covenant vows we spoke before God and all those witnesses in the ARP church in 1961. You have been so faithful to your vows, and you have made room for me when I came up short some of the time. This journey is a wonder and joy that cannot be expressed in written words alone. The lives we have touched together and individually are numerous and it has been because you have responded to the gift of God that He placed in you.

You have been obedient to His call and gifting and have not only touched my life but many, many others. I love you dearly my beloved wife for eternity. From Jerry to Judy – We were in Israel: My Judy, I have observed your walk with the Lord. It is so unique there is none other like it. He has truly chosen you for this hour, for this place and the timing of His anointing is so exact in you. Your children and grandchildren have never had the joy of seeing you flow in the Holy Spirit the way I have. I see how God has used you in the work of His kingdom. The hour is here, the time is now to do all the Father tells you.

I pray that you will receive a clear vision of His plan and purposes for us all the rest of our lives. Thank you for being so sensitive to me and caring so much for my needs. I love you dearly and forever.

From Judy to Jerry - Christmas: You are in the kitchen breaking pecans for the tipsy cake. You are so handsome in your red shirt, bib overalls and the Wake Forest hat. I love watching the beauty of Jesus in you, the hope of glory on your face as you prayed Psalm 91 this morning. The name of Jesus written in lights that you placed at the entrance of the farm is shining brighter this season in this dark world reminding us that Jesus is the light of the world and in Him there is no darkness.

From Judy to Jerry – This was Jerry's birthday: This year the breath we breathe together in our prayers, and in our silence, is molding us into the image of Christ. As we share His word, He brings us closer and closer to where Jesus, God and the Holy Spirit dwell in eternity. Here, there, everywhere From Judy to Jerry – We were in Galilee: My darling, beloved husband. God called you husband, and me wife. Becoming one flesh was His idea of eternity of reproducing sons and daughters in the Earth to fellowship with Him, here, now and forever. Your eyes shine brighter. Your father's hug is more powerful, your words echo streams of light and care and strength to this generation, the many spiritual children the Lord has given to us. You constantly watch and pray over those the Lord has given you to love and bless. They are bearing fruit like your garden. Neither crows nor vultures come near. You fire Psalm 91 and the blood of Jesus at them, and darkness goes.

We have by His grace and forgiveness and His abundant love and mercy made it through the black holes, the burning, and the threats that were ignited by jealousy, hate, bitterness and ignorance. Tears, rain bubbles and oceans of love wash up as we watch hand-in-hand together. Our feet are dug in the sand and our hearts are beating with an eternal melody of love, joy and thanksgiving for years in the name of the Father, the Son and the Holy Ghost. You, my darling, have a crown, an eternal reward for saying "Yes' ' to the Lord everyday of your wonderful life.

Prophecies

1 Thessalonians 5:21 – Prove all things; hold fast that which is good, prophetic words that have proven to be legitimate. Hold fast and keep them as a guidepost to navigate our journey through good times and bad.

Archbishop Bensen Idahosa-Africa: "Breaker of Dawn will bear fruit that will remain." Bishop Bill Hammond: Father, we bring your servants before you, and we speak with your authority and anointing – and we set in motion your divine purposes and plans oh God and we gang up on the devil like he's tried to gang up on them and the Lord said what I have joined and what I have begun – I shall begin to finish and the Lord says the devil thought if he could nip it in the bud – he thought if he could destroy it before it really got off the ground that it would never launch and never go into orbit, but the Lord says even though the countdown was delayed there for a while, yet the blast off has now happened and you're not going to explode and scatter but you're going to go in orbit around my divine purpose and everything in family and relationships and other areas are going to come into line said the Lord so get ready for the alignment for I put angels on assignment even to handle these situations and

I'm going after those who look like those who are scattered from you and looks like they are not going to relate but the Lord says do not judge it by the present because I am in control and God by the way you ought to go My grace I do bestow – so I'll show you my glory as you tell the story – you will not faint – you will rise and demonstrate my anointing said the Lord. Rise oh man and woman of God, arise in this new grace, run this race, for I am with you and I will open the doors and I will shut doors. I will open hearts and I will shut hearts. I want you to not complain. I don't want you to look at the natural things but I want you to see my hand and my control. I will move and do what needs to be done at the right time at the right place and I will even cause like the story of the children Israel heading for the promised Canaan land. I hardened some so they would fight against them and win their victory. Others I set by the water and by your space, and through them you will know which ones to relate to and which ones I have hardened their hearts. If I have hardened their heart, it's not the place for relationship or for that to happen, but go on and possess your promised Canaan land for I have called you to a destiny you will fulfill saith the Lord. Amen.

Barbara Yoder: I just heard you are going to get into doors that other people wouldn't get into – unusual doors are going to open up to you and the Lord said even the financial thing. God says I'm going to give you wisdom with that and I'm going to multiply it because the Lord says you're going to have your bags packed day and night and you need money for what is up ahead of you. For the Lord said I'm going to send you here, I'm going to send you there for you are even going to be forerunners of revival.

The Lord said you are relationship connectors. The Lord said the fire and the seed of revival is in you. I am even renewing your physical body and even the doctor's report that you got a year ago I am causing that to come to not for the Lord said I have given you an assignment over the years and it is not finished and it is not going to finish soon and so the Lord said get ready, get armed and even look at your investments for the Lord said I'm even going to have you change some to even bring in that which you are going to need for the days ahead. You're going to go to places you never planned to go.

I see an Asian country that you never even imagined that God said you're going to go and you're going to go on before and lay the groundwork even in intercession. A fire is going to break out in that place and the Lord said, I'm going to show you what it is right on time and the Lord said you are a man of relationship. I'm going to link you up to many and the Lord said you are going to even make the way for your wife. Sometimes your wife is a little weird because she carries that anointing of revival and the Lord said they are going to be able to link her to you and you are going to be the door opener for her and she's going to get in there and the fire is going to fall. The Lord said even this day I do put a new mantle on the two of you. You shall carry it, for the Lord said, "I'm going to cause you to pave the way even for that which I am getting ready to do and you shall be the Sarah and Abraham of old and you shall live to be old, old, old and you shall see this move of God that I am getting ready to loose in magnificence across the United States. You will see many years of it, and you shall be in the middle of it declares the Lord." Amen Mary Lance Sisk: "I see you blowing the trumpet and calling groups of people to prayer." A prophet in Israel as he lifted Judy's hands: "God has summoned you to write for the nations. Listen and obey."

www.breakerofdawn.org

Chapter 11

Maryal Boumann

JOY in the Fire!

I was raised in the Midwest, third of eleven children with parents who are now present with the Lord in their heavenly mansions!

As a family, growing up we prayed daily before meals, we regularly attended Church several times a week, and we served wherever needed. I have fond memories of stocking the nun's pantry in the convent, helping Mom arrange flowers on the altar, preparing cookies for the Bake Sales, and working at the church bazaar…

Dad was an usher and they each 'adopted' an hour every week to pray in the sanctuary. I think they both treasured their quiet time in the Lord's Presence and away from all the household noise and activity!

I am truly grateful for such wonderful, God-fearing, Jesus-loving parents.

I was baptized as a baby and at age 12 was 'confirmed', dedicating my life to Jesus, and choosing St. Cecilia, known as a Worshiper, as my patron saint… For those not raised Catholic, that is a Saint whom you admire and want to be like… little did I know that I would eventually become a true worshiper!

My junior year in high school my parents moved us from Nebraska to Colorado and finally to California, thus I attended three different high schools in two years. I was blessed to have siblings as my friends!

About age 17 I began to pass out in church, and at age 18 I stopped attending, but I never stopped praying or celebrating Christmas and the Resurrection. Like many others, I thought I was saved and headed toward heaven. It was only through tragic circumstances that I came to know Holy Spirit as my Best Friend and Helper, and Jesus Christ in a personal relationship.

Here's what happened

I had several male friends throughout high school and college that I dated but nothing serious, none with whom I had thoughts of marriage. Then I met Bob. He was three years older, a pilot, a PGA golf professional, a contractor, and loved the outdoors. He could accomplish anything he set his mind to. Bob was my first love, the one (and only!) man I've been with which was unusual back then and now! But it is God's plan for His daughters, no sex before marriage.

After I'd known Bob for about nine months, he proposed in a beautiful, romantic way at the Ahwahnee Hotel in Yosemite. But I was hesitant to accept. In fact, I ended up encouraging him to take the diamond engagement ring and use it as a down payment to purchase a small airplane, which he did.

Time went by, we continued to date and on one occasion, he got angry about something. He would curse, and/or break an item, usually something of mine. I should have ended the relationship the first time he yelled or threw something. I wasn't raised that way, my parents never swore nor yelled, that's not a part of my character. I was naïve and would always accept Bob's apology.

During our time together, he was diagnosed with malignant melanoma on his forehead. The surgeon successfully removed it. Next I was diagnosed with breast cancer. The weekend before I was to check into the hospital for a mastectomy, we drove to Lake Tahoe and along with his parents and mine, we got married at 'Chapel of Love.' That's the real name of the place, it was charming! I requested a Christian ceremony; it was quite holy and lovely. My family and friends wanted to attend but my doctor had clearly stated 'no stress' before my surgery, so my girlish dream of a big wedding in a white beautiful dress fell by the wayside. I wore a pretty brand new two piece coral silk skirt with a jacket that a Sister lent to me, and some pearls from my Mother-in-love. I carried coral roses from Mom's garden.

The three men played a round of golf in Tahoe as we got ready!

Our marriage was good for a number of years but we had not made Jesus the center of our lives. That was a big mistake. We didn't even discuss it beforehand. His parents never prayed together nor attended church, even at Christmas or Easter. I should have known.

We would fly to different places in our little Cessna for breakfast on Sunday mornings. I would pray during the flight, enjoying the gorgeous scenery but we did not praise or pray <u>together</u> as my parents had.

Ah, if only my Dad had sat me down and showed me the Scriptures about fornication and being equally yoked! (I pray parents do that with their children, so important).

Bob was very healthy but as the years went by, the degenerative discs in his back and problems with a shoulder surfaced. He stopped being able to swing a golf club in tournaments, he stopped being able to build homes, and the commercial airline business began drying up. Anger began to rise up in him and he would vent his frustration toward me. He became verbally, emotionally, and ultimately physically abusive.

One day after he had left the house, I was in fear for my life after the angry threats of shooting me himself. I quickly packed my vehicle and drove away, weeping. I didn't know where I was headed. A longtime family friend invited me to stay with her. She lived hours away from Bob's and my home. I was constantly looking over my shoulder, terrified that he would find me! He was leaving phone messages begging me to come back.

I would go for walks and talks with the Lord, and through a stream of tears, one day I gave my life to Jesus with the desire to put Him first in ALL areas of my life.

During that time away, I had taken a one day job at a Country Club for a Christmas party. It was December; my favorite time of the year, but life seemed so difficult, empty, without joy. Except for a couple sisters, I could not let anyone know where I was, including my precious parents. If anyone asked they could truthfully say they did not know where I was.

On the drive to the one day job it was pouring down rain and I was pouring out tears. I caused an accident and totaled my car. It happened on an unfamiliar road where I had driven through a stop sign. A female doctor was in the other vehicle. I blacked out for a few seconds but I recall the doctor telling those gathered around not to try to remove me from the car. She thought I had broken my back.

I remember how compassionate the ambulance drivers were on the way to the hospital. Miraculously, I was released after a couple hours with only bruises from my seat belt.

Two weeks after the accident I left and came into mediation by one of my sisters and her husband who both loved Bob (I kept most of the abusive incidents hidden from my family), I agreed to go back to him. I had two conditions for my return. First, if he would go to Church with me and would get anger counseling. He agreed things were fine for about a month and then he started to try to entice me to fly to our favorite breakfast spot on Sunday morning instead of going to church. I declined, saying we could fly somewhere for lunch. He stopped going to church with me, yet I continued. He began to resent that I chose church over him (only on Sunday mornings) and began to resent that I was successful in my business, which paid our bills. Once while he was washing his truck, he turned the hose on me, drenching me as I was leaving for an appointment to meet clients.

The day after I told him I was filing for divorce, I was getting dressed for work. He came upstairs in a fit of rage, and began choking me. Separation had not worked. I thought he was going to put my head through the bathroom window. I looked into his eyes that were once a beautiful blue color, but now they were now dark and angry. I remember thinking "I'm going to die!"

Suddenly (I love God's suddenlies!) the phone rang. It was one of my sisters… I saw Bob turn from a raging maniac to walking over, picking up the phone and in the friendliest voice say "Hello." I recognized my sister's voice and yelled "Sissy, he's trying to kill me!" She asked to speak with me. He handed me the phone with an ugly, mocking smirk… My sister asked if I wanted her to call the Sheriff's office. I shouted "Yes!" She asked again, "Really?! You want me to call 911?!" "Yes!" Never had I responded like that. Within five minutes four Sheriff Department vehicles drove up, deputies with guns drawn arrested Bob. They could see I was hurt, and one of the deputies was a former client of mine.

Upon counsel from a pastor, I got a restraining order against Bob. Reader, realize, in my heart I still loved him! I knew who he *could be*: the kind, gentleman who helped me through cancer, the one who built a tiny house for a squirrel until it recuperated, and the one who rescued dogs and took groceries to the elderly, the one who taught me to fly, camp, and golf, the one who fixed things around my parents' home.

All his friends except one had stopped calling him. They had witnessed his wrath. I called the one friend and asked him to bail Bob out of jail. I gave him the money to do it. You may be shaking your head and saying "What? Seriously?" Yes, I did. I remembered that one time Bob told me he would never last in jail. His spirit was like a bird who hated being caged.

His friend arranged for Bob to meet with his business lawyer the following Monday afternoon. It turned out Bob was a no-show, and shortly after I received a call from the Sheriff's Department. Bob was at Marshall Hospital. I drove there and learned that he had tried to commit suicide. He had shot off half his face.

He had left a note addressed to me asking for forgiveness from me and from God. He told me how much better I would be without him and so on. I was taken to his side, told him I loved him and I was there for him. The Hospital Chaplain offered him comfort and prayer.

After about three hours, the doctor came in and told me Bob had died. He asked if I would consider donating his organs? I knew Bob would want that, so I said yes. The doctor let me know he would be back to discuss it with me. In the meantime, I called Bob's parents to let them know. They wept and wailed with severe heartache. They had lost their only other child a few years earlier, Bob's older brother.

After about an hour, the doctor came back in and said Bob wasn't really dead. "What!?" Apparently he was given meds to paralyze his body to keep him still but a brain scan showed he was alive!

Doctors decided to transport Bob to UC Davis (just over an hour away). My sister drove me there; once again I was taken to his room. He was settled in a bed with an IV. For four days I stayed with him. I only went home once to shower and get fresh clothes. I prayed and sang over him. The pastor of the church I attended at that time called and asked if I would like him to come. I said, "No thank you, but could you please give me the words to the song, *Holy Spirit, Come and Fill Me Up*?" He did, and I sang that over Bob. I told him how much the Lord loved him. He gave him life and He allowed him to live so Bob could invite him into his heart. I shared the salvation message and read Romans 10:9: *"if you confess with your mouth the Lord Jesus and believe in your heart that God has raised Him from the dead, you will be saved,"* I told him Jesus could read his thoughts since he was unable to speak.

Doctors had told me that Bob had shot off part of his brain. They were astounded and amazed that he could lift up a specific finger when they asked him to move it. This meant he could hear and reason! One side of his face was bandaged, of course, but other than that he looked fine. He could not move any part of his body except his fingers, and he could open his good eye. On that Friday morning nurse Mary shaved and sponge-bathed him, I thought "Oh my goodness, he looks radiant!" There was so much peace in his hospital room. You could almost hear a feather drop.

About noon that day, Bob took his last breath on earth… I was engulfed in the Lord's quiet love. I think it's important to let you know that about one and one-half years after Bob's death, as I was in deep worship, not thinking about anyone or anything except Jesus, I clearly heard the voice of the Lord say, "Bob did die that night." I asked, "That Monday night?" "Yes." But because of all the salvation prayers for Bob, He allowed him to live until he could hear the Gospel message and choose if he would invite Jesus to be Lord, repent and confess him as Savior. I believe Bob did and that one day I shall see him in heaven. It was a last-minute salvation, just like the thief on the cross with Jesus at Calvary.

I had made poor choices as a young adult; I lost my childhood dream of having my own large family and a devoted, godly husband. My choice of a husband did not align with the Word of God. Yet I would go through it all again believing Bob and his mom got saved! I also led her in the salvation prayer.

The point of me sharing all this is that the Lord has taught me so much through the fires in my life, whether it's cancer, abuse, manipulation by others, breaking my leg then a week later breaking my wrist in Spring 2020. I then lost most of my belongings in a house fire in the fall of 2020 and was physically hurt again as a result of the fire. I lived in a hotel for six weeks and hemorrhaged my eye. I stayed with a sister, then a friend, for 12 months until I could find a place to live, which was in November 2021. I rejoice knowing that nothing can happen to me that the Lord does not allow. Nothing.

I rejoice because shortly after my husband's passing, I felt set free to be whom the LORD created me to be. I no longer walk on eggshells, no longer walk in fear.

I learned to live with no regrets and to check my motives. Those two characteristics have helped me a ton.

For Example, No Regrets

I know I did all I could for my husband including praying for him and his salvation, encouraging him to fulfill his vocational desires, being a helpmate, forgiving him so I would never have a bitter heart, cheering him on! And on his deathbed, I asked him to forgive me for anything I had ever done to hurt him; not physically or verbally but other ways I may have hurt him. As I spoke to him, he gently squeezed my hand. We experienced another miracle, astounding doctors!

I am one of my parents main caregivers, I think I did all I could to make their final years as comfortable and as wonderful as possible. Living with no regrets slams shut the door to guilt or shame!

Checking Personal Motives/Intentions

Years ago as part of the Leadership Team at a Ministry Retreat, I was sitting in the front row. Those who know me know I am tall. On that particular day I was wearing heels and a red jacket and long skirt. During praise I heard the Lord whisper "Worship Me. Lift your hands and worship Me." I responded "But Lord, I am so tall and I will stand out." He said something like "Daughter, do not worry what others think. Be an example. Worship Me!"

I lifted my hands and entered into deep worship, with my eyes only on my Beloved. After a couple songs I felt released to go kneel in a prone position by the side wall. I was overwhelmed by His pleasure and His love. I sensed someone come next to me and also kneel, bowing low after worship ended, I looked up and the conference speaker was the person on the floor next to me.

Two days later at a meeting with the Leadership Team to discuss the retreat, the president accused me of trying to draw attention to myself by standing and lifting my arms in worship. The four others in the room gathered in a circle and began quietly praying. I looked at the woman's face. Her anger distorted it. I remained silent. Finally, I took a deep breath and quietly said "You are wrong. I was worshiping Jesus." She continued with her skewed view for a minute. Gently I repeated "You are wrong."

I could say that with great conviction because I knew my motives were pure. At that very moment, for the first time ever, all fear and intimidation of man fell off me.

She leaned over to pick up her purse and leave the room. That is exactly what the enemy would want. I told her that and asked her to 'please stay and let's pray.' She put her purse down and sat down. We prayed a little, and then ended the meeting. It was obvious she was still upset.

The following day, my accuser called and apologized. I imagine the Lord had spoken with her about the situation. The Lord looks at the heart. And the other ladies in the room knew my heart and my intentions. Praise God that woman and I remained friends until she passed into eternity.

Another Example of Following the Voice of the Lord with Pure Motives

A local church was hosting a well-known prophet. Our *Aglow* board I was on decided to attend together in support of the pastors. During worship the Lord told me to get my red flags and step up into the sound booth, the highest point in the room, and wave the flags as a prophetic act of covering everyone in the room with the Blood of Jesus. The sound man was a friend, and when I asked if I could come up there, he said, "Yes." I did as I was instructed, worshiping with flags, cleansing the room from demonic activity.

A few minutes later, the prophet walked to the middle of the aisle and lay down on his stomach, hands outstretched above him. The head intercessor and her team of three surrounded him as he lay on the carpet. I watched as the intercessor began quietly speaking over him, and then began moving her arms as if she was throwing knives and darts into his back.

This is what I saw in the spirit. I began praying in tongues, while still watching. Suddenly, that intercessor looked up at me. Her face transformed into a large snake with fangs that appeared to lunge at me. I had never experienced anything like that, nor had I heard about anything like that. My reaction was to lift the red flags even higher, pray and bind the demons operating through her.

Without going into more detail, one of our team and I were accused by the intercessor and pastors of foolish things which were lies from the pit of hell. We remained in the peace of the Lord. After all, He is our Defender.

A week later I received a 'Thank You' form-letter from the prophet for the donation I had made that night. He did not know me personally. At the bottom of the letter was a hand-written note from him stating, "You are being verbally attacked with lies. But remain steadfast, God knows the truth, and others will also." I wept tears of joy and relief, knowing God's Eyes were on us and the situation. He is our vindication.

Shortly after that the head intercessor was 'released' from the church. It was discovered that she was a witch. Not too long afterward the church shut down.

Many of us know witches are real and are assigned to churches and conferences where the gifts of the Spirit are allowed, encouraged, and taught, and where the Word of God is preached and proclaimed.

When I became Spirit-filled, I began praying for discernment, 'divine' discernment so I would immediately recognize truth from lies, life from death, and good from evil. Surely, we all need that these days.

Being in the ministry and working with all types of people and personalities can be challenging. There are those who want to knock you down so they can feel high and lifted up. Sadly, jealousy is rampant within the Church. And there are those who want to steal your assignment, as well as your mantle.

Hold tightly unless the Lord tells you it is time to release it. He may have a new mantle for you or simply want you to rest and listen to His Voice.

It can be easy to get our feelings hurt by those who think they could do a better job than us. One thing I have learned is to never pick up an offense. If someone says something to you that pierces your heart and you feel a stab in your back, take it to the Lord and ask Him if the comment or criticism is true. If not true, forgive that person and pray for them. If true then learn, repent, thank the person for sharing, and move forward. I pray I will always have a teachable spirit. We know that iron sharpens iron.

When I look back over my life, I am aware of many times the enemy has tried to take me out in various ways using accidents, depression, discouragement, or people who aren't walking with the Lord. What the enemy means for evil, God <u>will</u> use for good when we allow Him. Where is the enemy attacking you? Rejoice because our God has given us His authority to bind and loose, to cast out evil and call forth the opposite to fill those dark places.

Remember the hospital I mentioned near the beginning of my story? The Senior Chaplain brought me on as a Chaplain there and I served for seven years until family and new ministry obligations caused me to step down. What joy to share the love of God and the hope we have in Jesus with the hurting, the ill, the lost, the oppressed.

We can do that every single day, no matter what we face. I used to preach 1 Thessalonians 5:16-18, "Rejoice always, pray without ceasing, in <u>everything</u> give thanks; for this is the will of God in Christ Jesus for you." Then the Lord had me put those verses into <u>action</u>, not testing me but strengthening my roots in His Words. Last year I clearly recall sitting in the snow on a steep, icy driveway not being able to stand up because of severe pain which turned out to be a broken leg. I struggled to get up and then slipped back down. The Scripture above came to mind. I released joy and laughed and sang, praising the Lord even as icy pelts began falling, calling on Holy Spirit and angels to help me and declaring the word.

It took me at least 25-minutes to push upward to my vehicle at the top of the driveway with my older neighbor (and her bad back) watching me. She was unable to help. I was going to the post office and since she was snowed in, I asked if she needed any mail to go out. She did, and as I was walking up the driveway with her mail tucked inside my coat I fell. I wasn't worried, I knew it would be okay because the Lord was with me and He wasn't going to leave. I thought for a moment my neighbor may think I was a bit daft as I started singing in tongues but it seemed to calm her, as she watched and listened to me praising and praying. Don't you love it when God's word comes alive in you?

These days with so much confusion, stress and strife swirling around us can make it easy to get caught up in the negativity and darkness. But for those of us who know and follow the Lord, we choose to focus on things above and be that bright light shining in dark places reflecting the love of our King Jesus.

We are charged to speak words of life, truth-in-love, and hope as we trust in our magnificent and majestic creator and Father, our beloved Savior, healer, Messiah, our helper, comforter, and teacher. We have all that we need because we have Jesus in our hearts, and in our lives. His Word is alive; it is powerful, and released through us! Worship and His Word can shift the atmosphere wherever we go. We know Holy Spirit and the Kingdom of God live within us.

We are truly blessed to be part of God's royal priesthood, His ambassadors, grafted into His Heart and into His family for eternity. The Lord is not looking for leaders who will rule over people, but for those who will discipline others and help uncover the best in them so they too can fulfill their destiny.

May every single one of the good plans the Lord designed just for you overtake the enemy's plans to depress or destroy you! You, beloved, are more than a conqueror in Christ Jesus who loves you. Let's get out there, spread the gospel, dressed in the full Armor of God, and slay some dragons with great joy and victory with Jesus.

Maryal Boumann
Pray California, Director
www.PrayCalifornia.org

Chapter 12

Vicki L. Nohrden

"Launch Out Into The Deep."

As a new believer in Jesus, I was daily seeking to know Him with all my heart. He spoke to me in many ways through bumper stickers, out-of-the-Word, road signs, in my prayer times, and through dreams in the night. I'll begin with a dream that still speaks today.

I was walking on a dock toward the water and as I continued walking, I heard a voice say, "Be careful the water is very deep." I ignored the voice and kept walking, suddenly the dock broke out from under me, and I was being drawn out into the deep waters. I saw a hand reach out as if to help me, however, I did not reach back as I was now being pulled out further and further away from the shore, I exclaimed, "Oh Lord, I never wanted to drown!"

Jesus was calling me out into the deep waters. He was inviting me to let go, He would be my Teacher.

> *Jesus climbed into the boat belonging to Simon Peter and asked him, "Let me use your boat. Push it off a short distance away from the shore so I can speak to the crowds."* (Luke 5:4 TPT)

My relationship with Jesus was one of faith. I believed what he said, I didn't doubt it. I trusted His voice. I launched, quit my job, sold my car, and gave away everything I owned. I paid off all debts and purchased a one-way ticket to Malawi, Africa.

I was on a spiritual honeymoon with Holy Spirit leading. I was so free. He showered me with so many gifts and what an absolutely amazing adventure it was. I was like my three-year-old granddaughter, who listens and follows, childlike. Time after time the Lord showed up and demonstrated his kingdom rule.

> *The sheep recognize the voice of the true Shepherd, for He calls his own by name and leads them out for they belong to him. And when he has brought out all his sheep, he walks ahead of them and they will follow him for they are familiar with his voice.* (John 10:3-5, TPT)

I still recall one such amazing adventure when we were on the train headed back to the mission house after ministering for several days in an outlying village, and I was speaking with my interpreter about being filled with Holy Spirit. As I looked up and around me, the people on the train kept looking my way and listening to our conversation; of course, we stood out as the only two American women amongst them!

I said to Holy Spirit, "Why don't you tell them too? They're all listening" Well, that was His invitation, and moments later I found myself preaching to the entire train of people. When Holy Spirit was finished, I was aware that I was standing. Then I sat down in my seat and pulled my hat down over my head because now I was laughing joyfully. I thought they must think I'm crazy, laughing uncontrollably. Truly, I was filled to overflowing that day. It was one of my first of many deep-water encounters of letting go and letting God show up. This happened in 1987 before I had ever heard about something known as holy laughter. Honestly, I didn't know what to think. Faith is like a locomotive; it keeps moving.

"Believe in me so that rivers of living water will burst out from within you, flowing from your innermost being, just like the Scripture says!" (John 7:38, TPT)

Launching out into the deep is exactly where we are being summoned. Because you're reading this, then the summons is to you too!

Ezekiel saw this river as he was being led and measured out into the deep, a place where you can no longer walk but you have chosen to follow him; you've left the comfort and safety of the known shore to venture out until you are over your head. Now that's exactly where you need to be -- over your head knowledge. If you remain in the shallow water of your own understanding or even a religious mindset, you won't let go and trust Holy Spirit to lead you. You must and let the adventure begin. Control and fear will try to hold you back, but apostolic women are bold and courageous.

He measured off another thousand, but now it was a river that I could not cross, because the water had risen and was deep enough to swim in—a river that no one could cross. (Ezekiel 47:5 NIV)

I believe the Word of God, where we are told, "We can do all things through Christ," and "With Him nothing is impossible." I believe Him at His Word. Faith is believing and trusting He has the outcome, and has gone ahead of you.

If your dreams are bigger than you, most likely you're dreaming with God and He'll lead your every step. Jesus called to the disciples, "Follow Me." He taught them daily, revealing the Father's love, manifesting God's glory, opening the eyes of the blind, setting captives free, demonstrating the kingdom. He led them to the cross; He kept His promise, sending Holy Spirit to be our guide. Welcome Holy Spirit right now to lead you on.

> *And without faith it is impossible to please God, because anyone who comes to him must believe that he exists and that he rewards those who earnestly seek him.* (Hebrews 11:6, NIV)

I love dreaming with God and stepping out of the boat when others have chosen to remain at the shore of discussion. I love to pray and listen for the voice of God, to hear things I've never been taught of men. As you launch out into the deep you will have to let go of man's opinions and allow yourself to be taught of God. You too may be criticized, spoken about, mocked, and even misunderstood. At times finding yourself standing alone, and even feeling hidden or isolated for a season of time. But get ready; He's preparing you to manifest His glory. By the way, that's why you're here -- to discover who you are in Him and have you're being in the abundant life.

> *"Just remember, when the unbelieving world hates you, they first hated me. If you were to give your allegiance to the world, they would love and welcome you as one of their own. But because you won't align yourself with the values of this world, they will hate you. I have chosen you and taken you out of the world to be mine. So, remember what I taught you, that a servant isn't superior to his master. And since they persecuted me, they will also persecute you. And if they obey my teachings, they will also obey yours.* (John 15:18-20, TPT)

There are many times the Lord has directed me to keep moving out into the deep. One such time was when I raised a tent in Carmel, CA where I live. I have often thought of that "gate-taking" experience in 1992 when I first began to understand that I was walking in an apostolic calling. Day after day, the battle raged at that gate, but I never drew back. And spiritually speaking we took that gate and obtained the key.

A few weeks later, I recall driving by the corner where we had raised the tent and a cloud of glory could still be seen hovering over the land. The Lord was pleased at our faith to believe Him, even when the opposition swelled like a tidal wave against us. Many were saved and delivered impacting entire families, and yet others stood outside the gate wondering! The battle didn't stop after our two weeks of revival meetings, yet I'm thankful for having done all to stand. The anointing is costly; you must be willing and obedient.

> *"And this truth of who I am will be the bedrock foundation on which I will build my church-my legislative assembly, and the power of death will not be able to overpower it! I will give you the keys of heaven's kingdom realm to forbid on earth that which is forbidden in heaven, and to release on earth that which is released in heaven."* (Matthew 16:18-19, TPT)

A most recent adventure was when the Lord asked me to run for public office, not once but twice. I had a lot to learn. I have received several prophetic words about my governmental mantle and calling. Although I wrestled with getting involved in politics, I knew I had to say, "Yes."

*The Lord declared, "My people will be willing in the
day of my power."* (Psalm 110:3, NKJV)

This adventure was definitely going to take me yet deeper, not leaning
on my own understanding but trusting the Lord to lead me. My first
response was, *I don't know how to do that.* There was no further
conversation about not knowing how but instead His reply was, "Ask
me to show you." I prayed, then Googled how to run for office. I
researched and read until I felt faith and confidence arise in me, and
the day came when I said to my husband, "Ok, let's go file my papers."

*"Trust in the Lord with all your heart, and lean not on
your own understanding; in all your ways acknowledge
him and he shall direct your path."* (Proverbs 3:5-6,
NKJV)

My first campaign was for state assembly, and my second run was for
state senate. Running for public office was quite an adventure, perhaps
even one I may want to forget. Honestly, I enjoyed speaking, writing
speeches, researching, and standing up to represent the people, as well
as discussing policies that need common-sense solutions, not agenda-
driven, union-backed, lobbyist-influence party politics. I'm a justice
fighter, I enjoy taking on bullies and standing up for those who feel
their voice is unheard.

As you read this most likely you can feel the tugging. Is He calling you
to step into the faith and glory dimension to encounter his kingdom
calling upon your life? The deep waters are for those who want to
dream with God, they are pioneers, builders of the kingdom; they are
faith-filled believers, innovators, obedient, and willing to answer when

He calls. He says, "Follow me I will make you, I will do exceedingly, abundantly above all you ask or desire".

> *"I promise you if you have faith inside of you the size of small mustard seed, you can say to this mountain, 'Move away from here and go over there', and you will see it move! There is nothing you couldn't do.* (Matthew 17:20,   TPT)

Pray or sing this song of the Moravian missionaries with me. In 1727 they encountered a powerful move of Holy Spirit and answered the call. They sang this song as they boarded the ship and left the shores of their homeland. It was said of some that they were willing to sell themselves into slavery to go and preach the good news of the kingdom. They too launched out into the deep waters and answered the call.

> ***I lay my life down at Your feet.***
>
> ***To give to the Lord the rewards of His suffering, to give to the Lord the souls of the lost, to give to the Lord the rewards of His suffering, and take up my cross.***
>
> ***I_____, lay my life down at Your feet.***

Vicki Nohrden

Wind and Fire Ministries

PO BOX 6181 Carmel, CA. 93921

https://www.windnfireministries.com

windandfire@comcast.net

Chapter 13

Dr. Qaumaniq Robin Suuqiina

I have loved God since I was a little girl. You can say I have always been "God's girl." I was raised in the Methodist Church where I learned about God but my knowing and connecting with Him was something inside of me and not related to church.

My family did not read the Bible together or talk a lot about God. We said the prayer before our meals and at our bedside at night before we would go to sleep. And yet when our family had to evacuate our home in 1961 due to Hurricane Carla my mother remembers me begging her to stop the car so I could run back into the house to retrieve the Family Bible to take with us. It made me feel safer to have it along.

In 1967 a gentleman who was a member of The Gideon Bible Society taught a bible study on the Book of Revelation and I attended and it was the first time I had ever studied the Bible. I remember being so excited to find out that the Bible was really In 1976 after many years of doing my own thing at the age of 24 I walked the isle of Evangel Temple in Nashville Tennessee where I was welcomed by Pastor Jimmie Snow and I gave my will over to the Lord and asked Him to take over the reins of my life. That was a turning point in my life and saved my life as far as I am concerned.

Over the years as a wife and mother there were struggles and at times, I took the reins back for short periods of time but not for long as ``The Hound from Heaven" never let me stray too far off the path.

Yeshua who I affectionately call "The big Kitty" has always been right with me every step of the way.

My journey has been like a paint by numbers picture. To look at the blank canvas with all the numbered spaces makes no sense but once you look at the box it came in with the finished painting and read the directions by the artist that designs it, it comes into focus. God has numbered the canvas of my life and knows what color paint to put in each space and my job is to follow the instructions. As I follow the instructions the painting of my life comes into view.

From the time I was a child the calling on my life has been for the underdog and to pursue and administer justice. My greatest spiritual gifts are in the area or discernment, word of knowledge, and counsel. Looking back on my life at the age of 70 I can now see that calling and those gifts play out time and time again in everything that I do.

I have spent four decades walking with those in life crisis through the deep waters of suffering, helping them to make sense of their journey, witnessing their pain and allowing God to use me as a catalyst to connect them to Him in the midst of it all. It has been my honor and privilege to be a midwife in the process of rebirth in the lives of these individuals. My calling was not to knock on doors to bring the gospel message to strangers. Many are called to do so but not me. It took time for me to accept that and stop comparing myself to others with the gift of evangelism and preaching and allow God to use me where I was needed. I have often said that I have been called to the Dung Gate not the Fish Gate and accepting that allowed me to be who I was meant to be and where I was meant to be.

Some of what I have encountered behind the scenes as the Dung Gate of organized religion has not always been pleasant to experience. I have encountered those who have experienced much dysfunction and abuse even while living in faith-based homes and who are confused about how a loving God who they have heard all about could allow those things to happen to them by people they were supposed to be able to trust using His name in vain (bringing His name to nothing.) I have also walked alongside people who have endured spiritual abuse through organized religion and various denominations and churches. This journey has not been easy to make sense of even for me at times much less for the victims of this type of abuse that leads to disappointment in God Himself.

My calling has not always been understood by the religious systems because it is somewhat out of the box. So it is that those with a true apostolic calling will not be hirelings or sell out to any of the systems of this world, including the religious system but instead will be servants of the Lord and only concerned with His Kingdom and His people.

What I have learned over the years is that His Kingdom is not ego based and narcissistic ways are not the building blocks that are used by Him. The Apostolic kingdom of Yahweh is not built like the Tower of Babel where we are allowed to "make a name for ourselves." On the contrary, the apostolic kingdom of Yahweh is built on Chesed (Mercy/Everlasting Kindness) and it is built stone by stone as an altar to God.

I learned this lesson through my own experience from the school of hard knocks of being humbled by the hands of the Lord. When I was a little girl my favorite words to my Mom at age 2 years were, "Me do it me self." There was a whole lot of me in there that had to come into the right place before the Creator of the Universe.

I view the apostolic as qualities based on the Fruits of the Spirit not the Gifts of the Spirit or ministry titles and these qualities should work through us creating an apostolic life and a life of Godly character. I feel that Apostolic people should be willing to go into the world to serve God and lead people to Him, they should look to God alone for the direction that they should go in to fulfill His calling and purpose of their lives, they should be totally loyal to the Lord not sold out to a system, they should be willing to suffer and be patient in hardship, and they should be totally devoted to God alone. I believe that apostolic means that we should be teachable, that we should walk in humility, honesty, transparency and love from the heart. It does not mean being a doormat or a pawn to be used and controlled by people that are not operating in apostolic principals themselves.

All through my twenties and thirties I served the Lord faithfully as a Biblical Counselor and Therapist in para-church organizations helping the Body of Christ. My expression and understanding of my faith in God were predictable and unshakable. I was very content with this and really liked having it all "figured" out. In my mid-thirties I became very ill with a life threatening and life controlling illness that caused me to enter a new walk in my faith and learn that there are chronic life difficulties we are allowed by God to encounter and not everything is always "fixed" by Him.

After all these years of walking through deep places of suffering I can now see how God used those very places to make me into the woman that I am today. Because of having to trust Him for every ounce of strength and even at times my very breath I can now say with confidence that He alone is my "Keeper." I have been miraculously healed of cancer in 2007 but not the serious illness that I have contended with on a daily basis for the last thirty plus years. I consider His 'Keeping' me and showing me how to be an overcomer even more miraculous than the immediate healing from cancer was. I have no doubt that I am here today still prospering in the midst of this storm because He wears me like a glove. At times I am so weak that I ask Him to put His Spirit in me that raised Him from the dead. And He does. I call that wearing me like a glove.

In 1997 a trip to Israel transformed my whole life. When He called me to go to Israel as sick as I was, I said, 'No Way." But then He said, "You don't have to go. You will still be my girl. It's just that we are getting married and I'd like you to meet my people." The next thing I knew I was on a plane to Israel. How do you say no to something as sweet as that? When we landed in Israel, I got off the plane wearing a wedding veil. The Jewish people said, "Are you getting married in Israel?" I said, "Yes!! I am marrying a wonderful Jewish man. His father arranged the marriage. I have never seen his face, but I have heard His voice and I have been reading all His letters and now I get to meet His people!" I was never the same after that. I realized that Jesus was and is a Jew named Yeshua. I learned everything I could about His culture and began to honor the 7th day as Shabbat, the Sabbath, and began to honor and keep all the festivals. I wanted to do and honor everything He had done and like Ruth wanted His people to be my people.

This opened new doors to me in my faith and my calling. I became the North American representative for a Messianic ministry that was stationed in Tel Aviv Israel for 9 years and during that time I was called to bring together the Jews from Israel and the First Nations leaders and

Chiefs into a relationship with one another. June 1999, I organized a meeting in Nashville Tennessee where there was a cultural and spiritual exchange between First Nations and Israel. It was a profound experience. We raised the Cherokee and Israeli flags on the land where I lived with the leaders present and now my calling was not only to Israel and the Jews but also to the Native Americans.

In December 1999 we gathered the Israeli leaders and the First Nations leaders again for Chanukah in Nashville Tennessee for seven days. At the end of that assignment, Dr. Suuqiina, one of the First Nations leaders came to me and told me that he felt I was to be his life partner. This was a shock to me because I barely knew him and had hardly ever spoken to him. However, I prayed and asked the Lord what I should do? I had no attraction for Dr. Suuqiina and could not imagine being in love with him, so I was perplexed.

The Lord told me that I didn't have to do so and that I would still be blessed and also showed me the script of my life and all the times I had stood for justice. He said that this assignment with Him would be another opportunity to do so. I answered yes to Dr. Suuqiina's proposal and yet I was still very leery because I had no love for him. When I went to pick him up at the airport December 25, 1999 I prayed and asked God to supernaturally download me with love and passion for him and He did. When he got off the plane I flew across the lobby and grabbed him and hugged and kissed him and I have loved him fiercely ever since that moment. I am not advocating for arranged marriages or marrying someone you don't know. This is just my experience and it has worked for me because God was in it, it was not of my own doing and I was not "Looking for a man." I already had one. His name is Yeshua.

After Suuqiina and I married in March 2000, my life diversified. I was now called to Israel and First Nations and then God added a calling to women and the arts to my plate. Suuqiina and I ministered together teaching on all of these things and we traveled the world doing so. One year we did 300 meetings in that year. You might say that grass was not growing under our feet. We were privileged to stand before various governmental, tribal and religious leaders across the globe. In the midst of this I never allowed myself to forget who I was and who I was NOT. As impressive as all of this was, my first love was still to dive deep into people's lives in one-on-one conversation with those who were willing to be real, authentic and transparent. Guess you could say," Once a Dung Gate girl always a Dung Gate girl." My heart's passion has always been those one-on-one divine appointments where you get to really connect with God's precious people.

Because of that my counseling ministry is always active and I continue to this day to walk with people as a midwife through the most challenging times in their lives. I was made for this and I thrive in this environment. I am a deep-water person and I love the deep waters where people get real. In the deep waters I meet people who have bottomed due to trauma and tragedy in their lives and I have the honor to abide with them in the deep while they learn to grow gills and breathe water through the process of transformation. I sit Shiva with them until they are born again through these trials and adversities in their lives. They do so because the Creator of the Universe dwells in the deep and religion cannot keep you in the deep only He who made the deep can and does.

Recently my husband Suuqiina was diagnosed with Dementia and can no longer travel and teach so I am now traveling alone and at almost 70 years of age this is quite challenging, but I have learned over the years to trust the Lord with the process. I know that He has sustained me all these years and will in my old age as well.

Some things that have now become even more important to me during this winter season of my life are the following: eldering, integrity, creating a legacy and finishing well. All of these things should be a part of an apostolic lifestyle. I am more convinced than ever that what is most important is the way we live behind closed doors, not how we live in front of the masses.

Over the years I have seen the brokenness of the Body of Christ. We are all broken but not all are willing to bring that brokenness into the light and be made new. Until the climate of the system-based church creates a safe place that is process based rather than performance based I fear not much will change. It is my dream and desire that the Remnant Bride of the Messiah will find safe havens in which to reveal their struggles to people of integrity and empathy so that true healing can take place.

I will continue to use what gifts God has bestowed upon me in service to Him and His people. I will show up and be present and do my best to live a life of honor that reflects the character of Christ. I am grateful for all I have encountered along my journey, the blessings, and the challenges for them have made me the woman I am today, and I like her.

Dr. Qaumaniq Robin Suuqiina

Chapter 14

Sondra Martin Hicks

A Trail of Hearts

Aristotle said, "The whole is greater than the sum of its parts." I think as humans our sum, or who we are today, is a result of not only our genetic makeup, environment, relationship with God, but the influence upon our lives by those significant people that have been placed in our path as we travel our unique journey. We are indebted to the "sums" that have helped us become our "whole." I call these significant influencers in life my trail of hearts. Individually, I call them my heart stone.

Like too many of us, feeling loved and cherished as a little girl was not in my resume. I struggled with believing I mattered. Although I feel God has healed my heart in many ways, a few years ago I had an unusual thing happen. I was sitting in a service when I felt God drop this question in my spirit, "Would you like to know one way I have been loving you your entire life?" I was taken by surprise and immediately responded, "Yes!" One by one God showed me the people He sent to lead me down the path to Him and to my destiny.

He sent my first heart stone when I was only six years old. Her name was Ruth Springer Asper and she was my first grade school teacher. She was a teacher that influenced my life for that school year. She remained in my life until she passed away when I was twenty-two years old. Why did she remain so faithfully in my life when she had literally hundreds of students over the years? I believe it's because she knew how badly I needed her.

While in her class, she was kind, patient, attentive, and loving to a little girl that needed TLC. In my mind, she was a valiant warrior protecting the little ones in her care. As I grew older, she became a steady source of encouragement. I still have every note she ever sent to me. Every time I had a significant accomplishment she would send words of affirmation like, "I've always believed in you" or "I'm not surprised at what you have accomplished, I always knew you would." Every letter included, "I'm so proud of you. Love, Ruth."

Ruth Asper was a very petite woman, not quite five feet tall, and had suffered through polio as a young woman. She walked with a limp when I was in her class but a little more than a decade later she was forced to retire when her legs weakened causing her to fall often. This broke her heart. The students she taught were her children and she was somewhat lost without them. She kept every school picture and treasured them the rest of her life.

I will never forget the day I graduated from high school. Her husband, Roscoe, drove her to my house. Because she couldn't walk very well, I went out to the car to see her and slid in the seat next to her. She handed me a gift. It was two identical necklaces, a long gold chain and a shorter silver chain. It came with a note. She explained that the longer gold chain was me, not just because I was taller but because in her eyes I was gold. She wore the shorter silver necklace because she had silver hair. She went on to say that every time I wore the necklaces it would remind me that she was always with me, cheering me on and loving me. There was no stopping the big tears that flowed down my face. What else can you do in the presence of unconditional love? That day

I sat in the car next to my heart drop was forty-four years and seven months ago, but the emotion I remember even now makes it feel like yesterday.

We continued our special friendship until she passed from this life on June 24, 1981. It was a sudden death, at least to me. I attended her funeral to say goodbye. Her husband was very kind to me and honored me with some of her possessions that I treasure to this day. I got married six months later. I longed for her to be there on that special day but that was not to be. In her absence, I wore her 1937 high school graduation ring around my neck underneath my wedding gown.

God, can you do me a favor? Would you please tell Ruth Springer Asper that she made an eternal difference in the life of a little girl 56 years ago and the effects are still playing out.

Mrs. Asper was the beginning in a trail of hearts that God would send my way.

The next significant heart stone came during my eighth grade school year. I had a new boyfriend and he was in the youth group at First Baptist Church Chickasha, Oklahoma. My family was members of this church but we hadn't gone in many years. Joining the youth group seemed like a great way to see this boyfriend so I went. What I didn't expect was the forever life change that was about to happen. To help guide me on this radical change that was coming, God sent heart stones - two of the most beautiful people I would ever know. Duane and Sylvia Boothe were the youth leaders and choir directors. They had been missionaries to Thailand and were back home in Oklahoma while their kids were in high school. Their presence was so powerful to me because they were full of love and kindness.

It wasn't long after I met them that the church held a Lay Witness Revival service. It was the first time I heard that Jesus was to be Lord of your life not just your Savior. I felt something in my spirit wooing me. It was the spirit of God. I wanted Him. Sign me up. Jesus radically changed me in a moment. My scared, angry heart was suddenly full of joy and peace. I wasn't done with all the anger that had stored up in my heart from past wounds - not by a long shot - but the relief I felt made a huge change in my behavior. It also changed the way I saw my world.

Over the next four years, Duane and Sylvia would spend many hours encouraging and guiding me. They taught me how to love God. They modeled the love of Christ. I consistently felt their love. Rest assured, I wasn't the only one they gave so much to. They loved Jesus with all their hearts and it was evident. They believed in me and they knew my passion for God was real. I was growing spiritually. I was pursuing God and all He offered with all the zeal I had.

The summer I turned fifteen, Duane and Sylvia took our youth group to North Dakota for a mission trip. Weeks before we left, I felt God impressing upon me to be ready, that He was going to require something out of the ordinary for me on this trip. I prayed and asked God often what this was. I received no answer but the feeling didn't let up either. Time came and we took off. We were holding a revival service in the church we were visiting. It was the last night of the trip before heading home and nothing out of the norm had happened. I couldn't believe I was wrong. I had been so sure God was speaking to me. The young man with us who was to preach the sermon that evening came to the church upset. He had lost his Bible and sermon notes. We prayed for him and for God to come through and then the service started. I was in the choir singing when all of a sudden I felt intense anxiety in my stomach. I would describe it as powerful and sudden stage fright feelings. After a moment of this, it was as if someone lassoed me and pulled me out of the choir. I went straight to Duane. I was shaking, short of breath, and freaked out. I said, "Duane, I have no idea what is going on but I think God wants me to say something but I have no idea what it is!" Very calmly, he said, "It's ok, don't worry. Right after Stan, (another guy in our group,) gives his testimony, go to the microphone. Ask Timmy to pray for you and everything will be ok." Timmy was the one with the missing sermon. I went back to the choir and waited... feeling like I was going to lose my dinner. At the appointed time, I went to the microphone. I looked out at the packed audience, shaking like crazy.

After Timmy prayed, I put my hands on the pulpit and I was as calm and collected as I am right now. I didn't pause, hesitate, or consider what I should say. I spoke for forty minutes. When I finished, I had no idea how long I had spoken. Without saying a word, the pastor came to the front and the piano player went to the piano and they issued an invitation. People began to come to the front and pray, others were making up with one another where there had been problems. I'm not sure what all God was doing but I remember that Duane gave me the space to let God pour through me. That was something I had not experienced before.

Duane's impact on my life continued in a surprising way. At the beginning of my junior year in high school, the church organist moved to another town after many, many years. This left a vacancy. Our church was the biggest in town. We had about twelve hundred members, and maybe half of that came weekly.

We were also on the local cable television station. Remember this was 1975. I could play the piano a little bit. I played chords because I couldn't read music with my left hand. If you aren't familiar with sheet music, the notes for the left hand are different from the notes for the right hand. In spite of this big handicap, I had the courage to ask Duane if I could be the new organist. I'll say this. I must have been born with courage because it sure wasn't common sense. Anyway, he thought about it and said yes, I could be the new organist on one condition. I had to agree to take organ lessons from a very accomplished teacher that lived in our town. I did just that. I didn't want to let Duane down so I practiced literally eight hours a day. I became so much better that I even majored in organ my first year in college. One more time, Duane believed in me and encouraged me and I grew. I did something I never thought I would do.

My senior year in high school, my heart stones went back to the mission field. I cried a lot when they left. A year after they left, I had a very painful experience in church and that began a fourteen year period of straying away from God. I have two messages today - our love and our actions can draw people to our heavenly Father and our lack of love and mean spirited actions can push people away from Him. During this dry fourteen year period, the hole in my heart grew bigger and bigger. I got involved in the New Age despite my belief in Christ. I was definitely a sheep gone astray.

In the meantime, Duane and Sylvia came back from the mission field and moved to Atlanta, Ga. Sylvia had taken a position with the Southern Baptist Home Mission Board. She had been the director of their first Crisis Pregnancy Center in Oklahoma City. She left an indelible mark in the area of saving unborn children. She also had a beautiful singing voice. I will always remember her singing 'My Tribute'.

By now, I was married and lived in Houston, Texas, working as a filmmaker. In the midst of my spiritual struggle, I had a client send me to Atlanta to shoot a video for them. I went. I also took the opportunity to see my old friends while there. I confessed my involvement with New Age, sure they would have a fit. They didn't. They didn't even seem worried. They calmly looked at me and said, "We know what is inside of you. And you are coming through this and making the right decision." That's all it took. I came home and turned my back on New Age, never to return. My heroes saved me again. By the way, my client never did anything with the footage I shot. I believe with all my heart it was the hand of God … sending me to his faithful servants to speak truth to me.

I continued to see them from time to time over the years. In 2012, while I was in production for our film, *Faith Under Fire*, I received word that Sylvia had gone to heaven. She passed from this life on February 8th. That is the day that was established for pro-life advocates to take roses to the state capital to present to our legislators. Wow. Only GOD!!

I was heartbroken that she was gone. I shutdown production and headed to Oklahoma to pay tribute to my hero. After the service, I went to give Duane a hug. I tried to talk but all I could do was sob. He thanked me for everything I had done to help him while he served at the church we went to. I was speechless. How could he be thanking me? It was I that owed him thanks. How do you adequately express the feelings in your heart and the gratitude you have for people that make such a lasting difference in your life. Duane and Sylvia taught me how to love God. I still hold their love for me and my love for them in a very special place in my heart.

The next two heart stones guided me to the path I would walk on for the remainder of my life. They are both wonderful men that I still think of often, always with love and gratitude. The first was Darrell Harms, my high school drama teacher. We affectionately called him Pop. I'm getting tears in my eyes thinking of him now. He was a bright shiny beacon to me. He loved God, he loved life, he loved teaching.

He had worked as a professional clown in the rodeo before teaching, so we were delighted with the opportunity to form a clown troupe that performed in parades and other events. I was president of the Thespian troupe my Junior and Senior year and worked closely with him. He directed three plays a year and I was in every one of them for four years. What made his influence on me so great was that he gave me tremendous freedom to explore the gift that he saw inside of me. I was the queen of ad-libbing and he let me loose to grow and develop. My sense of humor and comedic timing had lots of opportunity and practice. I felt his respect for me. I felt his friendship. I even felt his pride. I also felt his appreciation for my humor. This is very important to a comedian!

There was a musical from the 60s called, *The Roar of the Greasepaint and The Smell of the Crowd*, that also became an expression in theater. That sums up the feeling I had every time I stepped out on stage. Drama class, theater productions and the clown troupe were by far the highlight of my high school days. It helped me flourish as a person, gain self-confidence, and experience success on a level I had not previously known. I thrived on stage and I felt the audience's approval. Those days will remain some of the most fun and exhilarating of my young life. It was so outstanding, that I decided to follow this as a career path. My life's ambition in those days was to be the next Carol Burnett. I went to Hollywood and studied but God would eventually tweak this path. I have spent the last nearly forty years behind the camera as a writer, producer, director. I don't believe I would have found my path in life had it not been for Pop. He gave me so many opportunities to discover what God had put inside of me.

The second man God used to shape my career that led to my destiny was Dr. Scott Parry. I don't know a better word to describe him than extraordinary… as a person, as my friend, as a way maker. I was only twenty-five years of age when he gave a green, eager filmmaker a chance of a lifetime. He was thirty years older than me and lived in Princeton, NJ. He was the CEO and founder of Training House, a company serving the human resources sector. He hired me to create a video based program that would launch his company into the new world of video based programming.

This began an unlikely thirty year friendship that was incredibly special. Scott was hailed as a highly respected expert in the business arena. He was later inducted into the Human Resources Hall of Fame. He constantly opened doors for me and helped me get clients. His endorsement carried a lot of weight. I had no idea at the time what a giant of a man was opening doors for me to build my production business above and beyond anything I could ever have asked. I would not have had a career as a filmmaker and learned my craft if my dear friend had not paved the way. Because of God's favor, he was drawn to me, found me entertaining and worthy of his support. He became very special to both me and my husband. We did a lot of work together over the years. Very few people have ever made me feel as special as he did. He was also a creative genius and I admired him greatly. He marched to his own drum, another quality I love. He made an enormous difference in my life and always treated me with such value. God worked through Scott to help me learn the craft I needed for the mountain I was called to the media and arts and entertainment mountain. He also taught me there is joy in promoting others and living selflessly.

The last heart stone I want to tell you about came when I was thirty-eight years old. I was a mother of two young children when I heard passion and fire coming out of this petite woman that I was hearing for the first time. She had such passion for Jesus. Her name was Alice Smith and she was teaching the audience about intimacy with Jesus. I had never heard of anything like this. I literally scooted to the edge of the pew to lean into her words. She told of being in her prayer closet for hours at a time. I struggled to pray for five minutes without repeating myself. I couldn't imagine how hours were possible but I knew that I had to experience what she was describing.

She had a booklet titled *Beyond the Veil* and I consumed it. She later enlarged on it and it became a bestselling book, *Beyond the Veil; Entering into Intimacy with God Through Prayer*. What she was describing was not a formula but a posture of the heart towards God. I was eager to go into my new prayer closet with this fresh attitude and understanding. This first encounter completely and totally wrecked my world. It was the biggest spiritual life change I ever had since meeting Jesus when I was eight years old. There aren't words in the English language to adequately express what I felt. The best I can describe it is to say that my spirit felt intertwined with Holy Spirit. I even felt elevated off the floor. I knew I wasn't but yet it felt like it. I remember thinking that if near death experiences people described were like this no wonder they didn't want to come back. The hours I stayed there before him felt like mere minutes. It was the most glorious, all-consuming experience of my life. I would never backslide again. It birthed in me a passion to pursue Him the rest of my days. I found the loving Father I had been hearing about for years.

After that, Alice and I became friends. She and her husband were the founders of the U.S. Prayer Center in Houston, Texas. They asked me to produce a video on a prayer initiative for the United States called *PrayUSA*. I was so honored to do something for Jesus. The fear of the Lord was so strong on me that I literally pushed my chair from the desk and edited on my knees. That put a desire inside of me to produce stories that focused on the love of God. I now spend all of my time producing stories of ordinary people living extraordinary lives partnered with an incredible God. He finally had me on the path I was created to walk on. Alice changed my life simply by living hers sold out to Jesus.

For the next twenty years I told God "I will go wherever you want me to go, but not Africa." So in 2016, God sent me to Africa. I took a production crew to Pemba, Mozambique, to produce a series of stories called *Walk with Me* about Heidi Baker's walk with God. Heidi and her husband Rolland have been missionaries since 1980, first in Asia, then England and now Africa. I had followed Heidi from afar through their ministry, Iris Global. I knew she was brave, courageous, giving and one of the heroes of the faith to many that know her. I had read some of her books where she said, "The poor made me rich." That sounded like a compelling sermon but I didn't really know if that was true or just a clever thing to say.

I spent two weeks at Iris Global in Pemba in November 2016, and went back for two months in the summer of 2017. On my first trip, Heidi introduced me to one of her favorite friends in Pemba. It was an older woman that lived in the village next to Iris' Global base. She and Heidi had been friends for a long time. Her name was Mamma Tina. Even though we didn't speak the same language I instantly fell in love with this little woman that had such a kind, tender heart. She told me through an interpreter that Jesus had appeared to her in a dream. She was homeless and starving at the time. In the dream, Jesus came to her and gave her bread and asked her to follow him. He told her to go to Pemba where someone would find her and take care of her. She did what Jesus instructed and as she was sitting under a tree, Heidi found her. Heidi took care of her, gave her food to eat, built her a home and watched over her from that day on. Heidi loved her very much. So did I. It wasn't hard.

On my second trip to Pemba, going to see her was first on my list to do. Not long after I arrived she became very ill. So ill, we didn't think she was going to live. Their food consisted mostly of beans and rice and she couldn't hold that down. Heidi went to see her and said her goodbyes. As I walked away from her home back to the Iris base, I thought about what my mother would do when I couldn't hold down food. She made us potato soup. So I stopped at the village market and purchased some potatoes and milk. In my room at the Iris base, I had a Bunsen burner that I used to make Mamma Tina potato soup.

The next morning I went back to see her toting the soup in hand. I found her lying lifeless on a straw cot. She couldn't sit up on her own, she couldn't feed herself. How was she going to eat the soup? This might sound a little crazy but I panicked. I was going to have to pick her up and hold her in my arms to feed her. But I was afraid and uncomfortable touching or hugging people or being so expressive with love. You see, even though God had sent amazing people along my path to love me and inspire me, I was still carrying fear of rejection and fear of truly loving and being loved. Wounds I had carried from my childhood had caused me to live for more than fifty years afraid of being hugged, afraid of really letting my heart go. I was faced with a line in the sand.

This was one of those moments that self talk was a good thing. I said to myself, "What are you going to do now? Get over yourself. Is Jesus alive in you or not? Let yourself love without reservation." I then thought of Heidi. Heidi loves and hugs everyone. She isn't afraid to touch anyone or anything. Love oozes out of her with no hesitation. That's the way I wanted to be. I thought, "I'm gonna do it." Love compelled me.

I sat down on the cot and picked Tina up and held her in my arms and fed her the soup. I went back the next day with more soup and held her again. I went for the third day. On the fourth day, she was sitting up on her cot and smiled the biggest toothless smile at me when I opened the door. She wasn't going to die. She continued to get better and on my last day in Pemba her family was there with her and I took them dinner as a farewell meal for us to share together. It was also my birthday. When I arrived, they were all dressed in their very best clothes to honor me. They gave me a *capalana*, that's their version of a skirt, covered in hearts. We cried tears of joy, we danced, and we hugged. It was the most spectacular birthday I've ever had. You see, the poor made me rich.

Momma Tina will always live in my heart. I am free to love, to hug, to give my heart away. No fear, no strings attached. I am forever changed. God knows what He's doing. Saying 'yes' to Him is the only way to live. Since that time, I have been to Africa many times and I can often be heard saying, "Lord, can I please go to Africa?"

The best way I know to honor my trail of heart stones and very special friends is to do for others what they did for me. They loved me and believed in me. I'm certain that none of them thought they were doing anything that was a big deal. They were just doing what they naturally do. What was simple to them was extraordinary to me. They changed my life. They offered it to me themselves. I will do that for another.

There are countless others that have influenced my life. Time and space doesn't allow the telling of them all. I believe every person has their trail of hearts. I encourage you to think back over your life and remember those special people that have made an important impact. Send them a note or give them a call and tell them. You won't regret it.

May I encourage you to be a heart stone for someone else.

Sondra Martin Hicks
HeartStone Network
www.HeartstoneNetwork.com
Sondra@heartstonepictures.com

Chapter 15

Sharon Parkes

Apostolic Women Arising

My husband Bob and I are Apostles with *Christian International* under Dr. Bill Hamon. We birthed and oversaw the Healing and Deliverance Ministry of CI. We call it prophetic healing and deliverance or PHD for short. I have been with Christian International for over 30 years. We were Pastors at Vision Church@ CI under Apostles Tom & Jane Hamon. We birthed the deliverance ministry at CI October 31st 1999. I function in that role as an Apostle. We trained 20 teams the first go round and that Friday Oct. 31st was Halloween Night. How awesome is that? We had a lady that was given only a few days to live. She had breast cancer and God supernaturally healed her that night. Since that night we have traveled to many nations and the US equipping and training in healing and Deliverance. We also launched a CI-Prophetic Healing and Deliverance Network February 2019. Several churches and ministers have come under the PHD network. We pray for them and are available to stand with them to see this ministry grow. We also minister Deliverance and Healing at Christian Internationals two major conferences.

The Watchman and International Gathering of Apostles and Prophets. (IGAP) The PHD teams from Vision church that we have trained and raised along with ministers from all over the world do the one on one ministry at these two conferences. It's amazing. We see people not only set free but miracles of healing take place. I have been blessed to be able to function in the role that God has given me because of my

Apostles Tom & Jane Hamon who saw the gifting and call in my life and provided a place for me to function and advance as an Apostle.

Most people know what an Apostle is but I will give the definition for clarity. Definition of apostle 1: one sent on a mission: or just a sent one. A. One of an authoritative New Testament group sent out to preach the gospel and made up especially of Christ's 12 original disciples, the first prominent Christian missionary to a region or group two a person who initiates a great moral reform or who first advocates an important belief or system. My husband and I are sent ones and travel nationally and internationally training, activating and equipping churches and people in the Deliverance and Healing ministry. Being a woman Apostle is challenged by religious leaders as well as they challenge that a woman could be a pastor or function in that role. The Bible mentions two women Apostles in Romans 16:7 Greet Andronicus and Junia, my fellow Jews who have been in prison with me. They are outstanding among the apostles, and they were in Christ before I was. I don't have to be called Apostle Sharon to operate in that role. It is what I am ordained in and operate in. I am not about titles but I also know my anointing and what authority I function in.

The Lord is so faithful to take a broken, rejected and abused woman and send her to the Nations to train and equip others to set the captives free. Sometimes knowing where I came from and all the battles I can only smile and thank the Lord for the restitution and restoration He brought me through. Recently I received a word in Jasper Alabama at Worship Life Church from Wayne and Jennifer Lee that it's not that I have a gift of Joy but that Joy carries me. The word talked about my battle scars too. I love John 10:10 when we speak of restoration, it is the process of bringing something back to its original state. Restitution means compensation for things lost or stolen. So I always say the devil stole so much from me and now it is time for restitution. The Bible says when the thief has been caught he has to give back.

My background is I was raised as a Quaker in North Eastern Ohio. But in 1985 I received the baptism of the Holy Spirit at a faith church. When I was spirit filled the Lord began to talk to me. But the faith church didn't believe or teach that. So it wasn't until I met a prophet at and Abortion Rally that I understood the 5-fold ministry. I received a 25 page presbytery at their church which led me to move to Christian International a few months after the death of my late husband. I first met my husband at a New Year's Eve party. I was not serving the Lord at the time. I was so excited to go because I had never been to a New Year's Eve party before. I grew up on a dairy farm. As I have already stated as a Quaker. You could say it was a humble life of having food, clothes, and a house, but it was not a very fancy life.

My parents had me when they were in their later years. My dad was almost 50 and my mom 43. I had a sister 26 years older than me and my brother 23 years older, then they had my other brother who is only 5yrs. older than me. I was the last and the baby of the family. My dad had worked in the coal mines in West Virginia before moving to Ohio to work on the railroad when I was just a toddler. They came to Ohio and bought an old dairy farm. We had an old two story farm house until it burned down when I was 12. Then we built a new ranch house. It was a blessing because the old farm house which we heated with coal was very run down. My parents both grew up in large families of 13 each. Both families were very poor and grew up in the mountains of West Virginia. My dad was the oldest in his family so he had to go to work to help support his brothers and sisters at the age of thirteen. When I was born, my parents provided all the things we needed but no frills. We went to MacDonald's a couple times a year. That was a big treat. As I grew older we may have occasionally eaten out, but that happened very rarely. I didn't even go to the movies. We lived in the country, and if you went anywhere it was to the store for groceries or clothes. My father and mother never spent money on anything that was just for fun. Say flowers for example. I had only seen such things on TV where a man would give a woman flowers. I had never seen my Father give my mother flowers. My parents had a good marriage but as far as being parents it was really like being raised by grandparents because of the age difference. I actually was embarrassed of them.

Most of my friends had young mothers who dressed very fashionably. Not my mom. She dressed very conservative. I remember once telling a friend that she was my grandma because I was ashamed of her age. Then I felt so guilty because I loved my mother very much. I knew she worked so hard to provide for me. As I got older she tried to buy things for me that I wanted like fashionable clothes. As a teenager I wanted to look cool and modern but my mom was very strict and religious. We went to the Friends Church (Quaker) but I got away from it when I was 18 and stopped going to church. I was an adult but I lived with my parents. So I really didn't date or go to activities that weren't in the church. I was invited to this party by a co- worker, so I deceived my parents and did not tell them where I was really going. It was at this party that I met my late husband and he began to talk to me. He introduced himself as Danny, "a good Irish boy," he said, and he began to tell me a little of his life. It sounded very exciting. As I said I had never really been anywhere outside of farm life. I joke today that I guess I ate organic for 10 years of my life because we had very little from a grocery store as we not only had cows and pigs we also raised most vegetables and fruits. My mom canned vegetables and fruit in the fall which is a lost art today. Today I would be called a latch-key kid.

My parents worked secular jobs and were not home during the day. During that time when I had no parental supervision or protection was when I was sexually abused. It was not by one person but by several, including neighbors and relatives. I did a teaching once on breaking off the spirit of fear and shame. My teaching came out of my personal experience of sexual abuse as a child and the long term effect of it. I never shared with my parents what happened because of the shame that I felt. As a child I was not able to understand that it was not my fault. I felt it was my fault and that I was defective and bad. Wanting to stop the pain and shame I felt from it led to me making a lot of bad choices as a teenager. I was in the Quaker church, but there was nobody I felt I could share this with for fear of being rejected. Once again shame kept me silent. But inside I so desperately wanted to share the guilt and memories I carried.

A spirit of shame entered me at a very early age along with abuse and rejection. The enemy set me up for that cycle and continued it with my late husband. I had never been around abuse before. I was 7 months pregnant the first time he hit me. I was asleep and he hit me in my back so hard it knocked me out of bed. This began a cycle of abuse that lasted for 17 years. Danny got saved and actually fell dead 3 weeks later at the age of 38 with sudden death cardiac arrest. I was really seeking the Lord for what I was to do and felt the Lord was relocating me. So I was led to move to Santa Rosa Beach, Florida to be part of Christian International with my three sons eight months after the death of my husband. I later wrote a book called Breaking the cycle of Abuse: How Forgiveness is a Key to Freedom to help others deal with abuse.

I was looking to become all that the Lord had for me. I wanted to start the process of destiny and restoration. I had received my first prophetic word from a church in Kinsman, Ohio. The pastors, Floyd and Sally

Smith, were ordained under Christian International (CI). Their team prophesied that I would move to CI and become part of the ministry there. I had no clue what CI was or anything about the prophetic. I sold almost everything I owned and moved to Santa Rosa Beach, Florida to be trained in the prophetic. My first job at CI was as principal and administrator of the Christian school for the staff children, Christian International Academy. Then a few years later, I went to work in the seminar department, where I worked until 1996 when I married my husband Bob. God truly is a restorer.

The word restoration in the Webster dictionary means this: To bring back to former, original intended or normal unimpaired condition. Bring back to a state of health, wholeness, soundness or vigor, renewal, revival, renovation or reconstruction for establishment. To give back or bring back something that was lost, to put back in a former place or position, reinstate, return to one's former position or dignity. To get back something that was taken away. My husband Bob is restoring it for me. He has brought such healing and joy to my life. After 17 years of abuse with my late husband, I now know how God wanted and ordained marriage to be. He is the love of my life. I used to joke that I could have been a LifeTime movie with all the abuse and torture from my late husband, but now my life is a Hallmark movie of the love and adventure I have with Bob. I would like to say that all these years there were nothing but blessings and smooth sailing in our lives. That wasn't the case. The Lord knew I would need Bob by my side to give me strength as the many tests happened, and there were many.

Many situations had me fighting death off my family and me. In 2002 I was diagnosed with cancer. I had an operation and they removed it all. In 2003 I had tumors that they weren't sure were not cancerous, so I had stomach surgery. During the pre-op tests, they found a mass in my left breast. Although the tumors proved to be benign, two weeks after stomach surgery, I was laying on the operating table because the mass showed up on the mammogram and in the ultra- sound. The Lord gave me Numbers 22:3-18 as I went through the test of cancer: The message here is that we cannot be cursed if God is with us, if there is no iniquity or wickedness among us. Numbers 23:21 says this: "He hath not beheld iniquity in Jacob, neither hath he seen perverseness in Israel: the Lord his God is with him and the shout of a king is among them." And if God has not cursed us then no false prophet can curse us. There are three conditions on us not being able to be cursed. 1. God is among us 2. God has not cursed us. 3. There is no iniquity or wickedness among us. I knew all these three conditions were met in my life. I knew it personally, and I also had several prophecies from others that declared that God was with me and that my problems were not a curse from God. I knew all of my sins were washed away by the blood of Jesus, and no iniquity or wickedness was in my life. Therefore these problems were from the devil, and in Christ's name and power, I had authority to destroy the works of the devil out of my life and my family's life.

We had prayer from our church and friends during the first surgery on my stomach to remove the tumors. Some people really felt we should not have the surgery and should trust God to heal the tumors instead. But our apostles Tom and Jane Hamon felt it was wise to have the surgery. As they and we have stated many times, God uses doctors also. But when the mass in my breast was found, and I was to be operated on again two weeks later, fear tried to come. Worship leader and Pastor Robert Gay wrote the song A shout of a King, based on the scriptures in Numbers 23:21 The lyrics were "We cannot be cursed because a shout of a king is among us. The weapons of hell will not prosper because a shout of a king is among us." Numbers 23:21 says "He hath not beheld iniquity in Jacob, neither hath he seen perverseness in Israel: the Lord his God is with him and the shout of a king is among them."

I was on the dance team at Christian International for eight years. I knew about warfare praise. I knew how to do that. So, I went to my closet and put on my dance shoes. I got out my hand banners and began to dance to this song. That was on the Saturday and Sunday before my surgery on Tuesday. I knew I was using warfare praise as a weapon against the enemy. As I praised and danced, I felt the Lord was healing me supernaturally. Psalm 8:2 says, "Out of the mouth of babes and suckling's hast thou ordained strength because of thine enemies, that thou mightiest still the enemy and the avenger." When they operated on me, God had indeed miraculously healed me, and the mass was gone. The doctor had no answer as to where the mass went. We know God supernaturally healed and removed it. They left a titanium locator in so it would show the place they saw the mass before, but I know it will never be there again because God doesn't do something halfway.

During this time of facing threats of cancer, my husband stood steadfast and declared over me life and that I would be healed. Even though he lost his late wife Barbara to breast cancer, he never wavered in his faith that I would be healed. He prayed over me and declared my healing to come forth. It was no surprise to Bob when we met with the doctor after the surgery and he said they found no mass. During this test of faith, we found that God was still in the healing business. Bob said when his late wife Barbara was diagnosed with breast cancer; they did not give in to the fears and limitations. They continued to be in church and even had outings, like going to Lancaster Pennsylvania to the Amish country. We always say that in faith, you don't deny the facts but rather the power of the facts. So a key for this test he went through was being plugged into church and having them stand with them in prayer. Another key was living as if she was already healed instead of retreating. Bishop Bill Hamon always asks, "How would you behave if you really believed your prayers were answered?" Now we have gone from my test with the cancer to a testimony of healing of cancer.

The battles have continued through the years. All three of my sons have gone through death experiences. My middle son Daniel died twice in one day in 2017. He actually died as his heart stopped. But God was faithful to bring him back and heal him. Another battle was when my oldest son Del contracted Necrotizing fasciitis or (Flesh Eating Disease) in 2009 and almost died. He was in the hospital for one month fighting for his life. It ate the back of his arm and ate a hole in his side exposing his organs. Necrotizing Fasciitis kills 1 in 4 people infected with it. We were opening a healing Centre in Prince Edward Island Canada and this was a heavy battle we walked through and stood on the prophetic words over my son Del's life. The Lord was faithful and did a miracle and he lived. In April of 2009 he had reconstructive surgery to heal the open wounds.

We opened our Healing Centre Beulah Restoration Centre June 2009 and saw miracles of healing. One man had pancreatic cancer and was given a 10% chance to live and God miraculously healed him on the opening night of the Centre. Be encouraged that we have covenant with the Lord concerning our family and no matter what the circumstances God's will for them prevails.

People have said I believe the devil is trying to stop you from ministry. This is partially true but I believe the anointing in my sons and grandchildren is even stronger than mine. I praise God for covenant and for his faithfulness. When I minister on restoration and restitution it is from the place of authority because I have walked through and am walking through it. Not only has there been opposition from the enemy against my calling and purpose but from people too. Whether it is competition, envy or jealousy doesn't matter. What matters is we keep our hearts right. We must continue to walk in forgiveness and let the Lord open the doors that no man can close. I am able to reach nations and see people's lives healed and restored because the Lord has used everything the enemy meant to destroy me with to bring a breaker anointing for joy and freedom. I not only minister deliverance but am able to train others to do the same.

I have written 4 books and 2 manuals that are available on Amazon or at Christian International to equip people in this important and valuable ministry. Our identity is in who God created us to be not our circumstances or lives but what He gifted and put in us.

Apostle Sharon Parkes
Isaiah624ministries.org
Isaiah624@aol.com

Chapter 16

Tonja Marie Peters

Not Abandoned

Tonja is a wife for thirty-four faithful years, a mother of four children, and "Grammy" of seven wonderful grandchildren! Tonja has served with great joy with her husband in ministry for over 31 years. Tonja is the author of Breaking Free Through God's Promises, A 22 Day Devotional. Her motivation in writing this devotional is to help individuals break free from dysfunctional cycles in their lives. Through Psalm 119 and meditation on God's Promises Tonja reveals her secrets to true freedom found in God's Holy Written Word. Tonja alongside her husband Ken Peters are the founding Pastors of The Gathering @ Corona, an Apostolic/Prophetic Reformation church, which was founded in 2007. Ken and Tonja have assisted in planting and covering many "Gathering" churches throughout California and the United States and they enjoy leadership development.

Along with pastoring, Ken and Tonja oversee Elijah Prophetic Trumpet Ministries, an International Ministry commissioned to build the Kingdom of God and bless churches abroad. Currently Tonja serves alongside her husband Ken in overseeing The Network of "Gathering" churches that are called by the Lord to be part of a transformational movement to restore the New Testament model / pattern of the church. "God has placed a burning desire in us to see Biblical Apostolic/ Prophetic Ministry restored and released throughout the entire body of Christ and to see Apostolic Government restored to the local church." Presently, Ken and Tonja have embarked on a prayer journey going to the fifty State Capitals praying for our Nation.

Tonja Marie Fischer It was 1964, my mom was 15 years old and found out she was pregnant with me. I'm sure her mind was racing as she began to think of her life changing drastically. I could only imagine what she must have been going through. Back in the early "60s," it was common to be shunned and identified as an outcast. I was told that a lovely family was going to adopt me and take her in until I was to be born. When my father realized that she was carrying his child, he went to find her and convince her to be his wife and start their family together. My parents divorced when I was four years of age and at the age of seven, my sister and I went to live with our father. I don't have a lot of memories of my life prior to that, only that of walking home from school unattended and being alone watching my little sister. My life wasn't an easy life, it didn't start off on the right foot, in fact, I followed in my parent's footsteps of premarital pregnancy, not once, but twice. I lived with the pain (before Jesus) of not choosing to keep my first baby. But for my second child, my life was forever changed. I chose to keep my son; although I didn't experience the same thing my mom did with the father of her child, wanting to father his son. I became a single mother at the age of nineteen and had a perfectly healthy baby boy, eight pounds, five ounces, 21 inches long, and named him Ryan Daniel Shain. I was very thankful for the support of my family during this time, my parents, aunts and uncles gave me the encouragement to keep going, and to make the needed changes of not giving up. During that time, my aunt shared with me "Tonja, everyone thinks you are going to fail, prove them wrong!" I think it must have been the Irish in me, maybe the German, but that day, I set a course to do just that, prove them wrong. I soon found out; I could not do this without the help of the Lord Jesus Christ. Being a single mother caused me to realize I couldn't be a good mother without God's help. I wanted to raise my son in the Fear of the Lord. I didn't want him to face the same things I did. So, I chose to turn my life over to the Lordship of Jesus Christ in full surrender to His will for both of us! I wish that my life could have been that of better choices, especially as a teenager. But the one choice I am so thankful I made, was that of giving birth to my son, Ryan. Even in the face of opposition and financial duress, the Lord kept us, and didn't abandon either one of us!

My Journey began June 2, 1986; 35 years ago I walked into a Sears department store to purchase a belt hanger. Never in a hundred years would I have known that my life would be forever changed! That day, unlike every other, was different. I was searching for more than what I walked into the store for. I was longing for more in life! I was longing for change, but didn't know how to find it.

As I approached the counter to pay for my item a joyous man named Bob greeted me. He had such kindness about him, that it caught my attention. He then proceeded to invite me to a bible study. He shared the name of the church he went to, in which I was encouraged about, because this is where my aunt and uncle were attending. He gave me his phone number and time of bible study the following day. I had no idea that that phone number would forever change my life. Without hesitation, I accepted his invitation! The following day I called to get directions to the bible study. When I showed up, I was greeted by such joy and peace that I knew I was in the right place. The night of the bible study was amazing. At the end of our study the singles pastor (Ken Peters) prayed for me to accept Jesus as my Lord and Savior asked everyone if they would like to be filled with the Holy Spirit. (Identified in the book of Acts- where Jesus told His disciples to go wait for the promise). The previous weekend my father had prayed for me to receive it, but nothing happened. The difference with this prayer was: The Singles Pastor says, I see pain in your heart and people you need to forgive, he had me open my hands and hold them together, and place all the people who had hurt me, all pain into the cup of my hands. When I was finished placing every issue into this cup, we gave them to the Lord. It was as if a 1,000 pound weight had been lifted off my shoulders, I felt so light and clean! He then led me in a prayer to receive my prayer language, and immediately I received. That night my life was forever changed! I began to speak in tongues every day! I was encouraged to read my bible, give to the Lord, pray for people, and reach out and save the lost. I was filled with that same "joy" that I saw on Bob, the man from Sears. I accepted Jesus, the power of the Holy Spirit, and began a journey of being close to the Father. I was set free from drug addiction, healed in my heart, and began walking in a new freedom to this day still amazes me! Thirty-five years of freedom never tasted so good! Thank you, Bob Eldridge for being willing to share your faith without hesitation! Thank you, Kenneth Peters for loving me through every hardship!

I Wasn't Like Most Girls

The following year was filled with so much change! I would never be the same. My singles pastor Ken Peters (everyone called him "Kenny") began to disciple me in the things of the Kingdom. I would attend Bible study each week as well as services on Wednesday and Sunday. I was immersed into a life change that was so invigorating. I was taught to evangelize my friends and be led by the Spirit of God, following His Voice! Then one day I was faced with a decision I had not contemplated… I had just pulled up to my babysitter's apartment to pick up my son. Ken had been working at a new construction site across the street and walked over from the job sight when he saw me arrive. I hadn't even gotten out of the car yet, and he opened my door, kneeled on one knee, and asked me to be his wife. The first feeling I received was total fear as my emotions ran through my body all at once! The second was complete confusion, then an overwhelming sense of being dumbfounded! Yes, dumbfounded, I felt like a mute, and couldn't speak. I wanted to say yes, but I was afraid, I wanted to speak, but I didn't know how to communicate all of the emotions that I felt. It was like I was going to uncork and explode all over the parking lot. I knew I needed to respond, so I asked him if I could tell him the following day? Well, tomorrow came, and I needed to give Ken an answer. I still didn't know how to respond. I chose to say "No." To this day I am not quite sure how it came out of my mouth, but that fear had overtaken me in such a way, I couldn't imagine how I could be his wife.

My parents divorced when I was four, and both remarried three times. I didn't want to get married, only to divorce. So, I knew that it would be for life when I chose to say, "I do." Most girls start dreaming of their wedding day, planning it, designing their dress, but I wasn't like most girls. I had no idea what that type of dream was. I had never imagined myself being a wife. So, when Ken proposed to me, it opened an entirely different world of something I didn't even comprehend. Through my entire life I bounced around from house to house, aunts and uncles, grandma, and grandpas, and then as I became a teenager, it was wherever I landed. So, the security of a husband, family, and a home of my own wasn't even a category I could comprehend.

All I could remember from that day was the great disappointment that Ken went through, his response was; "Well then, if you are not going to be my wife, then we can't be around each other." Ken had been teaching me the ways of the Lord, and now all of a sudden, "If you are not going to be my wife, we can't be seen together." I felt like I lost my best friend. I went for several months, still attending bible studies, but he was keeping his distance. Then one day, he realized I was missing him, and told me, "If you are going to be my wife, then you are going to have to ask me to marry you." Yes, the day came, and I had to ask him if he would still accept me to be his wife. He said yes. I found out later that he wanted to say no. I think because of pride and him being butt hurt...but he didn't. We lived happily ever after... NOT... without trials! My Best Friend Ken and I have now been married for 34 years, and have gone through many seasons of friendships in our life together. Some of our friendships have been blessed with learning to grow together. Some were with much difficulty, where we needed to process forgiving through painful situations. The one friendship that I am most thankful for is my husband! We have stood through thick and thin and through it all we continue standing in the covenant that we made to each other June 6, 1987. There were times that our friendship suffered much hardship. In those times I learned to grow closer to the Lord, and allow HIM to be my friend. I learned that I was placing expectations on my husband that only the Lord could fill. Once I was able to put the Lord in the proper place of my life, my life and our relationship flourished! I truly learned to have friendship with God, and my husband on a deeper level.

Through the storms of life Ken and I truly learned the value of our friendship, friendship with God and friendship with one another. I like how Ecclesiastes 4: 9-12 states it: Two are better than one, because they have a good reward for their labor. For if they fall, one will lift up the other. Again, if two lie down together, they will keep warm; but how can one be warm alone? Though one can be overpowered by another, two can withstand him and a threefold cord is not quickly broken. Ken and I took this scripture seriously when we quoted it in our wedding vows 34 years ago. We understood that the only way that we would be able to stand together was by putting our Lord Jesus right in the center of our marriage.

Moving From Dysfunction to Function

In 1989 I attended a support group for recovering alcoholics and drug addicts. As I listened to the testimonies of several individuals, I realized that my testimony was different from the others. I couldn't understand why many of them would say, "I only slipped a couple times," or "this time I am thirty days clean." I was set free from drugs and alcoholism, and I remembered that night so well: I had been invited to a bible study and at the end of the study when the Singles Pastor (now my husband) asked me, "Would you like to be filled with the Holy Spirit?" he then proceeded to help me forgive all who had violated me. That night I released forgiveness to those who had hurt, abandoned, and rejected me. I received the power to overcome every obstacle that would come my way. I have never turned back to that lifestyle and have now walked in the freedom of that power for 35 years. Later, as I was pondering my life, "I asked myself why I was different." I had asked my husband, "Why didn't I struggle the way these individuals have?" His response to me was: "You loved God, more than the sin, and the drugs that bound you." For now, thirty-five years I still think about my recovery, especially when I have gone through trials and difficult times. I have found that my love for my beautiful Savior, who saved me from a life of destruction, causes me to overcome every obstacle that the enemy would bring my way. He is beautiful beyond comprehension and greater than the drugs and alcoholism that was dragging me straight to the pit of hell.

Psalm 119:2b: *Blessed are they that seek Him with the whole heart.*

Supernatural Healing

It was the mid 90's, and my husband had taken a ministry trip to Vallejo, California while I stayed home with our children. (Now a mother of four) All of a sudden, I became overwhelmed with emotion. My thoughts were irrational, and I was very irritable. I couldn't seem to control my emotions; I felt abandoned, rejected, and completely alone. Irrepressible anger, bitterness, and resentment were widespread in my life in the early years of my marriage. I was unable to function when this anger would be aroused. I would fight depression horribly.

When my husband returned, he took the time to pray with me; suddenly, a well of uncontrollable sobbing tears arose from deep within my being. I couldn't stop crying. As my husband prayed for me, he held me as a father would hold his little girl. He asked our heavenly Father to reveal the root cause of my deep pain. In a flash, the Lord opened my spiritual eyes and gave me a vision of heaven. I suddenly saw a little girl with blue eyes and blond hair, she looked like my mother, and my grandfather was holding her. I immediately knew that this was my baby girl, the one I had aborted. I asked the Lord to please forgive me, again. Oftentimes I would repent for this sin over and over, but never felt the forgiveness or shame lift. But this moment was unlike any of the others. Immediately, I felt the Lord's forgiveness, healing, and unconditional love. He washed me of this horrible pain and shame. Seeing my little girl in the arms of my grandfather at the throne of God brought such healing to me. I saw joy and peace on my little girl as my grandfather held her in his arms. It removed the sorrow that had been bottled up within me for over fifteen years!

The Lord not only healed me of the pain that was engulfed in my shame. But He set me free of the depression that bound me. I was able to forgive myself, as well as others. I repented of unforgiveness, starting with myself. As I did this, the Lord began to show me the places of bitterness and resentment that I held so tightly, which I was now able to release. The Lord showed me that the cycle of these three together, un-forgiveness, bitterness, and resentment are what created the dysfunction in my life. These three lies disabled me and kept me from being able to function normally. I would literally not be able to get out of my bed, or off the couch. I was in complete dysfunction. Since that day, I have had the opportunity to share this testimony with hundreds of women and pray for numerous ones to be healed of this same type of pain. Each time I prayed; I had the amazing pleasure to see our heavenly Father touch each one uniquely and restore the deep places of their heart.

Revelations 12:11 *"And they overcame him by the blood of the Lamb and the word of their testimony."*

I've Never Walked Alone

As I grew in my faith, I learned to soak (worship) in the Presence of the Lord. I would get up every morning and meet with Him in my living room. I had created a spiritual altar right in front of our television. It stayed off most of the time. Some days I would be there for hours. My friends would come over, and we would soak and pray. My daughters would come downstairs and soak and pray. We created a spiritual pool right in the center of our living room. God's Presence would bring healing, life, and joy. When we would have prayer meetings, the Lord would answer without delay.

We encountered many times, with immediate answers to prayer, and amazing visitations. After several years of this going on, my husband was starting to get a little frustrated with me. Not about the praying, but that the housework was not getting accomplished to his liking. Dishes were piling up, laundry was overflowing - our home was completely out of order. So I did my best to start changing, with prayer/soaking less and accomplishing my housework; laundry, cooking, and dishes more.

A few weeks later, while I was doing my dishes and looking out my kitchen window, the Lord spoke to me loud and clear, "Tonja, you can't live here, but I want you to stay." My response was, "Ok Lord," but in reality, I had no comprehension of what He said. I pondered it in my heart for weeks, even months, repeating it over and over in my mind; I was heartbroken, did He want me to leave Him and His Presence? This was the last thing I ever wanted to do! Then one day, I got it. He was telling me that I can't live on my face every day, but as I go about my household chores and responsibilities that I could stay in His Presence continually. That day was very liberating for me! The revelation and understanding that I could stay in God's Presence every moment of every day was like taking a breath of fresh air of incredible liberation! The freedom of staying in His Presence wherever I went caused me to jump into the next season of my life. I now knew that I could access Him wherever I am and wherever I go, just like a best friend who never leaves me nor forsakes me. He has taught me that even though I walk through the valleys, and even some very difficult places, I have never walked alone. He is always with me wherever I go.

I Barely Made It

It was 1995; I was still asleep but slowly waking. As I was waking up, I started seeing myself walking down a long dirt road. As I looked at myself, my clothes were torn from head to toe. I was bloody as if beaten and was trying to walk straight ahead, but with all my strength, I was barely making it. Suddenly I looked up and saw an old rugged door surrounded by overgrown ivy. In fact, I was almost unable to see its door handle. As soon as I recognized the door, I was given a new strength to get to the handle, but before I touched it, it opened. I saw a glorious light shining; it was the Lord, my precious Jesus. He looked at me and immediately gave me a fresh new gown of pure white.

Instantly I was clean, and all the pain was gone. When I awoke from what I thought to be a dream, but later realizing it was a vision. I pondered what I saw and the one thing that I kept processing even to this day is: I was barely making it to the door. "I barely made it!" I started digging into the scriptures trying to find something to confirm this vision, and I found Mathew 7:14, because the gate is straight, and the way is difficult that leads to life, and few there be that find it. I then realized that being a Christian was more than just reading the bible to my children and going to services twice a week. I came to find out that it was learning to be forgiving when those closest to you betray you. I learned that I couldn't let the actions of others keep me from becoming like Jesus.

It is now 2021, and I have experienced many difficulties in my life, and I've had millions of opportunities to forgive, and forgive again. Learning to live a surrendered life hasn't been easy; in fact, it has been a painful one. I keep reminding myself to keep my focus on the Lord. To keep my eyes lifted up and on Him. I Know He will bring me through every circumstance, and every pain. Every pain was washed away in Him.

The Lord's Face

It was 1998, my husband had taken a new job at a church in Santa Barbara, but things weren't going so well. Ministry wasn't what it was at our previous church. We moved only one hour south of where we previously lived in Santa Maria, but the culture was completely different. My husband came home one day and said, "I think I need to quit my job," things aren't going so well. We prayed together, and the Lord gave him a strategy. He was to write two documents and address some areas. The first document, if received, was how he was to walk out his release from his job. The second was if it wasn't received, he was to leave immediately. I prayed all day the day he was to be speaking to his boss.

During this particular day, I was driving to pick up our daughter Sarah at Magic Mountain. This was a little more than an hour's drive. I had some worship going in the car, and as I started singing "If I could only see Your Face, I could make it to the end." All of a sudden, I had a full-blown vision of the Lord and His Face. I could see His passion in the fire of His eyes! I encountered a peace that flooded my entire body. When I gazed into His eyes, I became consumed by the same fire that I saw in His eyes. Suddenly, the fire shifted like beams moving up and over my head. Immediately in The Spirit, I could sense myself falling prostrate before Him, and as I looked to where the rays of fire were going, it went towards those behind me, to those that were persecuting me. I felt such divine protection and knew that no weapon formed against us would prosper and that whatever we were going to face, the Lord would be with us, and nothing else mattered!

As I returned home that day from picking up Sarah, my husband said to me, "I packed up my office today, what I had to say was not received." I remember the day so well; my husband was going through many emotions all at once. He said: "What are we going to do now? How are we going to survive with neither one of us having jobs?" I was able to share my vision of the Lord's Face and His All-Consuming Presence. This brought encouragement to him, knowing that the Lord would take care of us. Together, we knew the Lord was going to walk us through whatever we needed to face on the journey the Lord had for us. 2 Thessalonians 1:6-8 It is a righteous matter with God to repay with tribulation those who trouble you, and to give you who are troubled rest with us when the Lord Jesus is revealed from heaven with His mighty angels, in flaming fire taking vengeance on those who do not know God and do not obey the gospel of our Lord Jesus Christ.

Nowhere to Live

We left Santa Barbara, in fact, we were told: "Get out of town in 30 days." And because we were taught to submit to authority (through the religious mindset) we did just that, we packed up our family and left in 30 days. Our children were not allowed to say goodbye to their friends. People in the congregation were not allowed to say goodbye to us. They wanted to come to help us pack our home, and we were threatened not to have anything to do with, "their people." We had our home in Santa Maria, but we had leased it out for 1 year, and we still had several months to go before our 1-year was up.

We had nowhere to live! Thankfully our dear friends Bill and Linda Ward (Dad and Mom in the Spirit) allowed us to live with them until we could get back into our own home. Our children all shared one bedroom. (Thank you, Bill and Linda, for putting up with all of us!) This transition was very painful for our family, to think, these were "Christians" treating us this way? Had it not been for our personal devotion and relationship with the Lord, we may have been shipwrecked for life. (Others had also encountered this same treatment.)

As we pursued the Lord with what to do, He began to lead us to what He desired for us. During this time, Ken had a previous commitment to travel to Texas and speak at a small church. So we followed through with what was before us. We went and ministered, and then after the services, Ken shared what we had just encountered. Thankfully this wonderful Pastor, Pastor Benny Haun (total cowboy!) had been through something very similar. Pastor Benny was able to encourage us to, "Get free from religion." This was a new concept for us, but the pain that we were encountering was so real, we knew that we needed to embrace the freedom that he was sharing with us. God truly blessed us on that ministry trip, and that church took up an offering and sowed over $5,000.00 into our ministry! This was able to sustain us until we were able to figure out what the Lord had for us in the next season of our lives.

The Nation's Lord!

When we returned to Santa Maria, we received a phone call from our Pastor. He asked Ken if we could have a meeting. He then communicated that our previous Pastor from Santa Barbara would like to bring some resolve to things that happened while you were in, "his church." Ken agreed that we would meet with him. The day of our appointment to meet with our current Pastor and the Pastor from Santa Barbara was very unusual. Another brother was brought into the meeting with us, and he began to bring false accusations against us. This Pastor's motives were intended to remove us from the ministry completely. Under the mediation of our Pastor, he took my husband out into the hallway and said to him, "Just agree with him, and apologize," which my husband graciously submitted to and we went on our way. Immediately following this meeting, we headed out of town to a prayer meeting in Barstow for the weekend. As we entered into worship, a prophet identified that he saw arrows in our backs. This man had no knowledge of where we had just come from, or what we had been going through. He then said I see the spirit of Doeg chasing you, trying to kill you.

The leadership prayed for us and brought an incredible refreshing portion of the Lord's Spirit, healing our hearts. It was like a beautiful flow of water washing over us, healing our wounds and restoring our children.

After leaving Barstow that weekend, I started researching Doeg . I had never heard of Doeg before. I like to identify scriptural basis when someone says "I see a spirit." This person Doeg is found in 1 Samuel 21:7, he was an Edomite that pursued David to kill him. In 1 Samuel 22:18 Doeg killed all the priests and their families for protecting David. This was an evil man, and he had no fear of God whatsoever. My husband and I realized that we were not dealing with a person, but a demonic force that wanted us cut off from any form of ministry. We submitted ourselves to the Lordship of Jesus Christ, knowing that it was He who called us, and not a man. Shortly after this time, we found out that we were no longer licensed under our denomination because of this individual. It was heartbreaking, but we were receiving invitations to minister, so we knew that we needed to continue on ministering

The Gospel of Jesus Christ

As we sought the Lord as to what to do, the Lord spoke to Ken through a vision of a birdcage, and a bird being released from its captivity… and the Lord said to him; "Do you want the nations or a denomination?" We said, "The Nation's Lord!" Since that day, my husband received a formal apology from the denomination, which restored his heart completely from this season of our lives. And we have been free to preach the Gospel to the Nations! He Wants It All Learning to live by faith was such an incredible adventure, as the Lord was showing Himself so amazing in taking care of us. Even though we were spoken about evil, God's hand was still blessing us. Then one day, the Lord tells my husband, "I want you to give all of your savings away into the offering." The following weekend, we were to minister in Vallejo, California at our friends church. And the Lord gives Ken a message about destroying the Goliath's in our lives. Goliath means "debt," and God wanted to destroy the bondage of "debt" in His people's lives.

That day, we were tested to give it "all away." We now knew this was an act of obedience that was required of us. In agreement, we did so. That day was a monumental day in our lives. We learned that God doesn't want just a portion of us, He wants it all. We learned that day that being obedient to give what God requires us to give, brings the guarantee that He will always provide for our every need and desires too. Our heavenly Father has been so, so good to us. He has always provided extravagantly above and beyond everything we could ever ask, hope, or imagine. But, it has not come without living a life of obedience, to give what God wants, and when HE wants it. We learned that all that we have is His, and as we steward what He gives to us, by His direction that He causes us to live in a place of supernatural provision, and the course that He has for us in all that we do

Following His Voice

Romans 1:17 (TSB) "for in it the righteousness of God is revealed from faith to faith. As it is written, the just shall live by faith." Giving it all away was walking into the realm of faith by giving the Lord what He wanted, when He wanted it. It was an amazing journey. We would travel to churches; the Lord would speak to my husband to sow the offerings the churches would have for us. He would sow back to the church or individuals in their congregations. After about a year of this happening, we looked back and reflected upon all of the supernatural provision, especially when God would say, "Give it all away!" So many testimonies upon returning home, there would be checks in the mail from strangers, or someone who met us three years before would tell us, "The Lord put it on our hearts to send a thousand dollars." That would pay our house payment. Not once were we late on our bills, not once did we go without, not once! Then one day the Lord speaks to Ken and says, "I want you to quit traveling." Ken's response was; "Lord, how will I provide for my family? This is how you have been sustaining us." As Ken and I conversed, I was able to show him our financial books. And for one year, we had not been living on what God was bringing in through traveling, because he had been giving all of the offerings away. God had already been supernaturally providing for us. We were truly being fed like Elijah when he was in the cave. God fed him by the ravens. During this season in our lives, we learned to trust our Father in a new realm of faith. It is one thing to see it in the Word, and a completely different realm to walk it out, truly feeling His mighty right arm leading. and providing for our every need.

Making All Things New

It was around 9:00 PM on February 18, 2004. My husband, and our youngest 2 daughters and I were driving home from church, Southbound on the 101 Highway from Nipomo, California when a drunk driver hit our vehicle. The next thing I remember is being upside down, and my husband calling for our daughter Rachel, "Oh God, where is she, is she ok?" Ken immediately called 911, and then started calling everyone he could think of to start praying for our family. Paramedics arrived shortly after that, and my husband was hollering at them to please go find our daughter, she isn't here. Ken and Candice were removed from the car quickly, but when it came to get me out, they had to use the Jaws of Life. They started pulling on the door, and it was causing the safety belt to choke me. My husband then made them stop, and they were able to cut the seatbelt and then pull me out.

I remember the paramedics placing me on a gurney and putting me inside of the ambulance. They started cutting my clothes off from my body. I immediately asked the Lord "why is this happening to me, where are You, Lord, what are you doing"? I heard him loud and clear, and His words to me were: "Old things have passed away, behold I am making all things new". I sure didn't feel new at that moment, but with those Words came an overwhelming peace and comfort that surpassed the pain that my physical body had sustained.

Rachel was found half of a football field away from our vehicle on the side of the highway, just feet away from oncoming traffic. Rachel's left leg was broken, and her spleen had been punctured, and she couldn't move. Somehow an oncoming vehicle saw her on the side of the road and pulled over. Those individuals sat with Rachel and covered her until paramedics arrived. Considering how small she was and it was so dark in this area of the highway, I believe this was our first miracle. The left side of my head was scalped from the top of my left side down to behind my ear, my neck, and back broken in six places, almost all of my ribs broken, lungs punctured. My right arm was broken in three separate locations and shattered at my elbow.

I went through the darkest hour of my soul. Being bed ridden, there wasn't much that I could do for myself. My husband cared for me in a way we never would have ever dreamed of, from showering and dressing me, to cooking, cleaning and doing all of my regular chores.

Rachel and I began physical therapy together, her for her broken leg, and me for my broken arm, neck and back. The first thing that we were informed about regarding Rachel's broken leg was: that because she broke her leg during a time of growth in her life, she would grow her, but her broken leg would not.

Rachel walked with a slight limp, and I struggled with this until one day, I was at her water polo game, and a man with a peg leg walked by me (I think to be an angel because who has peg legs in this day and age?) and the Holy Spirit brought to my attention; she still has both her legs. To this day I am so thankful for God sparing her life. So many things could have happened to her that night.

Within a few months, my Physical Therapist informed me that he had never seen a recovery so quick as mine. I had stopped taking the pain pills eight days after being home from the hospital (with help from my husband). And as I came back to the rightness of mind outside of the influence of the pharmaceuticals, the first thing the Lord led me to do was to release forgiveness to the drunk driver. My therapist identified my quick recovery was due to the absence of the pain meds. I believe it was the combination of the two; releasing forgiveness and receiving the healing of the Lord to help me be free from the drugs. The recovery that I went through lasted one year with physical therapy, and several more years before I emotionally felt somewhat normal again. The one thing that I can say is that even though I walked through what felt like the darkest hour of my soul. I always knew deep inside; God was making all things new.

Keep My Focus

It was July 2004, five months after the drunk driver had detoured our lives, and the Lord spoke to us about moving across the country. We had just purchased a new home and moved to Holland, Michigan. yes, all the way across the United States, while I was still in recovery of some significant medical issues. We had to find new doctors, new banking, a new church, a new school for our daughters, and new relationships.

As I entered our new home, I started trying to put furniture where I thought I would like it to go. I started looking for furniture that we had when we first got married, as well as furniture we didn't own. I couldn't make sense of things and was very confused. At this time, I started realizing the mental effects of the brain injury that I had experienced. It was as if 10 years were erased from my memory. I knew everyone, but some of my memories were just gone. I continued to draw near to the Lord, knowing He said, "If you draw near to Me, I will draw near to you."

I was now living in a new region and what should have been an easy transition was very challenging. I had to learn a new address, new banking, and new doctors. It is normally a challenge for an average person, but for me, it was doubly challenging. I was determined to not make any excuses for myself. I started this journey of recovering my mind, body, and spirit. I have found that my daddy God is so faithful.

He takes everything that the enemy meant for harm in my life and turned it around and used it for good. My recovery didn't take place overnight, but one thing I realized was: if "I keep my focus" on the Lord Jesus Christ, He would be faithful to get me to the other side of every difficult place. It has now been 17 years since the drunk driver disrupted our lives. I can tell you that time and time again, God has shown He is so faithful!

The Fivefold Ministry

Six months after moving all the way across the United States, my husband informs me that he has been given a job opportunity back in California. He says, "Honey this is an opportunity to do what God has placed in my heart, to do church differently." We had been serving the Lord together now for almost twenty years in ministry, and we were beginning to see the "dysfunction" in The Body of Christ. We believed God didn't intend for everyone to rely upon

"The Pastor"

In 2002, The Holy Spirit had opened up the book of Ephesians to my husband in an open vision and spoke to him about the ministry of the Apostle, Prophet, Evangelist, Pastor, and Teacher, with this Fivefold Ministry moving and working together, for the equipping of The Body of Christ to do the work of the ministry. No longer relying on "The Pastor" to do everything, but relying on one another, and Christ Jesus as the center of it all. We did just that! We took the job and moved back to California. Ken wrote the vision, made it plain, and began this journey of implementing the fivefold ministry to the body of Christ. He taught and training people to do the work of the ministry which gave them the confidence to rely on Holy Spirit themselves, and not man.

We identified each office gift in our church body and then released them to function in their God-given authority. We taught them as Jesus did, and not as the Scribes.

24/7 Prayer

In 2005 our family moved to Southern California. It was one year after the drunk driver hit us, driving us off the road. This left our family in devastation. I found myself in the middle of a culture shock. My husband and I had lived in Santa Maria, California, which was a very rural small community, and then had moved to Holland, Michigan for one year, also a very small community. Facing the lifestyle of a very fast-moving concrete jungle was so overwhelming. At the time we had been in the ministry for fifteen years, so our life was centered on serving the Lord and His people. Of course, we enjoyed pleasures, but in comparison to going every weekend and keeping up with the lifestyles of our new region was uncommon and a challenge.. This was a new adventure.

Still, in a place of recovery, I didn't know how to acclimate to such a busy lifestyle. If I went anywhere, I would be stuck in traffic for two or more hours. I didn't have any close friends. Our daughters were navigating a new high school and hating their father for disrupting our lives. I was mad at my husband (and even God) for moving us to what seemed like a God forsaken land, filled with such perverseness, and compromise, even in church. I didn't know how to navigate my "new life." Then one day, I was invited to a conference in Kansas City, Missouri, it was just a weekend away. I was so desperate; I went on this adventure alone. Once I arrived, I checked into my hotel and ventured to the conference. I found that as I stepped into the building, the presence of the Lord was so strong; I had to go back outside and repent for my wrong attitude and call my husband and apologize for not supporting him in our new assignment.

As I entered the place of worship and centered into the Lord, I was filled with an overwhelming sense of peace. When the main speaker opened his mouth, the first thing he said was, "We need to stand in the gap for California!" God took me all the way to Missouri to pray for California. He spoke the very words that my husband had been telling me. "We need to stand in the gap and pray for California so that God's judgment against it would be held back."

As I traveled back to California that following week, I had such a desire to create an atmosphere of prayer like that in Kansas City, Missouri. I believed in the same type of conviction that came to me when I entered their campus. So I submitted the desire of praying 24 hours a day, 7 days a week, to my husband. His response was, "Tonja, they don't know how to pray for one hour, how can they pray 24/7?" That day we started a journey of teaching God's people to pray at The Gathering in Corona, California. We have consistently scheduled prayer. We do not have a 24/7 house of prayer, but we have people committed to praying continually. We had been in Southern California for 15 years, and God has stayed the judgment on our land!

Finding Freedom & Building Lives

There were so many challenges I faced in preparing for our move from Michigan back to California! The thought of being a part of another church denomination pained my heart. Just thinking of the rejection our family had encountered before was the last thing in the world that I wanted to embrace, nor see our daughters have to go through that kind of pain again. Then one day, the Holy Spirit spoke to me and reminded me of a movie that I had seen years before, "Matrix." At the end of this movie, Neo recognizes his authority, and the agents that were chasing him no longer had power over him. Neo then runs at Agent Smith and destroys him from the inside out. Incredible beams of light explode the agent like a sunburst discharging. At that moment, I realized the religious spirit would not have authority over me, or my family, but that we would be able to go into it, and change it from the inside out. Well, two years later, we were faced with the denomination not wanting us there (Go figure). The difference this time was, that even though a few leaders didn't want us, the congregation did (There was a congregational vote of 98% in favor of us). We prayed about leaving the region to find out what the Lord had for us. This time was unlike the last. The Lord spoke to my husband and said, "I sent you to this region to pastor these people." So that's what we did. This was the day we were delivered from every fear of man and chose to follow the Lord in the face of uncertainty. We were able to start our own church, and named it, Thegathering@corona. We are now 15 years later, with a network of Gathering churches, finding freedom and building lives.

The Ancient of Days

I was on my face one Sunday after Apostle Isaac Ramirez preached to the Gathering at Corona, California. I had been crying with everything within me for this next move of God, that an actual reforming would take place and that we would be those that would truly embrace all that God has for us, with no traces of a religious spirit. We wanted people entirely free to be all that they were created for. When I didn't think I could cry anymore, I started having an open vision and I was caught up in the Spirit. I was completely disconnected from everything that was going on around me naturally; The Ancient of Days came to me. He was all in white and surrounded with this beautiful Glory covered in gold. It was so bright and consuming that as soon as He picked me up, I was covered with the same glorious gold. His hair was white and long, He had this consuming fire in His eyes that appeared like an ocean, a fiery red and midnight blue ocean. The depth was so amazingly deep, it was as if I could walk into His eyes and step upon the seas. He picked my limp body up and carried me to the Throne and sat me on His Fathers lap. I grabbed him like a little girl would grab her daddies' neck, and He held me like a mother would hold a newborn child. I looked into His face, and it was the face of a Lion, with Consuming Fire in His Eyes. Immediately, He stood me up right in front of Him, (facing outward). As soon as He stood me up, I was overwhelmed with arrows coming at me from all sides. It seemed like hundreds of them all at once. As I looked to see where they were coming from, I saw that they were coming from our very own congregation of people. So many thoughts rushed through my mind all at once. I couldn't understand why God put me in front of all of these arrows. Why wasn't he protecting me? Immediately, my right arm went up and caught every arrow, and I was able to shoot them back to where they were coming from. With one exception, the arrows that I was shooting back towards every person that originally shot them at me, were taking out the demon that was standing behind the individuals, that was influencing them.

The Lord spoke this word following the vision: The Glory of God is rising in this hour to reveal, to heal, and to restore the broken hearted. We must be found in the arms of the Father. In that place, the Ancient of Days, the Lion of the tribe of Judah will arm you with strength. He is arming us in this hour with the strength from the Most High, to take out the enemies and not each other. God is turning us to not fight each other, but to take out the enemies that are influencing us. The Lord says

I am revealing my heart in this hour; I am arming my sons and daughters with weapons of war and weapons of love.

Walking in Freedom

During this season in our lives, we had been in transition to train leadership in the revelation received about raising up and releasing the five-fold ministry for the equipping of the body of Christ. There had to be steps of rising up leaders and releasing them to function in their God given authority. This took faith, faith to believe in people, and faith to release them. Unfortunately, in the midst of it all, my husband had been diagnosed with fourth stage kidney failure, and had to go onto emergency dialysis. His struggles were very real. Some days he did not want to live, but he kept forging ahead with the vision God gave him through the book of Ephesians.

At this point in our ministry he had established an amazing eldership team (which included us). We oversaw the business of the church and fivefold teams, along with a lead pastor. The beautiful thing about our team was that wives were included. We had the opportunity to help make decisions right along with our husbands.

One day, one of the wives was influenced by a Jezebel spirit, and started influencing the lead pastor, to not include the apostolic oversight of my husband and to literally take us backwards spiritually. While in prayer I could see how we were being divided by a Pharisaic spirit. The long and short of it all came through prayer. The Lord gave me a vision of two doors; Vision and Prophecy were the two doors. There were two doors placed before us, one a fiery door, and the second a whitewashed door. The fiery door will give you access to the Father, and it will take you through the purification process and purge you with hyssop. There will be many trials and tribulations through this door. The one thing that will remain will be the love of the Father. The heart of the one true lover of our souls. Our friend Jesus will be with us in this fire, for He is our access point. The only way to the Father is through the Son. Shadrach, Meshach, and Abednego were delivered to the furnace of fire, but they were not burned, for the Lord of the most high was with them in the flames.

The white-washed door has a cliff right where you enter. It leads to the gates of hell. This door is very difficult to get through, and it stands before the fiery door, where many cry out and say this is the way to go. They make many plans, meetings, and counseling sessions to help prepare people for this door. They have rules, regulations and many laws, burdens, and yokes that they place on people to get them through the door. They even say this is the way to heaven. They don't know where they are going, is not heaven. They are leading their flocks through the wrong door. Why are they going through the wrong door? "It's because they are filled with fear and are more concerned with filling their own treasuries rather than mine," says the Lord. "They don't know that the day is coming that I will require an account for all they have done, and not done."

"When I told them to feed my sheep, they ate till their bellies were full. When I told them to clothe the naked, they clothed themselves with jewels and glamor to be seen by men. When I told them to sell all that they had and follow me they were filled with every kind of fear and said that I was very difficult to follow. I require an opening of the books at my appearing, and I will require that all give an account. It is in this hour you are given an opportunity. It is in this hour you are given a choice. Will you be those that will choose to save your own soul, and let those around you suffer in hunger, being poor and naked? Will you lay down your life for mine? Will you take up your cross and follow me? I desire you to break through the lies that the Pharisaic spirit tries to clothe my bride with. I desire you to come to me and find rest. I will give you peace. I will bring you to the place of my bosom," says the Lord. "You are mine, and I am yours. I purchased you with my very own blood. I made a way where there seems to be no way. Come, come, come to me and I will lead you into complete truth. I will lead you to the desire of all nations, and I will cover you, and I will keep you. Even though you pass through many waters, they will not overtake you, even though you walk through the fire, you will not be burned. I am a covenant keeping Father, and I will not let you be overtaken by the enemy of your souls. I will not let you fall by the wayside. Stay close to me, and my heart and you will see that I will cover you completely. Let go of everything that tries to hold you back. Draw near to me, and I will draw near to you, and deliver you in times of famine, disaster, and every form of trouble. It is in my heart that you find the safety you yearn for."

After receiving this Word, I realized that part of our team had the religious mindset, not the mindset of the Apostle who set the vision of the house. Just like many stories that you have heard before, the enemy's tactics are always the same in regard to dividing God's people, and churches. Our eldership team became divided; the elders' wife who was influencing the lead pastor left the church along with many families (primarily where the women were stronger than the husbands). Shortly after this the lead pastor resigned for other reasons. This was a sad time for our congregation, but, we kept our focus, and learned to press the "reset button" (Thank you LuAnn Mast for your prophetic ministry to the Gathering). God used all of that trial to reveal the hidden motives of individuals.

It didn't stop what God wanted to do. We had to keep forging ahead with the Vision God gave, knowing that He would be faithful to complete it.

A Commitment to Prayer

During this season of our lives, I had to learn to walk alone. You see, the elders' wife that divided our congregation, was my best friend. I had trusted her with everything: my family, our women's ministry, our children's ministry. We did everything together. but, thankfully my relationship with the Lord was greater. Even though I did put trust in my friendship with her, the Lord was always first. He walked with me through a very painful time. He began to show me that even though I walk through the valley of the shadow of death that I would fear no evil, for He was with me. During that season Psalm 23 came alive to me: Psalm 23: "The Lord is my Shepherd; I shall not want. He makes me to lie down in green pastures; He leads me beside still waters. He restores my soul; He leads me in the paths of righteousness for His Name's sake. Yea, though I walk through the valley of the Shadow of death, I will fear no evil; for You are with me; Your rod and Your staff they comfort me. You prepare a table before me in the presence of my enemies' You anoint my head with oil; My cup runs over. Surely goodness and mercy shall follow me all the days of my life; and I will dwell in the house of the Lord forever." I love the Word of God! Next to my love for the Word, I love spending time with the true Lover of my soul, in prayer. As I learned to embrace the process the Lord had for me, I started down a narrow road of freedom and prayer. Each day I would arise to a new adventure in Him. Typically I would go for a morning walk and have a time of prayer and process through my daily activities. This would help my mind be able to have clarity of thought. Some days would be a time of pressing in and praying for my family, and friends. Other days would be times of strategy with the Lord, where He would reveal Himself with what we were to be doing in the days ahead. I always love seeing what's next! The Lord has always been faithful to reveal Himself to me in ways that have brought comfort, joy and provision for all that we needed. Some days He gives such clarity, and other day's it is walking in a place of complete faith. Faith knowing that He is there walking with me every step of the way, faith in his words "I will never leave you, nor forsake you." Faith in not being able to see, but to believe.

Tonja Marie Peters

The Gathering

680 East Parkridge, Suite 101

Corona, California 92879

PastorTonja@thegatheringcorona.com

Chapter 17

Joyce L Lane

Yah/God has always communicated with me in the supernatural. Around the age of 9/10 yrs. Living with our biological mother in Dos Palos, CA., I had gone out to get a bucket of water at the hydrant (there was no running water in the house), I was waiting for the bucket to fill (my first encounter with Yah/God), Yah/God spoke to me and said, "Joyce, I want you to preach my gospel." I responded with 'Kay, Lord!' Even though I did not know Him, and I did not fully understand, I knew it was good! Something stirred inside of me (I believe Yah/God preserved a place/spirit within us, his creation, that whenever He speaks our spirit responds and acknowledges his presence, his voice, whether we know him or not). Remember, it was His Breath, His Life, which was breathed into us in the first creation of mankind. Our First Life! (Genesis 2:7) A most intimate moment occurred when the Creator breathed into his nostrils the breath of life. "In Him was life" (John 1:4), and He gave humankind the precious life that only Yah/God has to give.

I Was Excited!

It was an extremely hot day, I ran into the house to share with my mother, (I called her Ma)" Ma, Ma, guess what just happened? She responded, what baby? God just asked me to preach His gospel!" She laughed, patted me on my head, and said 'yes, baby.' I was still filled with excitement! (Mom did not have a relationship with Yeshua/Jesus) But I was in awe of what had just happened!

We, (my siblings and I were raised by our father in Phoenix Arizona), and I do not know if our dad believed in Yah/God. There were no Bibles in our home, we did not go to church, and we had a 'story book evil stepmother.' Our father was a hard worker/construction worker but was gone to union meetings Friday evenings until Sunday evenings. (You figure it out)! The six of us kids suffered under the hands and the pain of our stepmother. (Our stepmother had one son).

After The Call on My Life the Enemy Tried to Take Me Out

Our Dad brought us to live with our biological mother when I was nine years old. His logic was the girls (my sister & I) should be with our mom at our age. I became extremely sick. I was diagnosed with Rheumatic fever, enlarged heart, Saint Vitus Dance/Sydenham Chorea. We were told that I had had heart attacks according to X-rays. In one eventful crisis, I had asked to be taken to church across the canal, near the house for prayer. (I was carried in by my mom & brother), An Evangelist Boom was there running a revival; our need was made known to her/our request for prayer; you could see my hands turning pink again. She gave me a little white New Testament and told me about the 91st Psalm and instructed me to use it when I was afraid. I was in the Merced Community Hospital for three months, complete bed rest, special diet. According to the doctors the nerves had died/were dying in my left side of my body and they had no cure. I was afraid of being separated from my family, so I hid the uncontrollable jumping/jerking of my left arm & left leg, by rocking all the time, hoping nobody would notice. Finally, my mom asked why I rocked all the time; I told her, and she panicked. That was when I was taken to Merced Community Hospital. The doctors had given my mom no hope and prepared her for a funeral, my fear of separation had become a reality! But Yah/God said, "she shall live and Not die" (Psalms

118:17) *"I will not die, but I will live and proclaim what the LORD has done."*

Atwater Children's Hospital

Psalms ninety-one became my Lifeline. My stay at the Atwater Children's Hospital was one and one-half years of complete bed rest; I attended school on a hospital gurney. It was the wheelchair, bed, and gurney. Later, I had to learn to walk again. My family could only visit once a week on Sunday afternoon, after our naps. We were anxious to take our naps so that we could wake up and our families would be there to visit with us.

Finally, I was strong enough to return home but with many restrictions; I my Jr. High years I attended half days in class & half days in the nurse's office lying down until it was time for the bus to take us home. No sports or normal activities. But during this time; this was a time of Holy Spirit Training, learning to Trust & depend upon Yah/God for absolutely everything. This was my time on the back side of the mountain; discovering who Yah/God was & is!

Is There Anything Too Hard for Yah/God?

The Holy Spirit and I had many conversations & classes. The Holy Spirit was an Excellent Teacher, Counselor, & Guide. John 14:26-28. I cannot tell you when my left side was restored back to normal, and my heart no longer covered the cavity of my chest. But Yah/God had miraculously healed me. Jeremiah 17:14 *"Heal me, O LORD, and I shall be healed, Save, and I shall be saved; for you are my praise."* I loved basketball and I wanted to play, but this was impossible unless Mom would sign a release, releasing the school from the liability of my playing. I pleaded with Mom for some time, finally she gave in saying if I could trust and believe Yah/God, she would match my faith, but she was afraid. I understood, but I knew Yah/God would take care of me. I was overjoyed, playing basketball!! I excelled in the game to a certain degree, they started to call me 'Sure Shot' until someone threw the ball and it hit me in my chest and down, I went, it knocked me out or at least knocked the wind out of me. When I came to, my mom was there with a very worried look on her face. I reassured her I was ok, and if she had been hit with a ball in the chest, she too might have gone down. My basketball playing was over. But my healing and restoration was intact!

Fast Forwarding ... Kingdom Authority

My brother's baby was born having Seizures, they brought the child to me and asked for prayer for healing; we prayed, Yah/God healed the child & she had a Seizure free life. We have pointed many to Christ. Some are serving as Pastors, Teachers, Bishops, Evangelists, Worshipers, & etc. I was reminded by my sister in one of our Bible Studies she received healing of a blockage she had to her heart. (Mark 16:17-18). Bless Yah/God! While ministering in Zimbabwe Africa (2017), We prayed for a young man scheduled for surgery (hearing issue), We received word from the Apostle, Pastor of the church that the young man was healed and no longer in need of surgery, he is hearing very well. Acts 1:8. Bless Yah/God. We have an invite to return.

Dreams and Visions and the Voice of Yah/God

As I was going into my Prayer Room (War Room), I heard the Holy Spirit say; "there's Snipers in the Land. Take cover; and I responded, how do I do that? He said 'the 91st Psalms.' "Pray Madera" the Heart

Affects and Governs Every Part of the body:" (both physical and spiritual)

The Lord asked me a question; "Who told the story and who painted the pictures?"

While preparing for a Mission Trip to Accra Ghana, (2019), I had a dream of a compound of white buildings and the strange part of the dream there were caves, many caves. I shared this dream with my husband, Ken. I did not understand it. While in Ghana, we went on a tour of the "The Castle" upon our arrival, we discovered this was a holding place for the African Slaves, a place of disbursement, torture, and death. A place of "No Return!" As we toured the Compound with the Narrator; to my amazement; I let out a shout to my Honey, Ken, these are the Caves I saw in my dream!! These were the Caves my African People were held in pitch black, no windows, no ventilation, as the narrator explained; spit, tears, blood, feces, urine, sweat, having to walk in a stooped position, pushing, and crushing one another, no place to stand or breathe, in chains & shackles around their hand, necks & feet; every cruelty was used to rob a people of their dignity their will, and their hope, and no way of escape!

"Tell them because it's a 'Yah/God' Fix, I will increase their capacity to (of) AGAPE …, I will increase their Capacity to Love!" "That is why I said to Love Me with all their heart, soul, strength, & mind; because you are incapable of loving in this Dimension to this degree- within yourselves – but you must be willing and choose to be obedient in Yah/God's Agape and the Holy Spirit will empower you to allow me and my son, Yeshua to agape/love through you and you will be Able/Equipped to agape/love all people."

Joyce L Lane, Apostle

The Glory of Zion Ministries

P.O. Box 594, Madera, CA 93639

praymadera089@gmail.com

(559) 661-4656

Made in the USA
Columbia, SC
24 July 2022

63887275R00157